DESIGN AND MAINTENANCE OF ACCOUNTING MANUALS

Second Edition

**THE WILEY INSTITUTE OF MANAGEMENT ACCOUNTANTS
PROFESSIONAL BOOK SERIES**

Jack Fox • *Starting and Building Your Own Accounting Business, Second Edition*

Harry L. Brown • *Design and Maintenance of Accounting Manuals, Second Edition*

Gordon V. Smith • *Business Valuation: A Manager's Guide*

James A. Brimson • *Activity Accounting: An Activity-Based Costing Approach*

DESIGN AND MAINTENANCE
OF ACCOUNTING MANUALS
Second Edition

Harry L. Brown, CPA, CDP

JOHN WILEY & SONS, Inc.

New York • Chichester • Brisbane • Toronto • Singapore

SUBSCRIPTION NOTICE

This Wiley product is updated on a periodic basis with supplements to reflect important changes in the subject matter. If you purchased this product directly from John Wiley & Sons, Inc., we have already recorded your subscription for this update service.

If, however, you purchased this product from a bookstore and wish to receive (1) the current update at no additional charge, and (2) future updates and revised, or related volumes billed separately with a 30-day examination review, please send your name, company name (if applicable), address, and the title of the product to:

Supplement Department
John Wiley & Sons, Inc.
One Wiley Drive
Somerset, NJ 08875
1-800-225-5945

Library of Congress Cataloging in Publication Data:
Brown, Harry L.
    Design and maintenance of accounting manuals / Harry L. Brown.—
    2nd ed.
        p.   cm.—(The Wiley/Institute of Management Accountants
    professional book series)
        Includes index.
        ISBN 0-471-59643-4 (cloth)
        1. Accounting—Handbooks, manuals,
    etc.—Authorship.   I. Title.
    II. Series.
    HF5657.B75   1993
    808'.066657—dc20   92-45032
                                                         CIP

Printed in the United States of America

10 9 8 7 6 5 4 3

In memory of Phyllis Marie Baguley Brown, the best first and only wife any man ever had, who worked with me on my first Wiley book and would have enjoyed working on this one even more.

PREFACE TO THE FIRST EDITION

It has been proven that one of the greatest fears among business people is public speaking. The next greatest fear must be writing for publication, particularly writing and publishing accounting documentation. In a career of almost 40 years as a certified public accountant, systems consultant, data processing specialist, and controller, the single most glaring weakness I have encountered in reviewing and using accounting systems has been the lack of adequate documentation.

One of four excuses is usually given: (1) nobody reads it, (2) the hands-on approach in which each person teaches another is a better method, (3) written policies and procedures are too confining, and (4) nobody here has the time; we're too busy "doing." In a constantly changing accounting world, none of these excuses can stand very long.

Throughout this book about designing and maintaining good, acceptable, and readable accounting documentation, my message is that you should write much as you speak—clearly, simply, and understandably. As the old saying goes, there are two rules for good documentation. Rule 1 is "Write to be understood by a reader you may never meet face to face." Rule 2 is "Follow Rule 1."

The world of auditing is changing from voluminous testing of transactions to procedural reviews of internal controls, tests of conformance to acceptable accounting principles, and reviews of the application of rules and procedures to insure consistency and reliability. This type of auditing makes written documentation and mandatory. Also, accounting in the United States is inundated with written materials from outside. Examples are FASB (Financial Accounting Standards Board) and GASB (Government Accounting Standards Board) pronouncements, AICPA (American Institute of Certified Public Accountants) guidelines, federal regulations, Internal Revenue Service rules and regulations, and technical articles in journals such as the *Journal of Accountancy* and *Management Accounting*.

If an accounting staff and company executives are to be fully informed, this flood of material must be read and, when necessary, related to the accounting operations at your company. The dissemination of information on this scale cannot be handled orally or with periodic meetings and brief letters to the staff involved. Thus there is a need for clear, consistent documentation to describe the accounting system being used, the principles involved, the policies that executive management wishes enforced, and the procedures described what is to be done and how it is to be performed on a daily basis.

In this manual on manuals, I have used titles such as *Chart of Accounts, Policy/Procedure Statements, Administrative Releases, Information Releases, Forms Manual*, and so forth. These are just good descriptive words. If you think of titles more meaningful in your situation, by all means use them.

This book covers the development, implementation, and maintenance of seven different accounting manuals or systems. Two of these manuals are almost mandatory: the *general accounting manual* that describes the accounting numbering scheme and how the numbers are used to code transactions to be processed by the accounting systems and subsystems, and the *policy/procedure statement* system that can provide full information to anyone with the need to know the organization's accounting policies and the procedures to maintain those policies.

The other five manuals are optional, but as you read about them you will find that they supplement and complement the primary accounting documentation. They are the lubricant of the system, keeping the wheels in motion and turning in the same direction. If none of the following optional manuals is developed, certain portions of each of them will show up in the basic manuals but in less depth.

The *forms manual* describes every accounting form in detail—its use, its limitations, and how it is completed by various users in the accounting stream.

The *year-end manual* describes the actions, reports, and schedules to be completed in sufficient detail to assure that the fiscal year-end closing is accurate, consistent, usuable, and timely.

The *data processing manual* is a condensation of the portions of the technical computer processing instructions the accountants must handle. Examples are batch input control forms, record layouts to enable errors in coding to be corrected, and the contents of accounting reports with the meaning and use of the report fields and summaries included therein.

The *user manual* provides information to nonaccountants in the company who are involved in initiating or adding to an accounting document. This manual provides a list of accounting personnel by function, a condensed chart of accounts and accounting codes, and instructions for completing accounting forms used within the organization.

The *information release system* provides instant reporting of events that may affect an accounting policy or procedure, smoothes the daily operations of accounting, and supplies information that may be of interest or help to the accounting staff and outside users.

Some of the manuals may have a fairly significant development time, possibly several weeks. The general accounting manual, the forms manual, and the data processing manual are in this category. All the other manuals have a very limited start-up time or none at all. These last manuals merely require that you put pencil to paper, have the output typed, edited, copied, and distributed—probably no more difficult than writing a lengthy letter of explanation to a friend. In any case, documenting accounting systems can be exciting and is always rewarded if done well. It is often the case of the teacher learning as much or more than the pupils who use the written materials.

Once developed, even the more difficult manuals require little maintenance unless a very significant change in the accounting system occurs. This book discusses the three levels and types of maintenance tools: the interoffice letter, the policy/procedure statement, and the rewrite of the manual or sections thereof.

Finally, the documentor (I like that title) should remember this: If you publish something with one or two spelling or typing errors, that's no problem. If there are one or two grammatical errors such, as suddenly splitting an infinitive or madly misplacing a modifier, that's no problem. But if the reader of your writing effort does not understand what you have said, that *is* a problem.

Once the documentation systems are in place, the small amount of time needed to keep each of them current is time well spent, and I am sure the effort will be appreciated by both internal and external users of the accounting systems of your company or organization.

As you study the many exhibits included in this book, you will understand that I did it my way. I certainly hope that you have as much chance to design and maintain accounting manuals as I have had, and that you also have the opportunity to do it your way. Good luck. And happy writing.

HARRY L. BROWN, CPA, CDP

Hattiesburg, Mississippi
January 1988

PREFACE

The new chapter in this second edition is a series of documentation illustrations covering computer hardware and software studies. It includes a classic System Development Process, a work plan outline for replacing both hardware and software, and a series of survey forms used to study an existing computer operation when planning to improve or to consolidate it with another operation.

Also added in this edition are information releases on dealing with the media and on the basic rules for preparing visuals for a speech or presentation, as well as a list of redundant or obsolete phrases.

I continue to hope you enjoy documenting accounting systems.

HARRY L. BROWN

Traverse City, Michigan
April 1993

CONTENTS

CHAPTER 1
ACCOUNTING MANUALS: HOW TO YOU DO

Many speakers at workshops, seminars, or conferences mention poor communication as the number one business problem. Communication, written and oral, is the documentation required to produce information, measure results, and facilitate planning. Lee Iacocca has said, "Chrysler operates with people, product, and profit—connected by communication."

The current trend in manufacturing is to use "quality circles" or "involvement circles," both of which refer to workers *communicating* with each other to perform specific tasks in the most efficient and effective manner.

Ask a dozen accountants to name the major method of communicating in their accounting operations and they will probably describe the accounting manual. However, you will get 12 different answers of what the manual is, varying from a simple listing of account names and numbers to an academic treatise of the philosophy and practice of accounting as used in that particular environment.

In its simplest form, the accounting manual documents the meaning of sets of descriptive numbers used in an organized manner to record, summarize and report data and information. It may contain descriptions of one or more of the systems and procedures that explain the basic accounting structure of the enterprise.

However, the manual can be much more than numbers and definitions. It may contain organization charts to show responsibility and lines of authority, policy, formulas, clerical procedures, special industry terminology, data processing rules and procedures, forms descriptions and uses, and so on. It is the general map within which travel will take place.

Every business enterprise has an accounting system, from the self-employed person operating a small business out of his or her home to charitable, not-for-profit institutions and agencies, educational institutions, governmental agencies, industrial and service companies, and so forth. The system may be completely undocumented, possibly just a checkbook and a list of receipts, or it may be an elaborate, difficult-to-maintain, small library of books and manuals used by large national and international companies.

An accounting manual has three basic purposes: to answer questions, to instruct accounting personnel, and to provide consistent reporting of business transactions. As a printed document, it must be useful and, more importantly, *used*. Therefore, it should be *formal*. Not in the sense of being rigid and unyielding, but in the sense of being complete and consistent.

It should be *available* to all who need it or think they need it. Certainly the accounting staff needs the manual. Also, line supervisors, managers, and others who submit accounting data should have the manual available to them.

It should always be *current*, a condition requiring a method of publishing changes, additions, and deletions very quickly.

Finally, the manual should be *easy to use* as a tool to answer questions of consistency, accuracy, and clarity of presentation.

To summarize, an accounting manual should be:

Formal
Available
Current
Easy to use

Throughout this book, the theme will be FACE it.

A word of warning! Unless the contents of a manual are to be used exclusively by accountants in our accounting operation, the accountants must turn *our* terminology into *their* terminology, that is, the terminology that will be understood by nonaccountant users of the manual. Avoid accounting jargon at all times.

For reference purposes, *accounting manual*, as used in this book, includes all the *modules* described. The reader has the choice of developing selected modules and combining them into one accounting manual or maintaining each one as a separate manual. The seven modules are:

General accounting manual
Policy/procedure statements

Forms manual
Year-end manual
Data processing manual
User manual
Information release system

GENERAL ACCOUNTING MANUAL

The general accounting manual includes a general description of the overall accounting system, the chart of accounts, numbering scheme, account descriptions, and, if desired, the general accounting principles and policies being followed. Parts of the general accounting manual are usually included in the user manual to provide account coding information to outside departments such as purchasing, receiving and others to code transaction documents or otherwise provide accounting information. The general accounting manual is covered in Chapter 2.

Developing the Accounting Manual

If your accounting system is functioning, even fairly well, some kind of accounting documentation is being used. It may be scant, scattered, highly variable, and incomplete. Much of it is probably unwritten, handed forward to replacement employees orally as instruction takes place. However, informal systems cause inconsistent treatment of similar transactions, incomplete subsystem reports, difficulty in analyzing comparative statistics, and so forth. In this situation, as consultants say, we must first define the problem, which is the need to develop an accounting manual for a specific business entity. The source of materials is the existing staff who operate the system. Each operating unit within an accounting operation has developed some workable procedure. It may be slow, cumbersome, and devious but it always works!

The axiom "A committee of one gets things done!" is never more true than in this development phase of an accounting manual and that *one* should be at a fairly high level within the group. As this is an action program, there is no time for deference, hesitation, or subservience. The available information must be captured quickly and efficiently.

General Procedures

If the goal is the accounting manual, start with the general accounting operation. Every accounting operation consists of related but disparate units such as:

Payroll

Accounts payable

Cost accounting

Inventory control

Accounts receivable

Cashier

Physical plant and equipment

General accounting (Controller)

Purchasing (included here because of its close relationship to accounts payable, cost accounting, and inventory control)

An easy beginning is to have every person in each unit write a detailed job description with particular emphasis on actions related to procedures. Ask for more, not less, and do not bother with fine editing or consolidation. What they do is more important than how they do it.

Chart of Accounts

At the same time, prepare a list of every account number and name, such as asset, liability, ownership, income, expense, clearing, and special purpose. Now the hard part: Define each account number in one or two sentences. The final glossary developed here will be the primary reference of permitted actions and, more importantly, those not permitted, in each account being used.

If divisions, regional, or branch operations are used, define each of these and show which accounts are used by each region, division, or branch. For example, if one specific division has 10 exclusive expense codes, show these as part of the branch description. Also, the 10 expense codes should indicate they are to be used only by the named division.

Many questions will be answered by the formal chart of account numbering scheme and the glossary.

Overall Descriptions of the Accounting Process

The introduction to the accounting manual should describe the transaction numbering method in detail. For example, if a transaction requires a 2-digit location (division, branch, etc.), a 3-digit department, and a 4-digit balance sheet or operating income or expense code, define the individual items. Chapter 2 will illustrate methods of explaining account sequences. The only requirement is to FACE it, that is, Formal, Available, Current, and Easy to use.

The next section, account names and numbers, is already in place for most enterprises. For new businesses, there are several sources for generally used numbering schemes, such as accounting textbooks, trade publications, specialized industry releases, and so on.

The final section for a minimum accounting manual is the account glossary. Chapter 2 will also illustrate usable formats.

Accounting Rules and Regulations

A more complete manual would contain a section on accounting principles and general procedures. For example, the company might indicate it follows a published industry account numbering and procedure format, or that it operates its accounting in accordance with an American Institute of Certified Public Accountants' *Audit Guide* such as the *College and University Guide, Hospital Guide, Health and Welfare Guide*, and so forth.

The relevant or important principles in the guide could be restated in the manual. The inclusion of this material makes the manual more usable by knowledgeable accountants.

The accounting manual may contain copies of accounting documents with brief descriptions, copies of reports, and accounting statements produced by the system. If there will be no forms manual, then forms contents may be described here. If there will be no data processing manual, then a brief description of computer processing input and output control procedures should be included as part of the general accounting manual.

POLICY/PROCEDURE STATEMENTS

This manual is unique to each institution or enterprise. The only thing to be said here is that these changes to other accounting systems should be easily understandable, should explain the background or reason for the change, the change itself, and a complete description of what the reader must do or plan to do.

Planning the Policy/Procedure System

The moment a manual is completed and published, it is subject to change. Luckily, there are only three things that can be done: add something, delete something, or change something to fit changing circumstances. This axiom is true of data also, and most packaged, computerized accounting systems provide a means of adding data, deleting existing data, or changing data fields. For example, in our payroll system, we can add a complete employee record, delete a record, and add, change, or delete almost any field within any record.

It does not seem feasible or practicable at times to reissue an entire manual, which may be 100 or more pages, for the addition of one or two new accounts or procedures, particularly if those additions affect only a few individuals or operations.

Also, the addition of a new form into the accounting process can be handled with a change-reporting mechanism. Such a procedure can be used for both of the manuals described so far, with the knowledge that each manual will be revised and republished in its entirety at some future date.

The change reporting format can be given any appropriate generic name; however, I prefer descriptive titles such as *Policy/Procedure Statement* (PPS), *Administrative Release* (AR) or *Administrative Policy and Procedure Changes* (APPC). All that is required is a standard format that will be recognized by the recipient as an important document in the overall accounting operation.

The minimum identification information of the P/PS form is a descriptive title such as *New Travel Reimbursement Form, Revised Shipping Procedure*, and so forth, the effective date, the unit or department issuing the release, and the distribution. Releases should be numbered for reference purposes and indexing provided at some prescribed interval. The release should also indicate if it supersedes a previous release on the same topic.

The policy/procedure statement system will be discussed in Chapter 3.

FORMS MANUAL

A third but related manual is the *book of forms*. Forms are the vehicles that carry data, information, and approvals throughout the accounting map. They contain the actions accomplished, the authority, and the purpose such as buy, sell, make, pay, bid, move, add, delete, change, and so forth. Forms are the foundation of computerized data processing in business. Developing and maintaining a forms manual need not be difficult or burdensome.

Starting the Forms Manual

The first step in this process is to gather a complete original of any accounting-related form. Attach a single sheet to each form and complete the following:

Complete form name
Form number
Revision date
Number of copies
Distribution of copies

Later we will add the printing source (in-house, vendor name, etc.), and the department responsible for acquiring the supply of forms and issuing them to other users. Chapter 4 will discuss a simple, workable 3-page form description layout.

YEAR-END MANUAL

The year-end manual is a once-in-a-company's-lifetime manual. Once prepared, it is updated annually for any changes in the fiscal year-end closing procedures. Such changes come about by a change in management, a change in auditors, or an expansion or contraction of year-end procedures caused by a change in accounting systems. This manual, probably better described as a *year-end assignments list* defines all the tasks that must be accomplished at the end of the organization's fiscal year to close the books and prepare the required accounting statements, schedules, and narrative for the annual report. There is no preferred format although a columnar style is often used with columns for a narrative explanation of the assigned task, the completion date, and the name of the accountant assigned to the task.

The completed assignment list is usually issued one or two months before fiscal year-end to every employee assigned to complete one or more tasks. The manual is sometimes assembled in cooperation with the independent auditors, and working papers or schedules needed by them are included as tasks. The year-end manual is discussed in detail in Chapter 5.

THE DATA PROCESSING MANUAL

The fifth manual to be discussed is the data processing manual. This manual has limited distribution, principally the general accounting staff members who are responsible for submitting forms and data to computer operations for data entry, processing, storage, and retrieval of the data for accounting use. Primary users are the data control clerks responsible for accumulating the information, submitting it for processing, and reviewing the output for accuracy and consistency.

This manual is unique in that it contains both forms descriptions and procedures. It may also contain details of file record contents and codes used, descriptions of output reports, and the data and calculations used to report each item on an output information report.

An example of one section of a data processing manual is clearly shown in an accounts receivable operation. Input records consist of sales invoices, cash receipt records, debit and credit memos, and so forth. One output is an aging report with several columns of descriptive data (customer, region, office, type, credit rating, address, limit, etc.), and columns of aged invoices. Each data field can be described by the contents of the field or fields of data in the computer file that were used to print the report.

Developing The Data Processing Manual

This manual is the most definitive and exacting of all the manuals. If an accounting system or subsystem is purchased, this manual should be provided by the vendor of the purchased system. Even then, the user manual will have to be customized to the installation, a process almost as difficult as writing the manual from scratch.

This manual has two or three sections. Required sections are the input record layouts and descriptions, and the computer file record layout with acceptable coding formats. Descriptions of computer-processed output reports may be optional; however, they are useful when employee turnover may be high or when the auditors arrive.

Many recently developed accounting systems utilize a data base dictionary program which describes data segments, fields, contents, and codes permitted, along with a detailed record description showing field sizes, locations, and codes used by the computer specialist or programmer. Many provide a detailed data dictionary for the accounting users of the system.

This manual requires cooperation between accounting and data processing personnel. To be successful, it must contain computer information written in accounting language. Further discussion and examples are in Chapter 6.

USER MANUAL

The user manual is most useful in enterprises where nonaccountants initiate or prepare original accounting forms or documents that provide accounting information to the general accounting operation. Perfect examples are the hiring or termination of an employee. Usually the immediate supervisor initiates both these actions, followed by a form that eventually gets the employee on or off the payroll.

This manual can be general in nature or may be specific abstracts from the general manual, forms manual, and policy/procedure statements. Other examples of user manual procedures are petty cash reports, receiving reports, shipping documents, branch sales and activity, requests for special vendor payments such as subscriptions, dues, itinerant labor, contractual services performed locally, and so on.

Developing the User Manual

As the user manual consists of parts extracted from the accounting manual and the forms manual, it is usually easy to prepare. This manual is designed for mass distribution to departments and individuals who use or prepare accounting documents, initiate account transaction coding, have some knowledge of the accounting process, or receive summary accounting reports.

The user manual has a listing of income and expense account numbers and codes, and descriptions and use of accounting forms. It can be used as a training tool for nonaccounting supervisors, secretaries, and others who are involved in adding or checking data on accounting input documents.

User manuals seldom exceed 50 to 100 pages. Further discussion of the user manual is in Chapter 7.

INFORMATION RELEASE SYSTEM

The information release system is not a manual at all. It is the public relations document of the accounting department. An information release (IR) relates to an event, either internal or external to the accounting department. In style it is similar to a press release or media release as it has a meaningful subject or title and a brief description of the event or action being announced.

Internally, an IR may announce a new addition to the staff, either by transfer or new hire, or the resignation or termination of an employee. It may announce the arrival of the independent auditors and their names and titles, or a minor change in an accounting procedure not significant enough to require changes in existing manuals. It may announce the holiday schedule, overtime requirements, and any other event that will have some effect on the accounting operation.

Externally, the IR is sometimes used as a transmittal cover sheet to announce a major accounting manual change, a new policy/procedure statement, physical inventory dates to departments involved, and so forth.

The information release is a simple, powerful tool to keep employees fully informed of company or department actions that may affect their job and their attitude toward their employer. The information release system is discussed in Chapter 8 with examples.

THE TOTAL PICTURE

Developing one or more of the manuals described so far is a time-consuming task; however, it should never be burdensome. A leader for each manual is suggested and target dates should be planned.

The ideal situation would be to present a draft of each new topic to all the present and future users of that subject and have them comment on its readability and usefulness. Since that is not possible, the writer must try to put himself or herself into the position of the users at all times.

Before starting, and frequently during the development and writing stages, some of the general questions to be asked are:

1. Have I explained new or unusual terms the first time they are used? Terms like lcl, F.O.B., or encumbrance have no meaning to the first-time user. (See Chapter 9 for avoiding repetitive use of a term, phrase, or proper noun.)

2. Is my writing too complex? If the writer's vocabulary is unusually large, the writing may be at too high a level for many of the users. However, there may be some fear of using a bigger and better vocabulary, even if the use is correct and meaningful to the readers. Understanding is far more important than the correctness of the language.

3. Am I using complex words? Use short, meaningful words that the reader can relate to.

4. Am I adding extra words such as "the," "that," or "which" when they need not be used?

5. Am I using passive verbs? Use active verbs. For example, "Here is" can replace opening verbiage such as "In reply to your letter of the 16th."

6. Have I expressed my thoughts in the same manner I would when speaking?

7. Do I start with a problem or do I hit the reader with a solution when the reader may not know what the problem is or was?

STYLE AND MECHANICS

Presentation is also important. Many manuals are broken into very small sections and each section starts with a complicated, unnecessary standard heading. Some headings use a third of a page or more to show distribution, several approvals, more than one date, and so forth.

I use a maximum 6-line heading regardless of the type of procedure, release, manual, or policy:

1. The item type, such as administrative release, chart of accounts, procedure, policy/procedure statement, or handbook.

2. A retrieval or reference number so the reader can refer to the specific publication.

3. Pages. "Page 1 of 15" on the first page tells the reader the length of the document. Each subsequent page is numbered 2 of 15, 3 of 15, and so on. The reader knows if a page is missing or if only the first few pages were received.

4. Issue date or effective date.

5. Originator, which may be a person, a department, or a total unit within the organization. The originator is the source of the information.

6. Supersedes. By entering a retrieval or reference number, the user knows the replaced item is no longer effective. Indexing will be discussed later.

Some organizations use color to designate different manuals, for example, blue for policy, pink for a personnel handbook, yellow for accounting. While color adds a nice touch it sometimes becomes restrictive and may complicate photocopying or later printing.

Numbering each copy of a manual, unless absolutely necessary, should be avoided. Numbering implies confidentiality and some degree of importance which may not be the case. Besides, the issuer must maintain a permanent record of the numbers and recipients. Changes make such updating onerous and, sometimes, quickly obsolete.

Avoid unusual art work or type styles. These may become difficult to continue over a long period. Strive for consistency in overall appearance by selecting a common typewriter element or word processing print wheel such as Courier 10 or Prestige 12 or 72. Do not use all-capital, computer-like printing or fancy typewriter script styles as these are tiresome and difficult to read. Also avoid photocopy reductions whenever possible. When a procedure begins to look like the directions on a small patent medicine bottle or a phone book the material will not be read.

For cost savings, avoid booklet styles with covers, spiral bindings, or center staples. Most manuals will require partial updating, and bound or fastened materials cannot be updated by section very easily. Manuals are not generally available to the outside public, customers, vendors, and so forth, and generally there is little public relations value in a working, internal document or manual.

CHAPTER 2
GENERAL ACCOUNTING MANUAL: I'VE GOT THE WHOLE WORLD

The general accounting manual is the heart of the accounting documentation. It is here that the system is described in enough detail for a trained accountant to prepare the proper coding for any acceptable accounting transaction. This manual contains the chart of accounts, described as the account numbers with meaningful accounting descriptions. For instance, if all cash entries, deposits, or checks, are to be recorded in account 100 and all amounts due from a customer are to be entered in account 200, we are beginning to prepare a chart of accounts. To make reference easier, a tabular display is used.

Account Number	Account Name
100	Cash in bank
200	Accounts receivable

The chart is normally divided into asset, liability, ownership, income, and expense groups. Account numbers should be assigned in some logical order with provision for future expansion. Account numbers can vary from three digits (probably the minimum for any business) to 20 or more. For simplicity, Figure 2.1 at the end of this chapter shows a 7-digit code, structured 1-3-3 for branch, department, and object, respectively. Figure 2.2 is a summary of account coding for a college or university. It could be used for governmental accounting.

Account attributes to be described are plant number, department, location, branch, type of account in governmental accounting, type of income or expense, and so forth. Some of the more common coding structures by type of organization are:

General Industry
Division
Plant
Department
Object

Government and Education
Fund Type
Department
Object

Retail
Store
Department
Object

Similar businesses and organizations tend to develop similar charts of account. As a test, define the following terms:

Encumbrance
Third-party reimbursements
Endowment
78ths method
Markup
Function
Origination fee

Each one is a commonly used expression in a specific industry. *Encumbrance* is fully understood by any accountant in government or education to be a purchase commitment. *Third-party reimbursement* is a hospital receivable due from an insurance company rather than from the patient. *Endowment*, used in higher education, is defined as an investment pool which permits only the investment income to be expended. The *78ths method* is the method of determining the interest earned on installment loans in a financial institution. *Markup* is used in the retail industry. *Function*, used in higher education, is understood to mean the recognized purpose of the account such as instruction, research, scholarship, and so on. *Origination fee* is used in mortgage banking and real estate operations to define the fee charged to the borrower to prepare and handle the mortgage papers.

The only purpose of this exercise is to emphasize that every business organization develops unique terminology to express more clearly its operations to the people in that organization. To the outsider, these terms are buzzwords or jargon. It is mandatory that the accountant preparing a chart of accounts and the related definitions of those accounts explain every unusual or unique term or expression used in the accounting operations of the organization.

The accountants are the interface between the company's operations and those outside the company who are interested in the company, usually in terms of dollars or production figures. These interested parties may be stockholders, lenders, auditors, regulatory agencies, and so forth, and it is the accountant's duty to define one to the other and be fully understood when doing so.

DEVELOPING THE CHART OF ACCOUNTS

The beginning of a chart of accounts for a typical organization starts with a general description of the numbering scheme and how the different numbering units are used. This is followed by the permitted codes in each group of numbers.

Account coding structures can be very elaborate. In addition to location (store, branch, division, city), coding can define product lines, expense groups, departments, buildings, and so forth. Account numbers with four or five sets of one to five digits each, a total of 12 to 25 numbers, are not unusual today. The permitted numbers in each set should be listed in the chart of accounts. Computer editing programs are usually designed to reject any numbers not permitted in the system and produce a specific error message for each number group error.

Placement of numbers should have some meaning to the users of the system and the numbers should be uniform across all reporting units of the total organization. If one unit does not need all the numbers, it is relatively easy to replace the unused sets with zeros.

In the account number xx-xx-xxx-xxx-x-xxxx, the various sets are defined as follows:

xx	Corporation
xx	Division
xxx	Location
xxx	Product line

x	Type of account (asset, liability, income, expense)
xxxx	Account name

Error messages would be reported as follows:

12-02-112-035-6-6250	Corporation 12 not in file.
02-02-112-035-6-6250	Location 112 not shown in Corporation 02.
02-02-122-035-6-6250	Account 6250 not permitted in this unit.

Account number documentation is very important in coding transactions, auditing and reviewing data entry transactions, and correcting coding errors reported by the computer editing programs. In the illustration, if there were no division numbers in this subsidiary corporation, the division number would always be zeros.

DEFINITIONS

The chart of accounts is the skeletal structure of the system. If only accountants used the system, few definitions would be needed. However, clerks should have some means of understanding the basics of transaction coding, and other managers need to know why something is recorded as it is. For training and to answer inquiries, we must add the muscle to the skeleton and this muscle consists of good definitions of every permitted account used in the system.

Definitions should be concise and meaningful. One or two sentences of definition are usually sufficient. The definition tells the user what can be recorded in a specific numbered account. However, if there is a confusing account usage, or if repetitive coding errors are being made, the definition can also inform the reader of what may *not* be recorded in this account.

Since the definitions are reference sources, they should be developed for quick and easy look-up. The account number and name should be on one line and may be underlined for emphasis. The definition should be indented slightly and follow a consistent pattern. If the account is part of a group, the group title should be at the top of the group or page. An example of definitions follow:

ASSETS
100—Cash on Hand
> Includes the petty cash and change funds held in various departments. This account is used only when a new fund is initiated or an existing fund terminated.

102—Cash in Bank
> Includes all cash held in the operating bank account of the branch. All withdrawals by check and deposits are recorded here. The reported balances are supported by a bank reconcilement prepared monthly.

Although this type of documentation appears to be elementary to the trained accountant, it is invaluable as a training tool for the clerical staff and as a source of answers to inquiries. In a large organization, there may be several hundred codes and combinations of codes. State and local governments and educational institutions typically have several funds, hundreds of reporting departments (even as high as 1000 or more), and as many as 200 or more revenue and expenditure codes. With account coding structures of a dozen or more numbers, memory cannot be relied on for accuracy in coding transactions. Under these circumstances, the chart of accounts is in constant use and frequent references are made to the definitions. Figure 2.3, at the end of the chapter, illustrates typical expense code definitions.

JOB CONTROL INSTRUCTIONS

If your accounting data is processed through a remote computer facility, there must be some communication method set up so accounting personnel can instruct the computer operator to process a specific job. Some jobs can be run at any time; others must be run in a specific sequence. In either case, the accounting department must control when each program is to be run. To accomplish this, it is the usual practice to fill in a job control card, processing card, run card, or whatever, which will provide the operator with the name of the system, the job number, date to be placed on the output, and possibly one of several selection codes such as sort sequence of output, records to be selected, and so forth.

The batch cards, as they are often called, are relatively simple. Some installations use terminal input screens to activate the processing of accounting programs. These screens are the same as batch cards and these program batch cards or screens should be described in the general accounting manual.

This section of the general accounting manual should follow a consistent pattern in describing each program and the related operating instructions. Unless the programs are closely related in sequence, each program should start on a new page. In this way, if different data control clerks are responsible for different sets of computer programs, the pages related to each of the clerks can be distributed individually.

JOB DESCRIPTION PAGES

Each job page should be titled with the system name such as "General Ledger" or "Payroll," exact job name, and program number. Although job control records can vary significantly, they usually follow a general pattern. Many use lines describing the input requested, followed by the required number of spaces to enter the data. The first line is usually the name and number of the program to be executed. One line may be the date of processing in a fixed order such as month, day, year, normally shown as MMDDYY. Following that information, there may be a provision for record selection such as "1" for all records, "2" for certain departments, and "3" for processing totals only. If "2" were selected, in this case, then there would be spaces provided to enter the departments or the range of departments such as "From" followed by the first department number, and "To" followed by the last department number to be selected.

A copy of the actual job control record or screen should be included in the instructions or attached thereto as shown in Figure 2.4 at the end of the chapter. The best job control or batch sheet contains the instructions on the face of the sheet so they are available every time the form is used.

If the company has a separate Data Processing Manual as described in Chapter 6, this section of the General Accounting Manual may be included as a separate section in that manual.

INPUT RECORD AND SCREEN LAYOUTS

The general accounting manual should include the layout of the input records or screen layouts for each type of transaction which may be entered as a transaction record into the computerized accounting system. Only a brief description will be discussed here as detailed descriptions of input layouts will be covered in Chapter 6.

The layout for accounting input records follows a fairly standard method developed in the early 1960s and which has remained relatively unchanged. Most input records include, as a minimum, the record type, the full accounting code distribution, a description of the transaction, a reference number such as check number, purchase order number, receipt, and so forth, the amount of the transaction, and whether the amount is a debit or credit.

One of the features that distinguishes a good, workable, computerized accounting system is the similarity of accounting record layouts for all input data. To determine the similarity, the record layouts should be listed in the 80-column format to be described later. Then review the layouts with these questions in mind.

1. Are identically described fields in the same location in each record?
2. Does each type of record handle all transactions of that subsystem, or must the user (accountant) switch to another layout for unusual transactions?
3. Is the description field adequate for the majority of transactions?
4. Are only one or two record layouts significantly different from the majority? If so, can these be changed for standardization?

While this section is a simple discussion of the maintenance of record layout documentation in the accounting process, it is a relatively important one. Accounting must maintain enough documentation to enable its personnel to have access to and understand how the system works. Accounting system changes are inevitable and this type of documentation permits the accountants to suggest and define possible or required changes in the existing systems.

ACCOUNTING PRINCIPLES AND PROCEDURES

To provide uniform financial transaction recording and reporting, many affiliated companies and not-for-profit institutions prepare manuals of uniform financial reporting. It is here that the accounting principles controlling the accounting results are described. This manual can be a separate manual in the accounting operation or it may be incorporated into the general accounting manual. The information here relates to the standards of financial reporting. There may be different manuals for foreign operations.

The effort to standardize fiscal year reporting is based on several principles, namely:

1. Requiring consistency among organizations and similar institutions to report like items in a similar manner. Examples would be product-line reporting, specified treatment of specific types of revenues, treatment of reserves for loan losses in a financial institution, and so on.
2. Requiring consistency in reporting from year to year and the use of comparative financial data.
3. Matching revenues and related expenditures based on the definition of a transaction event. Examples would be the reporting of warranty costs, depreciation and amortization policy, or the expensing of estimated cost of accidents which have been incurred but not reported to an insurance company at the close of its fiscal year.
4. Defining any restrictions or prohibitions which may conflict with generally accepted accounting principles.
5. Defining how revenues and expenses will be reported.
6. Avoiding inflation of reported revenues and expenses when one unit sells goods or services to a related unit.

The writing of principles must be very explicit—both what is required and what is not permitted. Avoid unusual or local terminology unless definitions are provided. Any deviations or exceptions, even minor ones, should be clearly noted. Reference to laws, regulations, pronouncements by regulatory agencies such as the Securities and Exchange Commission (SEC), the Financial Accounting Standards Board (FASB), the Government Accounting Standards Board (GASB), and the American Institute of Certified Public Accountants' audit guides and pronouncements should be referenced when necessary or when they provide additional detailed commentary too voluminous to be included in the manual itself.

BASIC STATEMENTS AND OTHER FINANCIAL INFORMATION

Copies of the statement of financial condition or balance sheet, the statement of operations, and pro forma footnotes to the financial statements should be included in the manual. The terminology used in the statements should be carefully written. For instance, if the accounts receivable were all from the federal government, then the title should be "Accounts receivable from federal government" and not the generic "Accounts receivable." If long-term debt is a mortgage, then it should be described as such.

If supplementary financial information is normally included with the basic financial statements, then these should be shown and the contents described. Examples might be a 10-year operating history, product-line reporting details, and, in not-for-profit institutions, details of assets, debt, investments, construction projects, and expenditure reports by function or department.

CHART OF ACCOUNTS

SM CORPORATION

January 1, 1987

The accounting structure at SM Corporation consists of seven digits in a 1-3-3 pattern:

1 - 234 - 567

1   The first digit indicates the branch. Normally, this digit would not be necessary but the Jackson Accounting Office maintains records for two branches and it is necessary at all times to keep the transactions separated.

234   These three digits are used to show the department within each branch. Departments vary among branches.

567   These digits are used to indicate the account number. Digit 5 indicates the type of account, as follows:

1 - Asset accounts
2 - Liability accounts
3 - Capital stock and earnings accounts
4 - Income accounts
5 - Expense accounts

Digits 6 and 7 indicate the specific accounts within each group.

Branch Codes

1 - Main Office, Hattiesburg
2 - Biloxi
3 - Oxford
4 - Starkville
5 - Jackson-North
6 - Jackson-North

Department Codes

100 - Office
200 - Outside Sales Department
300 - Store
400 - Outside Yard
500 - Custom Shop
600 - Rental Equipment
900 - Shipping and Delivery

Figure 2.1. Account structure for a small company with branch operations.

Account Codes

Asset Accounts

        100 - Cash on hand
        102 - Cash in bank
        110 - Customer Receivables - Wholesale
        111 - Customer Receivables - Retail
        120 - Inventory - Building supplies
        125 - Inventory - Retail merchandise
        127 - Inventory - Custom Shop
        130 - Prepaid expenses and deferred charges
        150 - Land
        151 - Building and building equipment
        152 - Vehicles
        153 - Store fixtures and equipment
        154 - Rental equipment
        161 - Allowance for depreciation - Building and
                building equipment
        162 - Allowance for depreciation - Vehicles
        163 - Allowance for depreciation - Store fixtures and
                equipment
        164 - Allowance for depreciation - Rental equipment

Liability Accounts

        201 - Accrued payroll
        210 - Accounts payable
        220 - Accrued expenses
        230 - Federal income taxes (Main Office only)
        235 - State income taxes (Main Office only)
        240 - Unearned income and deposits
        250 - Current portion of long-term debt
        280 - Long-term debt - Mortgage
        285 - Long-term debt - Banks

Capital Stock and Earnings Accounts

        300 - Capital stock issued (Main Office only)
        310 - Paid-In Capital (Main Office only)
        320 - Treasury Stock (Main Office only)
        350 - Retained Earnings

Income Accounts

        400 - Sales
        410 - Sales Returns and Allowances
        430 - Income from shipping and delivery
        440 - Income from rental equipment
        490 - Other income

Figure 2.1. Continued.

Expense Accounts

    500 - Cost of goods sold

    510 - Salaries - Office
    511 - Salaries - General
    515 - Fringe benefit costs

    520 - Depreciation - Buildings
    521 - Rental - Real Estate
    522 - Utility costs
    523 - Property taxes

    530 - Advertising
    531 - Travel
    532 - Advertising printing
    535 - Bad debts

    540 - Depreciation - Vehicles
    541 - Depreciation - Equipment
    542 - Depreciation - Rental Equipment

    550 - Consumable supplies
    552 - Legal and audit expense
    554 - Other taxes and licenses
    556 - Insurance
    558 - Other expense

    590 - Income tax expense (Main Office only)
    591 - Interest income
    592 - Interest expense

Account Code definitions are in Appendix A.

Figure 2.1. Continued

SUMMARY OF ACCOUNT CODING

The account coding structure consists of 18 digits with each digit or group of digits having a specific meaning.

Positions	Purpose
1-4	Fund/General Ledger Code
5-8	Revenue Source/Expenditure Object Code
9-15	Account Number
	9-10 Major Function
	11 Major Function
	12-13 School, College, Division
	14-15 Department
16-18	Restricted/Designated Project Number

Positions
1 - 2 = Fund

10	General Fund	60	Plant Unexpended
20	Auxiliary	61	Plant Renewals and Replacements
25	Designated	62	Plant Indebtedness
30	Restricted	63	Plant-Investment in Plant
40	Loan	70	Agency
50	Endowment		

3 - 4 = General Ledger

XX11	Cash in Banks
XX12	Cash in Offices
XX13	Temporary Investments
XX14	Accounts Receivable
XX15	Notes Receivable
XX16	Inventory
XX17	Expenditures - Deferred
XX19	Fixed Assets
XX21	Accounts Payable
XX23	Bonds Payable
XX24	Revenues - Deferred
XX26	Fund Balances - Allocated
XX27	Fund Balances - Unallocated
XX30	Revenues - Estimated
XX35	Revenues - Realized
XX40	Expenditures - Current
XX41	Expenditures - Prior year
XX45	Budgets - Current
XX46	Budgets - Prior Year
XX50	Encumbrance - Current
XX51	Encumbrance - Prior Year
XX55	Unassigned Budget Balance

Figure 2.2. Summary of account coding.

5 - 8 = Revenue Sources

0101	- 0199	Student Fees
0301	- 0330	State Appropriations
0501	- 0560	Federal Grants and Contracts
0601	- 0699	State Grants and Contracts
0708	- 0718	Local Government Grants and Contracts
0810	- 0884	Private Gifts, Grants and Contracts
0900		Endowment Income
1001	- 1043	Sales and Services of Ecucational Activities
1101	- 1157	Other Sources
1201	- 1202	Transfers between funds and within fund
1301	- 1399	Sales and Services - Auxiliary
1801		Agency Deposits
8030	- 8053	Loans Additions
9999		Closing Entry

5 - 8 = Expenditure Object Codes

1100	- 1899	Salaries
2100	- 2899	Wages
3910	- 3980	Fringe Benefits
4010	- 4070	Travel
5110	- 5995	Contractual Services
6010	- 6495	Commodities
6500	- 6900	Merchandise for Resale
7110	- 7500	Loan and Plant Fund
8110	- 8290	Capital Outlay
9100	- 9200	Transfers Out

9 - 15 = Account Numbers

01XXXXX	Instruction
02XXXXX	Research
03XXXXX	Public Service
04XXXXX	Academic Service
05XXXXX	Student Services
06XXXXX	Institutional Support
07XXXXX	Operation and Maintenance of Plant
08XXXXX	Scholarships and Fellowships
09XXXXX	Mandatory Transfers
10XXXXX	Non-Mandatory Transfers
11XXXXX	Auxiliary Enterprises
15XXXXX	Loan Funds
17XXXXX	Plant Funds
18XXXXX	Agency Funds

16 - 18 = Project Numbers for Funds 25 and 30

Digit 1 is fiscal year project started, 6 is 1985-86.
Digits 2-3 are assigned sequentially from 01 to 99.

Figure 2.2. Continued.

EXPENDITURE OBJECT CODES - 1

1000 SALARIES

Salaries represent amounts of fixed compensation paid regularly for services.

    1100   Executive, Administrative, and Managerial
    1200   Faculty
    1300   Professional Non-faculty
    1400   Clerical and Secretarial
    1500   Technical and Paraprofessional
    1600   Skilled Crafts
    1700   Service/Maintenance
    1800   Students

2000 WAGES

Wages represent amounts of compensation for services paid according to contract on an hourly, daily, or piecework basis.

    2100   Executive, Administrative, and Managerial
    2200   Faculty
    2300   Professional Non-faculty
    2400   Clerical and Secretarial
    2500   Technical and Paraprofessional
    2600   Skilled Crafts
    2700   Service/Maintenance
    2800   Students

3000 FRINGE BENEFITS

    3910   Employees' Retirement Matching
          The institution's portion of the contribution to the State Employees' Retirement System. Current rate is 8.75%.

    3920   FICA Matching
          The institution's matching contribution for FICA.

    3930   Workers' Compensation
          The cost of workers' compensation paid to the Insurer.

    3940   Health Insurance Contribution
          The portion of health insurance premiums paid by the institution.

    3950   Group Life Insurance
          The institution's portion of group life insurance paid for employees.

    3970   Unemployment Tax
          The institution's payment of unemployment tax to the State.

Figure 2.3. Typical expense code definitions.

4000 TRAVEL

4001 TRAVEL AND SUBSISTENCE

4010 Meals and Lodging
This includes meals and lodging costs (hotel, motel, etc.) in accordance with institutional policy for reimbursement. Per diem allowances for meals and lodging are included here.

4020 Travel in Private Vehicle
This includes travel in employee-owned vehicle at the currently-approved mileage rate.

4030 Travel in Rented Vehicle
This includes daily car rental from outside companies. See 4050 for motor pool charges.

4040 Travel in Public Carrier
This includes air, bus, and train travel.

4050 Travel in Motor Pool Vehicles
This includes charges for use of company-owned vehicles (motor pool) at the approved rates. Costs of air travel for company-owned airplane are charge here.

4060 Other Travel Costs
This includes incidental expenses such as separate tips, telephone, taxi, tolls, and parking. Tips on meals are included inmeal costs.

4070 Conference and Registration Fees
This includes conference and registration fees for seminars, workshops, conferences, and similar meetings. Tuition for schools such as NACUBO workshops or training sessions is included here. If meals and/or lodging included in the fee cannot be separated, they are charged here.

Figure 2.3. Continued.

5000 CONTRACTUAL SERVICES

5100 GRANTS, SCHOLARSHIPS AND AWARDS

5110 Grants
This includes financial aid payments to students from federal and state financial aid programs such as BEOG, SEOG, SSIG, and so forth.

5120 Fellowships
This includes specific grants to individuals to cover specific tuition and other educational costs. Graduate fellowships are charged here if no services are performed and the fellowships are non-taxable.

5130 Scholarships
This includes specific scholarships for tuition, fees, board, room and incidental educational costs.

5140 Awards
Cash awards to students for achievement, and the cost of trophies, certificates and so forth for academic achievement are included here.

5200 COMMUNICATIONS AND TRANSPORTATION OF COMMODITIES

5210 Postage and Post Office Charges
This includes postage charges for mailing.

5220 Telephone Local Service
This includes the basic monthly charges for all phones. See 5240 for maintenance and installation.

5230 Telephone Long Distance
This includes the charges for all long distance services, including WATS line or other similar services, line rentals, and telegraph charges.

5240 Telephone Installation and Maintenance
This includes the charges for installation of phones and maintenance of phone system.

5250 Cable TV
This includes all costs associated with the installation and periodic payments for cable TV service. Also included are any costs associated with the installation or any special equipment rental.

5260 Transportation of Things
This includes all freight costs including express delivery.

5000 CONTRACTUAL SERVICES - CONTINUED

5300 UTILITIES

5310 Electricity
This includes the cost of electricity for light, air conditioning and so forth.

5320 Heat
This includes the cost of natural gas, fuel oil and coal for heat or steam generation.

5330 Water
This includes the charges for water and sewer use.

5340 Sewage
This includes any separately-charged costs for sewage disposal.

5350 Garbage Disposal
This includes any costs related directly to garbage disposal.

5400 PUBLIC INFORMATION

5410 Advertising
This includes the cost for classified advertising for employee hiring, required advertising for publishing bids for purchasing and so forth. Printing costs are included in the 6100 series.

5420 Publicity and Public Information
This includes the cost of radio, television and live shows promoting the company as a whole. Layout and copy costs and special art work are included here. Printing costs are included in the 6100 series and direct advertising in 5410 above.

Figure 2.3. Continued.

5000 CONTRACTUAL SERVICES - CONTINUED

5500 RENTS

    5510 Rental of Buildings and Floor Space
        This includes payments to others for buildings, rooms for
        events, and floor space in buildings for special events.
        Rental of housing facilities and meeting rooms is included
        here.

    5535 Rental of Computer Software
        This includes the rental and/or lease cost of computer
        software packages to be run on equipment identified in
        object 5540.

    5540 Rental of EDP and Computer Equipment
        This includes the rental of computer and computer-related
        equipment, including payments on lease-purchase equipment
        not capitalized. Examples are computer hardware, terminals,
        word processing equipment, computer control equipment and
        any other equipment.

    5590 Other Rental
        This includes any rental which cannot be recorded in other
        rental accounts.

5600 REPAIRS AND MAINTENANCE

    5610 Repair and Service Streets and Parking Lots
        This includes repairs and other maintenance on roads,
        streets, drives, and parking lots.

    5620 Repairing and Servicing - Buildings and Grounds
        This includes wages and material costs of repairing, cleaning,
        and maintaining buildings and grounds. Outside contractor
        costs for this purpose are recorded here.

    5650 Repairing and Servicing Office Equipment
        This includes the costs of repairing and maintaining office
        equipment such as typewriters, calculators, terminals,
        furniture, chairs, desks. It does not include telephone
        maintenance or annual maintenance contracts.

    5660 Maintenance Contracts - Equipment
        This includes the annual contract costs for maintenance
        contracts on typewriters, calculators, data processing
        equipment, scientific equipment and so forth.

    5690 Repairing and Servicing Other Equipment
        This includes the costs of repairing and servicing machinery,
        engineering equipment, laboratory equipment, shop equipment,
        and other equipment not classified in other repair accounts.

Figure 2.3. Continued.

5000 CONTRACTUAL SERVICES - CONTINUED

5700 FEES, PROFESSIONAL

5710 Engineering
This includes out-of-pocket fees for professional engineering services.

5730 Auditing Fees
This includes the costs of auditing fees to outside independent auditors. Other incidental costs of the audit may be charged here. Examples are supplies, telephone, postage and printing charges directly related to the audit.

5740 Medical
This includes direct payments to others for medical services, including pre-employment physicals and lab tests.

5760 Legal Fees
This includes all fees paid to attorneys, appraisers, notaries, and witnesses, in addition to court costs and legal document recording fees.

5770 Laboratory and Testing Fees
This includes outside laboratory fees and fees paid to outside agencies for testing services other than medical services.

5780 Consultant Expense Reimbursements
This includes travel costs paid to consultants and other non-employees. See 5860 for employee recruitment travel.

5790 Other Professional Fees and Services
This includes fees to individuals not included in 5710 to 5780.

Figure 2.3. Continued.

5000 CONTRACTUAL SERVICES - CONTINUED

5800 OTHER CONTRACTUAL SERVICES

5810   Insurance and Fidelity Bonds
This includes the costs of all casualty and liability insurance and fidelity bond coverages.

5820   Dues
This includes approved dues for company memberships in professional organizations.

5830   Laundry, Dry Cleaning and Towel Service
The costs of laundry, dry cleaning services, and towel service are charged to this account.

5840   Subscriptions
This includes the cost of subscriptions to newspapers, magazines and periodicals not charged to libraries.

5870   Computer Software Acquisitions
This includes the initial cost of acquiring operating or systems software packages. Included is the purchase price, freight or shipping, if any, manuals, if separately billed, and other related costs except salaries and wages. See 5880 for relatd annual maintenance fees for software.

5880   Computer Software Maintenance
This includes the annual maintenance fees to maintain purchased software systems. These fees cover updates and corrections to the system.

5890   Other Contractual Services
This includes any contractual services which cannot be properly coded in other accounts in this series. The administrative charge for on-campus use of computer facilities is recorded here.

5891   Provision for Bad Debts
This includes the amounts of accounts receivable written off and the provision required to increase or decrease the allowance for uncollectable accounts at the end of the fiscal year. Any recoveries of bad debts previously written off are credited to this account.

5892   Cash Over and Short
This includes cash amounts over and short to balance deposits with recorded receipts.

Figure 2.3. Continued.

6000 COMMODITIES

6001 MAINTENANCE MATERIALS AND SUPPLIES - BUILDING, GROUNDS, IMPROVEMENTS

6010   Land Improvement Supplies
This includes aggregates, asphalt, cement, joint fillers, curbing, and so forth used in repairing or replacing roads, sidewalks, and parking lots on company property.

6020   Building Construction Supplies
This includes lumber, caulking, steel, fabricated metal parts, flooring, ceiling tiles, plaster, lime, and other materials used in repairing or renovating buildings.

6030   Paints and Preservatives
This includes all interior and exterior paints, wood preservatives, and road striping materials used for remodeling or maintenance.

6040   Hardware, Plumbing, and Electrical Supplies
This includes all hardware, plumbing parts or accessories, and electrical wire or parts, including lights used in maintaining or renovating buildings.

6050   Custodial Supplies and Cleaning Agents
This includes all custodial supplies of an expendable nature such as cloths, brooms, cleaning compounds, mops, pails, and so forth.

6090   Other Maintenance Materials
This includes maintenance materials not classified in accounts 6010 to 6050.

6100 PRINTING AND OFFICE SUPPLIES

6110   Printing, Binding and Padding
This includes the cost of printing, binding and padding paid to outside contractors or the Printing Shop on campus.

6120   Duplication and Reproduction
This includes the paper, toner and other supplies used in various offices' copy mahcines (Xerox, IBM, Canon, etc.).

6130   Office Supplies and Materials
This includes all office supplies and materials, such as pens, paper, pencils, adding machine tapes, staples, paper clips, in-out trays, and so forth, used in the normal course of business.

Figure 2.3. Continued.

6000 COMMODITIES - CONTINUED

6200 EQUIPMENT REPAIR PARTS, SUPPLIES AND ACCESSORIES

6210   Fuels
This includes vehicle fuels (gasoline, diesel fuel, propane) purchased from the institution's central service station or by credit card for motor pool vehicles and airplanes.

6220   Lubricating Oils and Greases
This includes lubricating oils and greases used for all vehicles and for machinery such as grounds equipment.

6230   Tires and Tubes
This includes the purchases of tires and tubes for all institution vehicles.

6240   Repair and Replacement Parts
This includes the purchases of vehicle and machinery repair and replacement parts and supplies.

6250   Shop Supplies
This includes the cost of shop supplies, such as shop rags, windshield cleaner, glues and cements, brushes, degreasers, solvents and so forth, used in equipment repair and maintenance operations.

6290   Other Equipment Repair Parts and Supplies
This includes repair parts and supplies not otherwise classfied in 6210 to 6290.

6400 OTHER SUPPLIES AND MATERIALS

6410   Small Tools
This includes small tools used in the operation.   Individual items must cost less than the capital outlay minimum.

6440   Food for Persons
Food purchases, other than travel meals for employees, are recorded here.   Examles are meals for employee meetings and food purchased for employee cafeteria.

6470   Fertilizer and Chemicals
This includes fertilizer for lawns and landscape plants. It also includes chemicals such as pesticides and other chemicals.

Figure 2.3. Continued.

DATA BASE MAINTENANCE

BATCH CONTROL FORM

	Number	Origin	Process Date		Trans. Count
B A T C H					
1 5	6 8	9 11	12	17	18 23

Field   Description

NUMBER: Enter the 3-digit number to identify the batch as it is processed.
                       Within a single update process, the same batch number can be used
                       only once.

ORIGIN: Enter any 3-character code which identifies the individual
                       preparing the batch.

PROCESS DATE: Enter today's date (MMDDYY) if the transactions within the batch
                       are to be processed during the current update process. If the
                       batch's contents are to be processed at some future time, enter
                       the date on which the transactions are to be processed.

TRANS COUNT: Enter the number of individual transactions which appear on the
                       forms in the batch. This number should not exceed 100.

Figure 2.4. A control form used to maintain batch control of computer transactions.

CHAPTER 3
POLICY/PROCEDURE
STATEMENTS:
YOU DO SOMETHING
TO ME

Policy. A definite course or method of action to guide and determine present and future decisions. Also, general goals and acceptable procedures.

Procedure. A particular way of accomplishing something, an established way of doing things, a series of steps followed in a definite regular order.

After the general accounting manual, the most important single documentation system for most organizations is the policy/procedure statement (P/PS) system. While P/PSs are issued singly and not as a manual, they accumulate and become a manual referred to by all levels of personnel in the organization.

It is this system that provides written company policy that governs the actions of the employees, and in which new or changed procedures are presented or old procedures eliminated. The use of the title *Policy/Procedure Statement* is deliberate. Almost every new policy developed within an organization causes some change in a current procedure or in a method of operating. Many procedures state or imply a policy change. The title covers both and eliminates the need to issue two documents: one with the broader policy change and another to explain the procedures which implement the policy.

An example of a policy/procedure statement release would be a new travel policy that changes a reimbursed mileage rate and sets a new per diem allowance for employees. The rate and the allowance are policy pronouncements; the implementation of changes in the travel expense report are procedural. Another example would be the statement concerning the control over the release of financial information. The P/PS would define the *policy* that such release to outside parties will be controlled and would specify the *procedural* method of control (who, when, and how).

PROCEDURE SYSTEM VERSUS POLICY/PROCEDURE STATEMENTS

If only procedures were to be documented, then *Policy/Procedure Statement* would be replaced with *Procedure*. A *procedure only* system implies a series of consecutive and related tasks by professional and clerical *named* positions. A P/PS, because of its policy nature, can identify the actual names of the people involved, while a procedural statement never shows names, only descriptive position titles.

Procedures also are oriented to numbered tasks accomplishing a specific function. They are not job descriptions, job outlines, policies, or form descriptions. Procedures name who and what, under captions such as "Employee" and "Task," or "Actor" and "Action." They document the flow of data and what each described station does to that data to process it and pass it forward to the next station.

Clerical procedure manuals are the most difficult and the most time-consuming to complete, if ever completed. A procedures manual may take one or two years to complete if every individual employee's job task is to be documented. The reason should be obvious. In addition to initiating, checking, approving, distributing, calculating, balancing, and other activities by many, many employees, there are many forms, many identifiable stations, and many departments involved. The average procedure, consisting of one accounting form being processed from initiation to final filing, may take 15 or 20 identifiable steps by a half-dozen or more clerical or approving stations.

A written procedure will fill one to two single-spaced, typewritten pages. The only method that produces consistent procedures is for a knowledgeable accountant to interview every person involved in processing a document from its beginning to its ending in the accounting cycle. The required interviewing, typing, editing, proofreading, printing, and publishing of a single procedure could consume at a minimum a week or more. A large accounting operation could have 100 or more separate procedures.

Procedures can follow several different layouts. Figure 3.1 shows who is involved

Procedure

- RETRIEVAL NO. 4005
- EFFECTIVE DATE August 15, 1985
- ORIGINATOR Business Office
- SUPERSEDES

THE UNIVERSITY OF SOUTHERN MISSISSIPPI

SUBJECT: CASH PROCEDURES-REGISTRATION

1. University Cashier

   Prepares a cash change fund sufficient for Registration. Gives to Main Cashier.

2. Main Cashier

   Signs receipt for cash. Prepares change drawer for each Station Cashier as the shifts begin. Has Station Cashier initial settlement sheet for receipt of change fund.

3. Station Cashier

   Opens station, collects cash, checks, and so forth. Prepares settlement sheet at close of shift. Brings drawer contents and settlement sheet to Main Cashier.

4. Main Cashier

   Counts cash in presence of Station Cashier, initials settlement sheet. Count shows amount of change fund and other cash. Returns change fund to Main Cashier Fund. Obtains acknowledgment of Station Cashier of count accuracy

   Prepares deposit ticket. Ticket may be for each Station Cashier fund or a combined ticket for several funds. Places deposit ticket (duplicate) and cash in bag for transport to bank.

5. University Cashier

   Takes deposit to bank. Has bank cashier count cash and initial deposit ticket.

6. Main Cashier

   Returns cash fund to University cashier at close of registration.

7. University Cashier

   Counts fund. Determines agreement with opening fund, signs settlement sheet, returns copy to Main Cashier. Places cash in main office funds.

Figure 3.1. Clerical procedure showing operations in narrative style by numbered positions.

by listing the job title in the heading, followed by a narrative task description. Figure 3.2 shows a columnar method with one column for the actor and another column for the numbered actions. *The New Playscript Procedure*, by Leslie H. Matthies (Office Publications, Inc., Stamford, Connecticut 06904) covers the development of this procedure method. Procedures are generally much more detailed and more restrictive in approach than the policy/procedure statements being discussed here.

In the research for this book, an operating procedure covering travel policy and rules was obtained from a major public institution. Each page was labeled *Operating Procedures* with three different titles for the three sections on authorization (19 pages), reimbursement (15 pages), and conference and convention travel (4 pages). These procedures were part of a much larger financial manual.

The heading of *each page* contained a letter denoting the series, a section number, a subject number (Dewey Decimal system), the page number, effective date, subject title, and one to three references to other sections of the series. In addition, every page ended with the statement that an asterisk denoted a change from the previous publication on this subject. Each of the three procedures had an approval signature at the end. Not only was the heading difficult to comprehend, the fact that it took 38 single-spaced, typewritten pages to inform employees of the travel policy was almost overwhelming. The whole package resembled a legal brief rather than a simple travel procedure. The policy/procedure statement system discussed in this chapter will be much simpler to write and easier to use.

DEVELOPING POLICY/PROCEDURE STATEMENTS

P/PSs are issued to specific employees at various intervals as required. Reasons for issuing a P/PS may be to explain a change in laws or regulations, or to define a regulatory agency pronouncement that the organization will, or must, adopt. It may be a change to an internal policy of long standing or a new form, a change in committee membership or lines of authority caused by reorganization, and so forth. Occasionally, a P/PS may be used as a cover letter to announce the issuance of a new manual, handbook, or a major announcement to selected employees. The P/PS system needs a distinctive letterhead to announce itself to the recipients as an important document. The standard heading should include the following minimum information.

> Official company logo
> Formal name of the company or institution
> Title *POLICY/PROCEDURE STATEMENT*
> Retrieval number for reference
> Number of pages
> Issue date or effective date
> Originator
> Reference to superseding a previous P/PS

THE UNIVERSITY OF SOUTHERN MISSISSIPPI

- RETRIEVAL NO.   4005
- EFFECTIVE DATE   August 15, 1985
- ORIGINATOR   Business Office
- SUPERSEDES

SUBJECT: CASH PROCEDURES-REGISTRATION

ACTOR		ACTION
University Cashier	1.	Prepares a cash change fund sufficient for Registration. Gives to Main Cashier.
Main Cashier	2.	Signs receipt for cash.
	3.	Prepares change drawer for each Station Cashier as the shifts begin. Has Station Cashier initial settlement sheet for receipt of change fund.
Station Cashier	4.	Opens station, collects cash, checks, and so forth.
	5.	Prepares settlement sheet at close of shift. Brings drawer contents and settlement sheet to Main Cashier.
Main Cashier	6.	Counts cash in presence of Station Cashier, initials settlement sheet. Count shows amount of change fund and other cash. Returns change fund to Main Cashier Fund. Obtains acknowledgment of Station Cashier of count accuracy.
	7.	Prepares deposit ticket. Ticket may be for each Station Cashier fund or a combined ticket for several funds.
	8.	Places deposit ticket (duplicate) and cash in bag for transport to bank.
University Cashier	9.	Takes deposit to bank. Has bank cashier count cash and initial deposit ticket.
Main Cashier	10.	Returns cash fund to University cashier at close of registration.
University Cashier	11.	Counts fund. Determines agreement with opening fund, signs settlement sheet, returns copy to Main Cashier. Places cash in main office funds.

Figure 3.2.   Clerical procedure in playscript format showing position titles and numbered tasks.

	Administrative Procedure	• RETRIEVAL NO.
		•
		• PAGE
		•
		• ISSUE DATE
		•
THE UNIVERSITY OF SOUTHERN MISSISSIPPI		• ORIGINATOR
		•
FINANCIAL AFFAIRS		• SUPERSEDES

SUBJECT:

Figure 3.3. Administrative Procedure with both institution name and department name.

If the P/PS system is to be used only by the financial operation of the company or organization, a descriptive department or function name may be added to the heading. Figure 3.3 illustrates an AP front sheet with both institution and department name.

Importance of Logo

The use of the company logo, if there is one, and the official name of the organization on the letterhead are very important employee relations tools. These make the P/PS *our* policy or procedure and not some boilerplate pilfered or adapted from another source. The top of the logo sets the upper limit for printing on this special front sheet. It is usually placed one-half inch from the top of a standard $8\frac{1}{2} \times 11$ sheet, and one full inch from the left edge of the sheet. This location sets the left margin at one inch for all narrative. The 1-inch margin is needed because P/PSs are permanent documents and are three-hole punched for retention in a three-ring binder.

Retrieval Numbers

P/PSs are released sporadically and consecutive page numbering would have no meaning. Also, a P/PS may be superseded and its removal would leave an unexplained gap in the page numbering. Thus an instantly recognizable number must be assigned to each P/PS when issued. This retrieval number should be on all pages of the release. An assigned series of five digits seems to be the most satisfactory numbering scheme. Because other systems yet to be discussed can also use retrieval numbers, an assignment of a fixed series to the P/PS system is suggested, usually 00001 to 09999, or 10000 to 19999. The use of a comma following the thousands position is discretionary; because the retrieval number is a reference number and not a "counting" number, the comma is usually left out. Retrieval numbers within one system are assigned when the document is approved and published.

Because the number will be used to index the system, someone must maintain a file of released P/PSs. This simple file may be maintained on 3 × 5 cards showing the retrieval number, date issued or effective date, the exact subject title, and if it superseded a prior retrieval number. The actual distribution may be listed here also.

Other Heading Information

Each page of a P/PS should be numbered. The use of "Page 1 of 5, 2 of 5, 3 of 5," and so on is the preferred page-numbering method. The first page denotes the number of pages that should be included and the reader is alerted quickly to whether a page is missing. Attachments, described on the last page of the statement, are never numbered as part of the P/PS.

Issue date is important. It should be the effective date of the policy/procedure statement. *Issue Date* is preferred because the body of the narrative may specify a past or future effective date, and the reader may be misled by the use of *Effective Date* in the heading.

The *Originator* section is used if the P/PS is to be related to a specific department or unit within a department. An accounting department usually consists of separate units such as payroll, accounts payable, accounts receivable, cashier, general ledger control, data entry, and so forth. The use of a descriptive unit name as the originator not only defines the audience for the release but may provide some overall meaning to the subject matter of the release. If the releases are to be segregated by specific department or unit, the 10,000 retrieval numbers can be further separated in units of 1000, and each series assigned, possibly as follows.

Accounting Unit	From—To
General ledger	10000—10999
Payroll	11000—11999
Accounts payable	12000—12999
Accounts receivable	13000—13999
Cashier	14000—14999
Budget	15000—15999
Inventory control	16000—16999
Future use	17000—19999

Because the only thing constant about accounting is change, there must be some means of deleting a previous P/PS documenting a prior policy or procedure now being changed. The use of *Supersedes* serves this purpose if the retrieval number of the prior release is printed here.

Subject

The last imprinted line on the preprinted P/PS front page is the word *Subject*. The use of good, simple, subject headings will help the reader of the policy/procedure statement. They should be descriptive without being too vague or wordy. Most subjects can be defined in five or six words or less. Remember, the subject printed here will appear in the index issued at some fixed future intervals and a meaningless subject description will not attract any readers. Avoid unusual words in the subject unless the words are part of that industry's terminology. Also remember that the heading has already told the reader that what follows is either policy or procedure, or both, is unique to this company, and was originated by a named department or unit. It would be redundant to state the subject as a *Payroll Change* when it came from the payroll department and the P/PS itself implies or denotes change.

Page 2 and subsequent pages have the retrieval number and the page number (2 of 5, 3 of 5, and so on) in the upper right corners.

THE BODY OF THE P/PS

The narrative information starts on the third line below the subject line. Margins on both sides and bottom are one inch. Pages 2 and beyond have one-inch margins on all four sides.

Although it can vary considerably, the general narrative pattern for a P/PS is an opening paragraph on the background of the subject and the existing problem. This first paragraph may be labeled *Background* or *Present Procedure*. This paragraph is followed by other paragraphs explaining the new policy or procedure.

If the P/PS subject is a new or replacement form, the purpose of the form and its contents are described as explained in Chapter 4 on the forms manual. The last paragraph may show the name and internal address or telephone number of the issuing unit if the reader needs additional information or explanation.

If there is an attachment, it is described at the end of the P/PS, using the exact major heading of the attachment. In some cases it may be desirable to show the distribution of the P/PS following the attachment line. If so, the word *Distribution:* is typed two spaces below the attachment line, followed by names or departments receiving this policy/procedure statement.

The finished draft is typed on the preprinted P/PS form, proofread carefully, and copies produced by photocopy or multilith. It should be issued on the issue date entered in the preprinted heading. More information on paper, print style, and other mechanical methods and procedures are covered in Chapter 10 on mechanics.

GENERAL POLICY/PROCEDURE STATEMENTS

Policy/procedure statements can be issued on any topic that may affect the organization. P/PSs will become the official voice of the company and they should not be used as a newsletter or the house publication for employees. If prepared carefully and published properly, they will be respected as the authoritative voice of company management. Following are examples of how four general P/PSs are developed, in what order the information is presented, and the probable distribution of each.

Example 1—Sales Department Reorganization

The first section always discusses the problem and/or the background of the topic. In this case, management felt the sales force was not covering adequately the needs of the three types of customers they dealt with. The company sells its products to original equipment manufacturers (OEM), to wholesale distributors, and to a few large regional retail operations in each sales district. Sales have fallen off and the managing committee has discussed the problem with the vice-president of sales. This information, and possibly more, would be presented in the opening section as background material.

The next section of the P/PS explains the action to be taken and how it is to be implemented. It has been decided to set up separate sales teams for each type of customer. The three large OEM companies would be assigned to three assistant vice-presidents, the distributors to the existing regional sales groups, and the large retail stores to a new retail sales group. To report the activities, three new cost centers must be set up for accounting. The centers would be:

230	Sales Costs—OEM Customers
240	Sales Costs—Distributor Customers
250	Sales Costs—Retail Customers

The P/PS might provide additional information on what costs would be reported in the new format and what internal reports would be prepared to show results.

The distribution of this P/PS would be to executive officers, possibly the entire sales force, accounts payable, travel auditor, and others as determined under the specific circumstances.

Example 2—New Corporate Committee

In this example, the P/PS is used to announce that the executive committee has authorized a new corporate budget committee. The subject of the P/PS would be *New Budget Committee*. The opening paragraph might state the general purpose of the committee and the expected benefits to the company.

The main body would describe how the committee is elected or appointed, the frequency and location of meetings, and the expected output of the committee. The P/PS would list the names of the charter members of the committee and the chairperson. Distribution would be made to all executive officers, department managers, and the committee members. This type of P/PS is very effective, particularly in large organizations where several committees are functioning on a regular basis. Financial institutions, colleges and universities, and governmental units tend to function quite effectively with the committee structure and employees should be informed of the changing memberships.

Example 3—Release of Financial Information

It is not uncommon to find that organizations receive many inquiries from outside agencies, the press, and TV and radio reporters about specific financial information. Many times the person receiving the request is not fully qualified to give such information but is flattered by the request and will usually attempt to provide an answer.

The policy/procedure statement is the perfect instrument to announce a corporate policy that defines the ground rules for such release of information and to name the financial executives who are qualified to release such information and under what circumstances.

The subject *Release of Financial Information* seems to adequately define the contents. The opening paragraph would again explain the problem and how it may adversely affect the corporation. The second paragraph, which may be labeled *Policy for Release of Financial Information*, would set up a procedure whereby any employee who receives such a request would forward it to one of the senior accounting executives listed. There may be further information on specific restrictions or prohibitions, and under what circumstances legal counsel may be involved.

Note again how the P/PS can be used to announce a new policy and provide the procedural mechanism to implement the policy.

Example 4—New Raw Material Receiving Report

In this example, the P/PS is used to report a change in an existing form to correct a potential problem which may be creating a dollar shortage in the raw material control system. The company buys large quantities of steel bars and rolls of sheet steel. Raw material inventories have been consistently short and a review of procedures disclosed that the receiving department always entered the weights from the mill tags on each bundle or roll received. The mill tag is attached to each item by the vendor.

The solution was to install scales at the receiving dock and to weigh each item when received and enter both the mill tag weight and the weight determined by receiving dock personnel. To complete the new procedure, the old receiving report had to be altered to provide space on the form for both weights.

The background paragraph would explain the problem of the raw material shortages and the probable cause. The second section of the P/PS would describe the weighing and reporting procedure and the changed form that provides designated space for the weights. It is usually very helpful to those employees involved in the procedure if a photocopy of the new form is shown as part of the P/PS or as a separate attachment. The location of the change in the form would be highlighted and the instructions for entering the weights would be described.

Again, the P/PS will provide a written policy, "We will weigh all raw materials," and the procedure for reporting the figures into the accounting system through a simple change in an existing form. Distribution would be to the accountants involved in inventory control, receiving department personnel, and the supervisors involved. A P/PS of this type might be expanded to include how the dual weight tags would be used when taking physical inventories.

USING THE P/PS

These examples show the versatility of the policy/procedure statement system. However, the P/PS system should not be used for trivial changes that might be handled more efficiently through memoranda. Any policy, even if developed and reported at a low level within the organization, does become company policy.

Because the policy/procedure statement is a powerful tool, the writer of any such statements should observe certain rules. First, if there is any doubt that major corporate policy is being developed or changed, there should be an executive approval requirement established. Second, a P/PS should not be distributed until another person in the organization reads it for clarity, readability, meaning, and possible impact on another operation in the company. Sometimes the person developing the P/PS material becomes so closely involved in its preparation that he or she fails to see a potential conflict or error in the policy or procedure being published.

THE MASTER P/PS FILE

During the development of a P/PS, background material is accumulated. This material may be other policy information, statistics, interview notes, research papers, and so forth. This material should be retained in a folder with a copy of the final published Policy/Procedure Statement. A copy of the P/PS can be reproduced from this permanent copy if there are future requests for it. The contents of the master folder are invaluable when another P/PS on the same or similar subject is being developed.

COVER SHEET AND REQUEST FORM

A simple cover sheet should be developed to show the pertinent information on the P/PS and this cover sheet should also be retained in the master folder. The cover sheet can be combined with a form to request a P/PS. Anyone in the organization may request a P/PS and this request form acts as an action transmittal letter. Once initiated, this form controls the editing, attachments, required approvals, heading information, and final distribution (see Figure 3.4).

Contents of the Form

The *Request for Policy/Procedure Statement* form is used when the person submits a new administrative release or a revision to a prior release. If the P/PS system is used throughout the company, the department title *Accounting Services* would not be imprinted on the form. The originator then describes the subject matter and writes a brief description of the requested statement. The full name of any attachment to the statement is entered, as well as the source of the attachment. An attachment may be a table from a periodical, a new law, a form, or anything that relates to the content of the proposed statement.

The request is signed, dated, and delivered to the person authorized to complete and publish the final statement. In this case, the director would review the proposal, complete the editing, approve it for distribution, and submit the draft of the P/PS to the originator to determine whether it provides the information the originator had in mind. When the originator indicates final approval, the suggested distribution is entered.

The director would enter the retrieval number, number of pages, date to be issued (which might be a future date), a descriptive name for the originator (usually a department or function), and the number of a previous P/PS being superseded, if required, by this document. At this time, the final distribution is set and the total number of copies to be printed is determined. When the final draft is edited for typographical errors, photocopies or printed copies are made and the distribution completed. Figure 3.5 shows the use of the P/PS system to announce its own initiation into the organization. Once started, it is this policy/procedure statement system that will announce all future accounting manuals, systems, policies, procedures, and forms.

Chapter 12 on maintenance will cover the use of the P/PS as a maintenance system in more depth.

APPROVALS

Approvals should be kept to a minimum. If only accounting information is released, a three-step preparation and approval system generally works best. The system consists of origination, editing for accuracy and consistency, and officer approval.

Origination is done best at the unit level such as the manager or supervisor of payroll, disbursements, budget, and so forth. The controller should review the pro-

REQUEST FOR POLICY/PROCEDURE STATEMENT

_____ NEW

_____ REVISION OF RETRIEVAL NO. _____

SUBJECT _____

BRIEF DESCRIPTION _____

_____

_____

ATTACHMENTS   SOURCE

   1. _____   _____

   2. _____   _____

   3. _____   _____

REQUESTED BY _____ DATE _____

DIRECTOR APPROVAL _____ DATE
                                                      RETURNED _____

ORIGINATOR - FINAL APPROVAL _____ DATE _____

SUGGESTED DISTRIBUTION _____

HEADINGS

   RETRIEVAL NO. _____

   PAGES _____

   ISSUE DATE _____

   ORIGINATOR _____

   SUPERSEDES _____

   DISTRIBUTION (Person, Group, Department)

     Director   1   _____   _____

     Managers   5   _____   _____

     Bursar   1   _____   _____

     Vice President   1   _____   _____

     Number of Copies Printed _____

Figure 3.4. Form for requesting a policy/procedure statement.

Policy/Procedure Statement

- RETRIEVAL NO.   10000
-
- PAGE   1 of 2
-
- ISSUE DATE   January 15, 1986
-
- ORIGINATOR   Corporate Accounting
-
- SUPERSEDES

```
┌──────────┐
│          │
│  LOGO    │
│          │
└──────────┘
```

L. O. GRANT ORGANIZATION, INC.

SUBJECT: POLICY/PROCEDURE STATEMENTS

To keep the Accounting staff informed of Company policy and major
procedural changes, the Policy/Procedure Statement (P/PS) has been
deeloped.   P/PSs define Company policy, administrative decisions, and
procedures to implement the decisions.

Such procedures are not clerical processing procedures, job descriptions,
or individual job task outlines.

Issuing Policy/Procedure Statements

Any employee can initiate a P/PS by completing an introduction and the
procedure details.   The draft of the suggested procedure and a Request for
a Policy/Procedure Statement form (attached) are submitted to the Director
of Accounting.   The Statement will be reviewed for real or apparent
conflicts with previous procedures or Company policy and, if approved,
typed in final form.

After the final draft is approved by the originator, the document will be
assigned a retrieval number and distributed to designated individuals.   The
Retrieval No. and other information described below under "Format" will be
assigned at time of distribution.

Printing and Distribution

The completed P/PS will be duplicated on white paper, 3-hole punched and
corner-stapled if more than one page.   All Unit Managers in Accounting will
be provided a procedures manual.   New P/PSs should be communicated to
employees whose actions may be affected.   The manual should be available to
all employees for reference.

Updating Prior Policy/Procedure Statements

A new P/PS must be issued if an existing P/PS is to be modified in any way.
The new P/PS (with a new Retrieval No.) will indicate it supersedes the old
P/PS and the old one will be purged from the manual.

Index

A numerical and alphabetic title index of all Policy/Procedure Statements
will be issued as needed (Retrieval No. = INDEX).   A copy will be sent to
all Accounting employees as notification on existing P/PSs which may
pertain to their job function.

Figure 3.5.   Statement announcing the policy/procedure statement system.

Format

RETRIEVAL NO. - A 5-digit retrieval number (Series 10,000-19,999) will be assigned when the P/PS is approved and issued. This number is located in the upper right hand corner on all pages.

PAGE - All pages will be numbered in the form Page 1 of 2. The page number will be located just below the Retrieval No. on all pages.

ISSUE DATE - Actual date the P/PS was issued in the form "February 1, 1985."

ORIGINATOR - The name of the individual or unit originating the P/PS. Usually unit names are used such as Payroll, Accounts Payable, Budget, and so forth.

SUPERSEDES - If the P/PS supersedes a prior Statement, the prior P/PS Retrieval No. will be entered. Superseded items are purged from the Manual immediately.

SUBJECT - A short descriptive title of the Policy or Procedure. The title will be used for indexing.

INTRODUCTION - A brief explanation of the background and/or purpose of the new P/PS. If related to Administration or Board policy, a copy of the policy may be attached for reference.

PROCEDURE - The body of the P/PS includes a complete description of the policy and/or the procedure, the methods to be used, form names and numbers related thereto, and so forth.

DISTRIBUTION - The original distribution can be listed at the end of the P/PS. Distribution may be "All Accounting Employees" or "Department Supervisors" as well as individual names.

Attachments

Any attachments to the Policy/Procedure Statement will be described, preferably by name of document and date such as "Board Minutes, January, 1985" or "Request for Petty Cash Disbursement."

Attachment: Request for Policy/Procedure Statement

Distribution: Accounting Staff
               President
               Vice Presidents
               Division Heads

Figure 3.5. Continued.

posed release for consistency and accuracy, make necessary edit changes and, if required, type in final form.

A photocopy of the final typed copy should be sent to the chief financial officer for review. This review checks for possible legal conflict, conflict with policy from another segment of the company, and general readability. If approved here, the release is printed and distributed.

This type of review serves three purposes. First, what makes sense to the preparer directly involved in enforcing the policy or conformance to a procedure may not be understood when read for the first time by someone not as closely involved. Secondly, both the controller review and chief financial officer review may prevent conflict with a directive published elsewhere in the company or with some policy or procedure still in the formative or discussion stages and of which the original preparer would have no knowledge.

A third purpose would be to eliminate the publishing and distribution of materials affecting only a small unit and which would be of no interest or use to others. Information at too low a level should not be upgraded to the status of corporate policy or procedure.

INDEXING

An Index of all active policy/procedure statements is issued periodically, preferably every few months or when more than five or six have been released since the prior index was issued. The index uses the preprinted P/PS form but does not use a retrieval number.

The subject is "Cumulative Index to (Date Issued)." Each retrieval number P/PS is shown on a line, followed by the date issued, the distribution, such as Departments, Designated (list), Accounting Staff, Officers, and so on, and the exact subject title. The index should be given a fairly wide distribution in the organization to alert those who may be affected that a listed P/PS may be related to their job or function in the company.

When a P/PS is superseded, only the retrieval number and date issued are printed, with the word "Superseded" in the distribution column. Those marked "Superseded" in the previous index are dropped (see Figure 3.6).

SUGGESTED PROCEDURES

A change in a policy caused by internal or external forces, a significant change in a standard or common procedure, or the adoption of a new accounting or accounting-related form can be documented with a policy/procedure statement. Distribution of a P/PS is unlimited and can be to as few or as many employees as necessary to implement the policy or procedure. Following are accounting topics suggested for possible policy/procedure statements.

Cash
Petty cash procedure
Bank relationship
Pooled cash
Purchase order draft
Check signing control
Foreign exchange

Investments
Investment policy
Investment committee
Short-term investments
Investment procedures

Accounts Receivable
Credit rating standards
Noncash credits control
Collection procedures
Credit control
Credit memorandums
Calculating allowances for uncollectibles

Other Receivables
Accrued investment income
Notes receivable
Employee receivables
Deferred income

Inventories
Receiving
Make or buy decisions
Just-in-time procedures
Economic order and minimum order quantity calculations
Scrap control
Stockroom procedures—small tools and supplies
Direct cost time recording
Raw material control

Deferred Charges and Prepaid Expenses

Physical Properties
Depreciation methods
Useful lives
Physical inventories of equipment
Capitalization policy—purchased or built
Book and tax differences control

Accounts Payable
Non-purchase-order procedures
Vendor analysis
Payable check with order—small purchases
Receiving reports
Check signing procedures
Travel expense reimbursements
Fixed contract payments

Other Accruals
Payroll and taxes payable
Fringe benefit procedures
Supplemental unemployment benefits procedures
Payments—pension and profit sharing
Short-term borrowing procedure
Warranty expense procedures

Income Taxes
State returns—income and other
Federal returns—estimates
Deferred tax procedures

Long-Term Debt
Record maintenance
Payment authorization

Stockholders' Equity
Issued capital stock records
Dividend control
Relationship with agents
Earnings per share calculation methods

Sales
Returns and allowances policy
Credit checking
Problem customers

Shipping and freight policy and procedures
Product-line reporting

Cost of Goods Sold
Annual inventory procedures
Purchase recording
Direct labor analysis
Indirect cost procedures

Operating Procedures
Payroll forms and procedures
Travel expense reports
Budget procedures—operating and capital
Audit committee
Organizational changes
Financial reporting control
Use of company vehicles
Use of company credit cards
Appointment of company travel agency
Charitable contribution policy
Fringe benefit changes
Scrap sales and control

Figures 3.6 through 3.18 are examples of policy/procedure statements and administrative releases. Figures 3.6 through 3.12 are for the L. O. Grant Organization; Figures 3.13 through 3.18 are for the University of Southern Mississippi.

Policy/Procedure Statement

```
┌──────────┐
│          │
│  LOGO    │
│          │
└──────────┘
```

L. O. GRANT ORGANIZATION, INC.

SUBJECT: CUMULATIVE INDEX TO SEPTEMBER 30, 1986

Retrieval Number	Date	Distribution	Subject
10,000	4/15/84	Accounting Staff	Administrative Procedure Manual
10,001	4/22/84	Departments	Petty Cash
10,002	4/29/84	Accounting Staff	Requesting Invoices and Receiving Reports
10,003	5/1/84	Departments	Outstanding Permission to Travel Forms
10,009	8/1/84	Designated	Entertainment Expenses
10,010	9/15/84	Departments	Deductions from Supplemental Wages
10,011	10/1/84	Departments	Interdepartmental Invoices
10,012	11/30/84	Designated	Required Graphics Review
10,013	12/8/84	Designated	Superseded
10,014	12/17/84	Accounting Staff	Mechanical Check Signers
10,015	1/10/85	Departments	New Remittance Voucher (ACC 14)
10,016	1/10/85	Departments	Multiple Vendor-Payee Attachment
10,017	1/10/85	Departments	Superseded
10,019	3/28/85	Designated	Travel Policy and Procedures – Aircraft
10,020	4/15/85	Departments	Departmental Deposit Ticket
10,021	5/16/85	Designated	Accounts Receivable Processing Form
10,022	7/1/85	Departments	Permission to Travel
10,024	7/1/85	Departments	Property Accounting Procedures
10,026	9/12/85	Departments	High Cost Cities
10,027	1/14/86	Designated	Superseded
10,028	3/15/86	Designated	Banking Policy
10,029	5/6/86	Departments	Use of Personal Vehicle
10,030	5/6/86	Designated	Review and Approval Summary
10,031	6/3/86	Departments	Superseded
10,032	7/2/86	Departments	Department Name Change
10,033	7/18/86	Designated	Price Variance – Small Purchases and Freight
10,038	8/9/86	Accounting Staff	Old Outstanding Checks
10,040	9/1/86	Departments	Equipment Inventory Change
10,041	9/2/86	Designated	Travel Procedures

Figure 3.6. Cumulative index of policy/procedure statements for an organization.

Policy/Procedure Statement

- RETRIEVAL NO. 10005
-
- PAGE   1 of 1
-
- ISSUE DATE   January 24, 1986
-
- ORIGINATOR   Controller
-
- SUPERSEDES

LOGO

L. O. GRANT ORGANIZATION, INC.

SUBJECT: RELEASE OF FINANCIAL OR STATISTICAL INFORMATION

Summary

To control the release of financial or statistical information to banks, investors, investment houses, other agencies or organizations, or to individuals, every request is to be referred to the Controller. Typical rquests are for additional information concerning details of the published financial statements, litigation progress or results, insurance coverages, name of investors, and so forth. Some requests require completion of a form with specific information about L. O. Grant.

Written Requests

If the request is by letter or requires the completion of a form or other document, the material is to be forwarded to the Controller who will decide what information may be released and who will be authorized to reply.

Verbal Requests

If the request is made by a personal visit to our office, the requestor will be referred directly to the Controller. If by telephone, the call should be transferred to the Controller.

If the call cannot be transferred, the person receiving the call should obtain the caller's name, company, telephone number and address, if possible. Also, the reason for the request and a brief description of the information asked for and the name of the person taking the call. The information obtained is to be forwarded to the Controller immediately for follow-up and reply.

Figure 3.7. Release of financial or statistical information.

Policy/Procedure Statement

L. O. GRANT ORGANIZATION, INC.

- RETRIEVAL NO.   10012
- PAGE   1 of 2
- ISSUE DATE   February 10, 1986
- ORIGINATOR   Controller
- SUPERSEDES

SUBJECT: REVIEW AND APPROVAL SUMMARY

Attached is a new Review and Approval Summary form which is to be used by Accounting for regulatory agency reports (HEW, DHHS, etc.), State reports, payroll deduction reports and other similar reports containing financial or statistical information of the Company.

The form covers preparation, review, approval, signature and mailing requirements for information disclosed to outside agencies. The completed form will be attached to the completed working copy of the return or report and retained in Accounting files in accordance with current record retention procedures. If the detail report is attached to the Remittance Voucher, then the Summary will also be attached thereto.

The forms are available in the supply room.

Attachment: Review and Approval Summary Form

Figure 3.8.   Review and approval summary.

REVIEW AND APPROVAL SUMMARY

(Tax returns, regulatory agency reports, tax payments, others)

TITLE _____

FORM NO. _____

FILE NOT LATER THAN _____ MAIL NOT LATER THAN _____

ACCOUNT TO BE CHARGED (IF AMOUNT DUE) _____

	SIGNATURE	DATE
1. Prepared by		
2. Reviewed by		
3. Approved by		
4. Signed by		
5. Remittance Voucher prepared		
6. Check enclosed-Check No. _____ Amount $_____		
7. Mailed by		
8. Copies mailed:		

Number
of Copies _____ Mailed to Name and Address _____

Figure 3.8. Continued.

Policy/Procedure Statement

L. O. GRANT ORGANIZATION, INC.

- RETRIEVAL NO. 10020
-
- PAGE   1 of 1
-
- ISSUE DATE   March 17, 1986
-
- ORIGINATOR   Information Systems
-
- SUPERSEDES

SUBJECT: INFORMATION SYSTEMS COMMITTEE RESPONSIBILITIES

General

The name of the committee has been changed from Management Information Steering Committee, to Information Systems Committee.

Membership and General Purpose

Membership consists of those appointed by the Board of Directors. The Director of Management Information Systems is Chairman of the Committee. The Committee purpose is to initiate, develop, implement and control the short and long-range systems development plans of the Corporation, subject to approval of the Management Committee.

Specific Authority and Responsibility

1. Establish the specific objectives of the systems and processing effort and forward recommendations to the Management Committee.

2. Review, evaluate, and approve the planned program, and establish priorities for the orderly accomplishment of systems projects in accordance with Project Initiation Request Procedures (Retrieval No. 0039).

3. Determine policy and revisions of policy as appropriate to the needs of the program and forward policy recommendations to the Management Committee.

4. Arbitrate and ratify the necessary decisions as required to insure efffective and timely development of the various projects.

5. Evaluate and monitor progress through periodic progress meetings and reports.

Figure 3.9. Information Systems Committee responsibilities.

60

Policy/Procedure Statement

LOGO

L. O. GRANT ORGANIZATION, INC.

- RETRIEVAL NO. 10028
- PAGE 1 of 1
- ISSUE DATE April 1, 1986
- ORIGINATOR Personnel
- SUPERSEDES

SUBJECT: KEY PERSONNEL PHYSICAL EXAMINATIONS

All Corporation officers at the level of Assistant Vice President and above, and all Branch Managers are required to have physical examinations on an annual basis.

Each individual is required to make his own arrangements for these examinations prior to December 31 of each year. Information on various local hospitals' diagnostic programs is available in the Personnel Department.

The out-of-pocket costs of the examination is 100% reimbursable to a maximum annual amount of $300. All bills should be submitted through the Expense Report System (Schedule 2, Line 15-17 Annual Physical Exam) with a separate memo to Personnel indicating that the examination has been completed for that year.

The results of the examination will be confidential and need not be disclosed to anyone within the Corporation. However, it is expected that any required medical services will be taken care of at the employee's expense.

The examination should consist of standard tests (EKG, blood count, blood cholesterol, blood sugar, etc.) plus any additional tests which may be required for diagnostic purposes (excluding eye and dental examinations).

Figure 3.10. Key personnel physical examinations.

Policy/Procedure Statement

L. O. GRANT ORGANIZATION, INC.

- RETRIEVAL NO. 10031
- PAGE 1 of 3
- ISSUE DATE May 7, 1986
- ORIGINATOR Management Information
- SUPERSEDES

SUBJECT: DATA PROCESSING PROJECT INITIATION REQUEST PROCEDURES

General

Policy/Procedures Statement 0023, Requisitioning and Purchasing Procedures, requires a Division Manager's approval to requisition new forms or to request an outside purchase of more than $100. On all individual purchases in excess of $1,000, Management Committee approval is needed and Board of Director's approval is required on single expenditures in excess of $25,000.

These approval requirements are now extended to Project Initiation Requests to Data Processing for new programs or changes to existing programs. The above amount limits also supersede the Estimated Cost amounts shown on the Project Initiation Form.

Project Initiation Form

Project Initiation Form (No. 6454) is used to request changes to existing computer applications or new applications. Any department head can initiate a project request if the appropriate approvals are obtained as described above.

The following information is required:

1. Requesting department name and cost center number.

2. Date.

3. Nature of the request that includes a brief description of the change needed to existing programs or new information which is not presently available on computer reports. In addition, the reasons for the request should be given. In general, little weight will be given to intangible benefits. Acceptable reasons include, but are not limited to:

    a. A requirement of a new law, regulation, or regulatory agency pronouncement.

    b. Error in existing calculations or report contents.

Figure 3.11. Data processing project initiation request procedures.

    c. More productive use of one or more present employees, a potential staff reduction, decrease in overhead costs for supplies or communications, and so forth.

    d. Major benefit to the Corporation in this Department or in other departments.

    e. Eliminating other reports which contain similar or related information.

4. Date desired. This should be a specific date. If mandated by a regulatory authority or law, a reference to such announcement should be made in the request section. A copy of the regulation or law should be attached to the request.

5. Department number to be billed.

6. User coordinator assigned to the project. The person named is to provide an adequate amount of time to the project until its completion.

7. Requestor signature (and Division Manager's approval).

The form is sent to the Data Processing Systems Manager who will assign a project number and hold the request for a meeting of the Management Information Committee.

Committee Procedures

The Committee will review each request for completeness and proper approvals. They will examine each request on its own merits, its impact on existing or planned systems or applications, and particularly its estimated costs and described user benefits.

If the project request is complete and no additional information is needed, the request and a brief memorandum prepared by the Committee is forwarded to the Controller for his review and approval. If the project is rejected (usually for lack of an adequate description of the project, user benefits, or other budgetary restraints) the form is returned to the Committee with the reasons for rejection noted.

The Controller may ask for additional information before approving or rejecting the project. If rejected, the request and attached documentation is returned to the user. Should the person requesting the project disagree with the rejection, additional information may be provided and resubmitted to the Controller or directly to the Management Committee. Approved requests are forwarded to the Management Committee ($500 to $25,000 estimated cost to complete) or to the Board of Directors (over $25,000 to complete). When this approval is received, the project is listed on the project Development Schedule and the Committee will assign a priority number to the project at its next meeting.

Figure 3.11. Continued.

Exceptions

If the request is based on a new law or regulation, it will receive special consideration and will be approved in time to meet the required implementation date.

If the request describes an existing error condition in which a file contains known errors or a report is misleading or erroneous, the request will be implemented as soon as the Committee review is completed.

Priority Assignments

Once a request reaches the Committee and is assigned a priority number, no officer in the Company can change or override the priority, nor can a new project be substituted for another project on the priority list. The original user requesting the new system or application may cancel the project or place it in a temporary hold status.

Feasibility Studies

As most projects have a cost to develop in the range of $500 to $10,000, a full feasibility study to determine development and operating costs, and benefits to the Department is not required. However, the user requesting the project should provide an estimate of the benefits such as a decrease in employee salary costs, either by eliminating an existing position or not filling a new position, decrease in supply or printing costs, or a decrease in the elapsed time to accomplish one or more functions in the department. If the request is considered by the Committee to be of considerable benefit to the Company, Data Processing may provide personnel for a full feasibility study. Because feasibility studies use Data Processing resources, any such approved study will be assigned a project number and a priority number by the Committee.

Comments

Any comments on this Statement or questions concerning its implementation should be directed to the Chairman of the Management Information Committee or Director of Data Processing.

Figure 3.11. Continued.

64

Policy/Procedure Statement

- RETRIEVAL NO. 10033
- PAGE   1 of 4
- ISSUE DATE   June 10, 1986
- ORIGINATOR   Controller
- SUPERSEDES

LOGO

L. O. GRANT ORGANIZATION, INC.

SUBJECT: CAPITALIZATION OF FURNITURE, EQUIPMENT AND LEASEHOLD IMPROVEMENTS

Summary

It is the policy of L. O. Grant Organization to treat depreciation, in general, for both financial reporting and tax purposes on a consistent basis.

With respect to specific items of furniture, equipment and leasehold improvements, the following depreciation method and useful life (one-half in the year of acquisition) is now utilized:

1. Furniture and equipment - Sum-of-the-years digits - 8 years.

2. Computers, typewriters, adding machines and similar mechanical equipment - Sum-of-the years digits - 7 years.

3. Leasehold improvements - Straight line - lower of the lease term and all option renewals or 30 years.

The lowest life permitted by the Asset Depreciation Range (ADR) regulations consistent with maximum utilization of the Investment Tax Credit will be claimed.

The revised procedure is effective June 1, 1986. If you have any questions, or if you have an expenditure for an item which does not appear on any of the lists, contact Mr. Ralph Miller, Manager of Corporate Accounting.

Leasehold Improvements

1. All expenditures (including painting) are to be capitalized under the following circumstances:

   a. If related to the occupancy of a new office.

   b. If related to a major renovation of an existing office.

Figure 3.12. Capitalization of furniture, equipment, and leasehold improvements.

2. Expenditures incidental to an existing office are to be recorded as follows:

   a. Any expenditure in connection with or for replacement of an existing facility should be capitalized as an improvement.

   b. Any expenditure in connection with maintaining an existing facility in good working order should be expensed as a repair.

   c. Any item (regardless of its nature) for which an invoice is less than $1,000.00 should be expensed as a repair (Painting or repairs as the case may be).

3. Specific items to be expensed (regardless of amount) except those in 1.a. and 1.b. above.

   a. Any incidental costs relative to painting such as moving equipment, etc.

   b. Invoices rendered for survey services relative to refurbishing are expensed as equipment maintenance.

   c. Relocation and moving of equipment are expensed as equipment maintenance.

Furnishings Expensed

The following items are to be charged to expense, regardless of amount:

Ash Trays	Mats
Book Ends	Name Plates and Holders
Calendar Holders	Paper Punches
Chair Seat and Back Covers Cushions	Picture Frames
	Rulers
Desk Pads and Blotters	
Desk Signs and Plaques	Scissors
Desk Pens and Inkwells	Smoking Stands
Desk Sets	Stapling Machines
Desk Tops-Glass	Step Ladders
Desk Trays	Step-on Cans
Drawing Equipment	
	Table Utensils
Glassware	Trays
Kitchen Utensils	Waste Baskets

Figure 3.12. Continued.

66

Furniture (Moveable) and Fixtures (Demountable)

The following items are to be charged to asset account "Furniture and Equipment" (8-year life). However, invoices for less than $500, net of taxes, are to be charged to expense. Sales and use taxes on all acquisitions are to be charged to a local tax expense account.

Benches	Mirrors
Bookcases	
Booths	Partitions
Breakfronts	Pedestals
Bulletin Boards	Planting Boxes
	Platforms
Cabinets	
Carpets	Racks
Chairs	Radiator Covers
Chandeliers	Railing
Chests	Rugs
Coat Racks	
Couches	Safes
Counters	Screens
Cupboards	Settees
Curtains	Shades
	Shadow Boxes
Delivery Charges	Shelves
Desks	Signs
Doors	Sofas
Draperies	Stands
Drawers	Stools
Easels	Tables
Electric Fixtures	Table Tops
Files	Umbrella Stands
Fine Arts (not depreciable)	Urns
Handling Charges	Venetian Blinds
Lamps-desk and floor	Wardrobes
Lockers	

Figure 3.12. Continued.

Portable Mechanical Equipment

The following items are to be charged to asset account "Furniture and Equipment" (7-year life). However, invoices for less than $500 net of taxes, are to be charged to expense. Sales and use taxes are to be charged to a local tax expense account.

Adding Machines	Mailing Machines
Addressing Machines	Microfilmers
	Multilith Machines
Baling Machines	
Bookkeeping Machines	Numbering Machines
Calculating Machines	Perforating Machines
Checkwriters	Postage Machines
Clocks	
Computers and Peripheral Machines	Radios
Copying Machines	Recording Machines
	Refrigerators
Delivery and Freight	
Dictaphones	Scales
	Stoves
Electric Ranges	
Endorsing Machines	Time Stamps
Excise Taxes	Transcribing Machines
	Typewriters
Fans - Electric	
	Validating Machines
Handling Charges	Vending Machines
	Water Coolers

Figure 3.13.   Furniture and equipment control procedures.

	Administrative Procedure	•	RETRIEVAL NO. 10,004
		•	
		•	PAGE 1 of 4
		•	
		•	ISSUE DATE March 25, 1986
THE UNIVERSITY OF SOUTHERN MISSISSIPPI		•	
		•	ORIGINATOR Property Accounting
FINANCIAL AFFAIRS		•	
		•	SUPERSEDES

SUBJECT: FURNITURE AND EQUIPMENT CONTROL PROCEDURES

Purpose

The purpose of maintaining the furniture and equipment inventory is to comply with the State-owned Property Inventory rules of the Mississippi Administrative Procedures Act and the Code of 1972. The Property Accounting Department will assist departments in accounting for all furniture and equipment purchased, donated to the University, transferred to or from other State agencies, sold, junked or transferred.

Responsibility

Department heads are responsible and accountable for all furniture and equipment in their departments and they are to maintain some type of control over furniture and equipment. Property Accounting will assist in and evaluate any department's furniture and equipment inventory control procedures.

Filing Reports

The Property Accounting Department will furnish each department a report showing acquisitions, disposals, and transfers of property. This report should be filed for reference and later use. All furniture and equipment transactions are reported monthly to the State Department of Audit.

Purchase of Furniture and Equipment

Furniture and equipment purchased through the Purchasing Department from budgeted departmental appropriations, restricted funds, or special appropriations will be assigned an inventory number, number attached, and the item accounted for. Items that cost less than $500.00 or with a fair value of less than $500.00 will not be reported on the Furniture and Equipment inventory records. The exception to the $500.00 rule are weapons and cameras. These items will be included as inventory regardless of the price paid to acquire the item or the fair market value.

Shop-Made Furniture and Equipment

Furniture or equipment manufactured in the Physical Plant shop will be reported to Property Accounting if the item cost was $500.00 or more. A complete description of the property, date manufactured, number of items, cost or value, and a statement that it is shop-made will be included in the report.

Figure 3.13. Continued.

Gift or Donation of Property

Policy requires the Vice President for Business and Finance be notified before acceptance of the item. The description of the gift, the name of the donor, and the intended purpose or use of the donated item must be included. If the item is usable by the University, can be placed in use without significant preparation costs, and can be maintained at a reasonable cost, a current market value of item will be determined. The Vice President will then acknowledge the gift without stating a dollar value thereof. Property Accounting will number the item and record it in the fixed asset file.

Transfer of Property from Another State Agency

Furniture or equipment received by a department through transfer from another State Agency will be reported to the Property Accounting Department. A complete description of the property, serial number, name of the manufacturer, number of items, original cost, original date of purchase, name of transferring agency and any other information about the property will be included in the report.

Inventory Numbering

Property Accounting is responsible for attaching the assigned inventory number where it can be readily located on each item of furniture and equipment. The department is responsible for locating the inventoried item with its number attached when requested by Property Accounting, the State Property Auditor, or Internal Auditor.

Trade-In of Property

Furniture or equipment may be used as a trade-in provided Purchasing has received written approval from the Commission of Budget and Accounting. When submitting a requisition for a purchase where allowance is given for an inventory item being traded in, the description, serial number, and inventory number of that item should be listed on the requisition. This will assist the Purchasing Department in completing the forms for processing the trade-in request. See Purchasing Policies and Procedures.

Property Accounting Department will receive notification from the Purchasing Department that the property has been traded in and the property will be deleted from the inventory records.

Sale of Property

Furniture or equipment may be sold after written approval has been received from the Commission of Budget and Accounting. Property to be sold should be reported to Property Accounting, with description, serial number, inventory number and condition. Property Accounting will verify the items to be sold and will submit this list to the Purchasing Department to advertise the property for sale and to obtain the necessary bids and approvals. See Purchasing Policies and Procedures.

Property Accounting will receive notification from the Purchasing Department that the property has been sold and will delete the property

Figure 3.13. Continued.

from the inventory records.

Worn-Out or Obsolete Property

Worn-out or obsolete property with no cash value will be reported to
Property Accounting with description, serial number, inventory number and
condition. Property Accounting should inspect all worn-out or obsolete
property before it is removed from the department and will secure the
necessary approval for disposition from the University of Southern
Mississippi Salvage Committee. The department will be notified of the
Salvage Committee's decision and the property will be deleted from the
inventory record.

Stolen Property

Furniture or equipment that is missing or has been stolen will be reported
in writing to the Public Safety Department and Property Accounting as soon
as possible.

The description, serial number, inventory number, and other information
about the lost item should be included in the report.

Property Accounting will secure the necessary approval for disposition from
the Salvage Committee. The department will be notified of the Salvage
Committee's decision. Property Accounting will then delete the property
from the inventory record and send a report to the State.

Temporary Transfer of Property

The loan or transfer of furniture or equipment between departments for
short periods need not be reported to Property Accounting. However, the
department head to which the property is assigned will be held accountable
for the loaned item and should, for his protection, require a memorandum
receipt for furniture or equipment loaned to another department. This
receipt should be available for presentation when requested.

Permanent Interdepartmental Transfers

Interdepartmental transfers will be reported to Property Accounting in
writing including the description, serial number, inventory number of the
property being transferred, the name of the department to receive the
property, and proof that the department has received the property.
Property Accounting will assist in transferring furniture or equipment from
one department to another. The department head to whom the item was
assigned originally will be held accountable until Property Accounting is
notified of the transfer. After being notified, the department head
acquiring the property assumes accountability. Form is available from
Property Accounting.

Surplus or Salvage Transfer to Stores

Equipment declared surplus or salvage by a department is transferred to the
East Stores Warehouse (Building 609), 2607 W. 4th St. The item may be
brought to this location if easily carried. A Transfer/Obsolescence Report
is needed.

There is no charge for picking up equipment and delivering it to Stores.
There is a charge for delivering equipment from Stores to a department.

Transfer of Property to Another State Agency

Furniture or equipment may be transferred to another state agency after
written approval has been received from the Commission of Budget and
Accounting. Property Accounting will be notified of property transferred
to another state agency, including the description, serial number,
inventory number, reason for transferring, and present condition of the
property. See Purchasing Policies and Procedures.

Property Accounting will receive notification from the Purchasing
Department that the property has been transferred to the other state agency
and will then delete the property from the inventory and send a report to
the State Auditor.

Inventory Listing

Periodically, each department will be furnished with a listing of its
tagged furniture and equipment.

Audit of Department's Inventory

Each department's inventory will be audited periodically by Property
Accounting. A report of this audit will be sent to the Vice President for
Business and Finance and the department chairman.

The State Property Auditor audits each inventory every two years. A report
is sent to the President, Vice President for Business and Finance, Director
of Accounting and Property Officer.

Change of Department Head

Whenever a change in department head occurs, all items should be accounted
for by the outgoing department head. The incoming department head will
accept the responsibility and accountability for the departmental inventory
when he/she assumes duties as department head. Property Accounting can
assist with this audit.

Suggestions

Please direct any suggestions or recommendations for improving the
furniture and equipment inventory system to Property Accounting, Southern
Station Box 5086. Telephone 266-4439.

Attachments: Completing the Transfer/Obsolescence Report
               Transfer/Obsolescence Report

Figure 3.13. Continued.

COMPLETING THE TRANSFER/OBSOLESCENCE REPORT

"FROM" DEPARTMENT

    A. Date transfer is authorized.
    B. "From" Information.
    C. "To" Information. May be another department, surplus,
       or salvage.
    D. USM metal tag number.
    E. Description of item being transferred.
    F. Condition of item such as good, fair, needs repair, junk.
    G. Approval signature and date.
    H. Signature of mover, date, and work order number, if
       necessary.

"TO" DEPARTMENT

    I. Receiving department verifies items received from movers,
       signs and dates the form.

FORM DISTRIBUTION AND USE

"From" department retains canary copy. Sends white copy to Property
  Accounting.
"To" department retains pink copy.
Movers send gold copy to Property Accounting.
Property Accounting matches white and gold copies and records transfer
  in equipment inventory file.

Figure 3.13. Continued.

TRANSFER/OBSOLESCENCE REPORT

PROPERTY ACCOUNTING
SOUTHERN STATION, BOX 5086
PHONE 266-4439

DATE _____**A**_____

THE UNIVERSITY
OF SOUTHERN MISSISSIPPI

FROM: ___**B**_____
      BLDG.   ROOM NO.   PHONE   DEPARTMENT   CHARGE CODE

TO: ___**C**_____
      BLDG.   ROOM NO.   PHONE   DEPARTMENT   CHARGE CODE

U.S.M. TAG NUMBER	DESCRIPTION	CONDITION
D	**E**	**F**

APPROVED BY: ___**G**_____   2854
                                DATE

THE ABOVE INFORMATION TO BE COMPLETED BY THE "FROM" DEPARTMENT

MOVED BY: ___**H**_____
              SIGNATURE   DATE   WORK ORDER NO.

RECEIVED BY: ___**I**_____
           SIGNATURE   DATE

COPIES:
WHITE—SENT BY "FROM" DEPARTMENT TO PROPERTY ACCOUNTING AFTER MOVER SIGNS.
CANARY—RETAINED BY "FROM" DEPARTMENT AFTER MOVER SIGNS.
PINK—RETAINED BY "TO" DEPARTMENT AFTER SIGNING "RECEIVED BY"LINE.
GOLD—SENT BY MOVER TO PROPERTY ACCOUNTING FOR VERIFICATION WITH WHITE COPY
     ITEM TRANSFERRED AND RECEIVED.

FORM PA-001 (6-82)

Figure 3.13. Continued.

SUBJECT: BANKING POLICY

Background

The University conducts most of its banking and investment operations
through five banks:

Bank of Hattiesburg
Citizens Bank
Deposit Guaranty
First Mississippi
South Mississippi

Effective January 1, 1985, certain deposit and check writing operations are
rotated between Citizens, Deposit Guaranty and First Mississippi. The
Hattiesburg Bank is used for the biweekly wage payroll on a permanent
basis, and South Mississippi handles the Bursar account.

The University has fixed amounts of certificates of deposit at eight other
local banks and savings and loans institutions (generally $100,000 per
institution).

Policy

The University can invest in certificates of deposit in Mississippi banks
and savings and loan institutions, bank money market funds, and in federal
obligations such as Treasury Notes and Bills.

Total investments in any one bank should not exceed 25% of the net worth of
the financial institution. State law requires a depository bank to pledge
securities equal to 100% of University assets in excess of $100,000 at that
institution.

Investments are to be distributed between the five major banks
approximately as follows (excluding the $100,000 certificates at local
institutions):

Bank of Hattiesburg	$12\frac{1}{2}$%
Citizens Bank	25
Deposit Guaranty	25
First Mississippi	25
South Mississippi	$12\frac{1}{2}$
	100%

Figure 3.14. Banking policy.

The five major banks are assigned to the following uses:

1. Rotated annually (July 1) between deposit account only, accounts payable checks and salary payroll checks:

    Citizens Bank
    Deposit Guaranty
    First Mississippi

2. Wage payroll checks: Bank of Hattiesburg (permanent)

3. Bursar account: South Mississippi (permanent)

The payroll accounts are maintained on an imprest basis and one bank is used to deposit all receipts. The deposit bank may receive an increased portion of temporary investments during the fiscal year to offset the lower activity that year.

The banks have agreed to the following:

1. No service charges for checks, deposits or statements.

2. No charge for stop payments.

3. Account balances over $50,000 are to be swept into a money market fund paying daily interest no lower than 1% less than that bank's CD rate.

4. No float holdback on deposits so deposits may be invested immediately.

5. Certificate rate must be competitive or the percentage division of investments will not be in effect.

Assignments Institution	1985 Jan. 1 – June 30	Fiscal 1985-86
Bank of Hattiesburg	Wage Payroll	Wage payroll
Citizens Bank	Accounts Payable	Deposits
Deposit Guaranty	Credit Card Receipts Salary Payroll	Credit Card Receipts Accounts Payable
First Mississippi	Letters of Credit Deposits	Letters of Credit Salary
South Mississippi	Bursar Account	Bursar Account
Hancock Bank-Gulfport	Gulf Park deposits	Gulf Park deposits
Lloyds Bank of California	NDSL Collections	NDSL Collections

Figure 3.14. Continued.

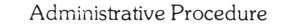

Administrative Procedure

THE UNIVERSITY OF SOUTHERN MISSISSIPPI

ACCOUNTING SERVICES

SUBJECT: NEW REMITTANCE VOUCHER (ACC 14)

Many expenditures for services do not require a purchase order and authority to pay has been processed through the use of a memo, a purchase requisition sent directly to Accounting Services, or by a remittance voucher. The new Remittance Voucher form is to be used by anyone authorized to approve disbursements for an account. The use of the purchase requisition for payment authorization is no longer acceptable.

Use of the Remittance Voucher

Items which do not normally require purchase orders and for which this Remittance Voucher is to be used are:

    Seminar and conference registration fees for employees
    Honorariums to non-employees
    Speaker's fee
    Travel expense reimbursement for non-employees (recruiting, speakers,
       professional fees and so forth)
    Stipends
    Agency accounts
    Items on contract (leases, land purchases, entertainment groups, Cablevision, etc)
    Legal, audit and other professional fees
    Payroll taxes and amounts withheld for payment to others
    Insurance
    Postage (Post Office only)
    Advertising
    Utilities
    Telephone
    Freight when shipper is USM
    Band and music awards (not trophies or plaques)
    Registration workers
    Officials - Athletic and Intramural Departments
    Sales Tax
    Refunds - housing deposits and Continuing Education fees

The form is used as a cover document for form ACC 14A - Multiple Vendor-Payee Attachment.

Supporting documents are to be attached to the accounting copy of the form. The preparing department retains the pink copy for comparison to the monthly budget activity report.

Figure 3.15. New remittance voucher.

Completing the Form

Department enters:

A. Department name
B. Account number
C. Telephone number of preparer
D. Name and address of vendor. If used as a cover form for the Multiple Vendor-Payee Attachment, enter "See Attached Forms". Social Security number must be supplied for payment to individuals.
E. Description of charge to be paid, including name of registrant(s) at a seminar or conference, purpose of payment and so forth. If registration form, document or letter is to be sent with check, indicate that enclosure is attached.
F. Amount to be paid. Attach supporting document, if any.
G. Total to be paid on this voucher.
H. Signature of person requesting payment and date signed.
I. Approval signature and date. Payments to individuals require two approval signatures if an invoice is not available.
J. General Ledger Code, Object Code and Department to be charged. If department is not entered, the charge will be made to the account shown at top of the form.
K. Amount to be charged to this account. Form provides distribution for up to eight accounts.

Accounting Services enters:

L. Vendor code number.
M. Voucher number.
N. Voucher date.
O. Purchase Order Number, if any.
P. Name of person processing the voucher and date processed.
Q. Name of person reviewing or verifying information.
R. Preprinted number of special check used to pay voucher.
S. Special handling required or enclosure to be mailed.
T. Amount of encumbrance to be liquidated, if any.

This form is available from Accounting Services, 201 Forrest County Hall. The use of unauthorized forms should be discontinued.

Any questions concerning this procedure should be directed to Accounting Services, Box 5143, Telephone 4084.

Attachment: Copy of Remittance Voucher

Figure 3.15. Continued.

REMITTANCE VOUCHER
UNIVERSITY OF SOUTHERN MISSISSIPPI
HATTIESBURG, MISSISSIPPI   39406-5143

THE UNIVERSITY
OF SOUTHERN MISSISSIPPI

DEPT NAME	(A)
ACCT NO	(B)
TEL NO	(C)

VENDOR (D) _____

_____

_____

| VENDOR CODE |
| (L) |

DESCRIPTION	AMOUNT
(E)	(F)

REQUESTED BY	DATE	APPROVED BY	DATE	TOTAL	
(H)		(I)			(G)

ACCOUNTING USE		GL	OBJECT	DEPARTMENT	LIQUIDATION	EXPENDITURE
VOUCHER NUMBER	(M)	(J)	(J)	(J)	(T)	(K)
VOUCHER DATE	(N)					
PURCHASE ORDER NUMBER	(O)					
PROCESSED BY: DATE	(P)					
VERIFIED BY:	(Q)	SPECIAL CHECK NO. (R)	ACCOUNTING USE (S)			

ACC 14 (REV. 1-83)   WHITE — ACCOUNTING   CANARY — VENDOR   PINK — DEPARTMENT

Figure 3.15. Continued.

 **Administrative Procedure**

THE UNIVERSITY OF SOUTHERN MISSISSIPPI

ACCOUNTING SERVICES

- RETRIEVAL NO.   10,016
-
- PAGE   1 of 1
-
- ISSUE DATE   January 10, 1983
-
- ORIGINATOR   Accounts Payable
-
- SUPERSEDES

SUBJECT: MULTIPLE VENDOR-PAYEE ATTACHMENT

The Multiple Vendor-Payee Attachment (Form ACC 14A) is used to process payments to several vendors or payees. Principal uses are:

Student Refunds
Payments to game officials
Fee refunds - Continuing Education
Stadium event labor
Registration workers

This form has no approval or account distribution sections and cannot be used alone to authorize expenditures. The Multiple Vendor-Payee Attachment forms must be summarized on and attached to a Remittance Voucher. (Form ACC 14)

The form is completed entirely by the department as follows:

A. Name of department.
B. Account number of department.
C. Telephone number of preparer.
D. Date form is completed.
E. Vendor code number, if known. For an individual, vendor code is the social security number.
F. Vendor-payee name and address, if needed. There is provision for 12 vendor-payees on a form; however, if only one line is needed for each vendor-payee, the designated spacing can be ignored.
G. Amount to be paid to each person listed.
H. Total of payments on the page. Each page should be separately totaled and the cover form show the page totals and the grand total of the amounts paid.
I. Page number as Page 1 of 5, 2 of 5, 3 of 5, and so on.

Payments to individuals require two signature approvals unless an invoice or other source document is attached. Payments to employees for any services rendered are not to be reported on this form.

Attachment: Multiple Vendor-Payee Attachment

Figure 3.16. Multiple vendor-payee attachment.

80

THE UNIVERSITY
OF SOUTHERN MISSISSIPPI

MULTIPLE VENDOR-PAYEE ATTACHMENT
UNIVERSITY OF SOUTHERN MISSISSIPPI
HATTIESBURG, MISSISSIPPI   39406-5143

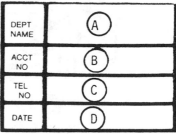

	DEPT NAME	Ⓐ
	ACCT NO	Ⓑ
	TEL NO	Ⓒ
	DATE	Ⓓ

	VENDOR CODE	VENDOR — PAYEE (Name and Address)	AMOUNT	
1	Ⓔ	Ⓕ	Ⓖ	
2				
3				
4				
5				
6				
7				
8				
9				
0				
1				
2				

ACC-14A (REV 1-83)
ATTACH TO COMPLETED REMITTANCE VOUCHER

PAGE_____of_____TOTAL   Ⓗ

Ⓘ

Figure 3.16.   Continued.

Administrative Procedure

THE UNIVERSITY OF SOUTHERN MISSISSIPPI

ACCOUNTING SERVICES

SUBJECT: TRAVEL POLICY AND PROCEDURES - UNIVERSITY AIRCRAFT

Travel by University aircraft only when feasible or upon recommendation by the University President or Vice Presidents.

These procedures will apply only to transportation furnished by the University aircraft. Other travel procedures will remain as they are now.

Dispatching will be made from the Motor Pool Office. Procedure for requesting use of the aircraft follows:

1. Call Motor Pool Office (4435) to see if aircraft is available on date needed.
2. If available, prepare Aircraft Request form, retain pink copy and forward original and yellow copy to Motor Pool Office (Box 5058).
3. Motor Pool will forward yellow copy to pilot.
4. Pilot will contact person making the request to set departure and return date and time.

Completing the Aircraft Request form:

A. Date - Current Date
B. Itinerary - Dates and places of trip
C. Purpose of Trip - Check one category and describe
D. Departure - Date and time of departure
E. Return - Date and time of return
F. Passengers - List of individuals going on trip
G. Department Name and Account Number
H. Individual Requesting - Name of person requesting the aircraft and phone number
I. Approvals - Department Chairman, and Dean or Director
J. Estimated Cost - Flight Time - From chart in aircraft procedure times rate per hour. Established rate is $185.00 per metered hour.

The completed form authorizes the pilot to dispatch the aircraft and charge the department.

The Aircraft/Dispatch Invoice is completed by the pilot as follows:

Heading
    A. Date prepared
    B. Department name
    C. Account number to be charged
    D. Pilot name
    E. Copilot name

Figure 3.17. Travel policy and procedures—University aircraft.

Section I - Trip Statistics

F. Date of trip.
G. Departure time.
H. Station departing from and arriving at.
I. Arrival time.
J. Flight time (not used for billing).
K. Mileage
L. Fuel, oil or repairs.
M. Quantity of fuel or oil or description of repair.
N. Passengers.

Section II - Billing Information

O. Meter reading of engine start and stop, used for billing.
P. Hours and tenths of hours.
Q. Current rate per hour of airplane use. Current rate is $185.00 per metered hour.
R. Extension (transfer amount to V and W below.)
S. Pilot and copilot meals, lodging, mileage, car rental and other
    expenses incurred on trip.
T. Total of pilot and copilot expenses (transfer to V below in detail and
    X in total).
U. Pilot's signature.

Section III - Accounting Information

V. General Ledger, Object, Department codes and amounts charged to user department.
W. Credit income to Airplace operating account.
X. Credit pilot and copilot expenses in total.
Y. Signature of person completing the form.

Motel, meals, mileage and car rental expenses are for pilot and copilot only.
Expenditures for passengers are reported on their Travel Expense Vouchers as
outlined in Travel Procedures.

Pilot and copilot expenses are charged to the department in addition to the
aircraft use charge.

The pilot completes the Aircraft Dispatch/Invoice, retains the pink copy and
returns the white, green and yellow copies to the Motor Pool Office. In addition,
he submits a Travel Expense Voucher for reimbursement of personal travel costs
incurred. Receipts attached to Travel Expense Voucher.

Trip Cancellation

If the trip must be canceled and the requester calls the Motor Pool Office by
1:00 p.m. on day prior to flight, no charge will be made. If later than 1:00 p.m.
the department will be charged $50.00 on the Aircraft Dispatch/Invoice.   This
charge may be waived if the user presents sufficient justification to the Vice-
President for Business and Finance.

Final Billing

The Motor Pool Office reviews and completes the Accounting information on the
Aircraft Dispatch/Invoice, forwards the white copy to Accounting, the yellow copy
to the requesting department and retains the green copy in a permanent file.
The white copy will be processed the same as an Interdepartmental Invoice.

Attachments: Aircraft Request
               Aircraft Dispatch/Invoice
               Aircraft Mileage Chart

Figure 3.17. Continued.

THE UNIVERSITY
OF SOUTHERN MISSISSIPPI

AIRCRAFT DISPATCH/INVOICE
UNIVERSITY OF SOUTHERN MISSISSIPPI
HATTIESBURG, MISSISSIPPI 39406-5143

DATE (A) _____

DEPARTMENT NAME (B) _____   ACCOUNT NUMBER (C) _____

PILOT (D) _____   COPILOT (E) _____

TRIP DATE	DEPART TIME	STATION	ARRIVAL TIME	FLIGHT TIME	MILEAGE	FUEL, OIL REPAIRS	QUANTITY OR DESC.	PASSENGERS
(F)	(G)	(H)	(I)	(J)	(K)	(L)	(M)	(N)

TRIP COST

Meter   Engine Start (O) _____

Meter   Engine Stop (O) _____   Hours & Tenths (P) _____ at $ (Q) _____ Per Hr = (R) _____

Pilot and Copilot Expenses

Motel (Receipt Required)   (S)

Meals B_____ L_____ D_____   (S)

Milage to/from Airport   (S)

Car rental (Receipt Required)   (S)

Other (Receipt Required)   (S)

TOTAL EXPENSES   (T)

COMMENTS:

(U)

PILOT'S SIGNATURE

CHARGES						CREDITS				
	G.L.	OBJ.		DEPARTMENT	AMOUNT		G.L.	OBJ.	DEPARTMENT	AMOUNT
AIRCRAFT CHARGE	(V)	40	5	(V)	(V)	AIRCRAFT INCOME	2035	1342	1127516	(W)
MEALS LODGING		40	1			EXPENSE INCOME	2035	1343	1127516	(X)
MILEAGE		40	2							
RENTAL CAR		40	3							
OTHER		40	6							

White—Accounting
Green—Motor Pool
Yellow—Requesting Department
Pink—Pilot
Gold—Motor Pool Ticket File

ACC 33 JAN 1983

(Y) _____
SIGNATURE OF PERSON COMPLETING FORM

AP

Figure 3.17. Continued.

THE UNIVERSITY OF SOUTHERN MISSISSIPPI

AIRCRAFT REQUEST
UNIVERSITY OF SOUTHERN MISSISSIPPI
HATTIESBURG, MISSISSIPPI 39406

Date _____(A)_____

Itinerary _____(B)_____

Purpose of Trip _____(C)_____

(C) ☐ In State Official Business - - - - (4035)

(C) ☐ Out-of-State Official Business - - - - (4045)

(C) ☐ In State Conference - - - - - - - - - (4055)

(C) ☐ Out-of-State Conference - - - - - - (4065)

Departure   Date ____(D)____ Time ____(D)____

Return   Date ____(E)____ Time ____(E)____

Passengers   1. ___(F)_____

                  2. _____

                  3. _____

                  4. _____

                  5. _____

                  6. _____

Dept. Name ____(G)_____   Account No. ____(G)_____

Individual Requesting ____(H)_____   Phone ____(H)_____

Approvals: ____(I)_____   ____(I)_____
                  Department Chairman   Dean or Director

Estimated Cost: Flight Time ____(J)____ Hrs @ ____(J)____ Per Hr = $ ____(J)____

Motor Pool Approval _____

Instructions:
1. Travel by USM Aircraft only when feasible.
2. Call Motor Pool to determine if Aircraft is available.
3. If available complete Aircraft Request Form—forward original and yellow copy to Motor Pool; maintain pink copy in Department file.
4. The Pilot will contact the individual requesting aircraft for exact time of departure.

WHITE—MOTOR POOL
YELLOW—MOTOR POOL/PILOT
PINK—DEPARTMENT FILE

Acc. 34 - Jan. 1983

Figure 3.17.   Continued.

AIRCRAFT MILEAGE CHART

The below distances are statute miles. The rate is figured at a crusing speed of 200 statute miles per hour in a no wind condition. The rate is computed at $185.00 per operational hour. This amounts to $0.925 per statute mile.

CITY - STATE	MILES One-way (Round trip)	Estimated flying time One-Way (Round trip)	Estimated dollar cost One-way (Round trip)
Atlanta, GA	340 (680)	1.7 (3.4)	$314.50 ($629.00)
Auburn, AL	246 (492)	1.2 (2.4)	$227.55 ($455.10)
Baton Rouge, LA	120 (240)	.6 (1.2)	$111.00 ($220.00)
Bay St. Louis, MS	66 (132)	.3 (0.6)	$61.05 ($122.10)
Birmingham, AL	220 (440)	1.1 (2.2)	$203.50 ($407.00)
Cleveland, MS	190 (380)	.9 (1.8)	$175.75 ($351.50)
Dallas, TX	480 (960)	2.4 (4.8)	$444.00 ($888.00)
Greenwood, MS	163 (326)	.8 (1.6)	$185.00 ($370.00)
Gulfport, MS	60 (120)	0.3 (0.6)	$55.50 ($111.00)
Houston, TX	400 (800)	2.0 (4.0)	$370.00 ($740.00)
Jackson, MS	92 (184)	0.5 (1.0)	$85.10 ($170.20)
Jacksonville, FL	468 (936)	2.3 (4.6)	$432.90 ($865.80)
Knoxville, TN	448 (896)	2.2 (4.4)	$414.40 ($828.80)
Louisville, KY	532 (1064)	2.7 (5.4)	$492.10 ($984.20)
Memphis, TN	272 (544)	1.4 (2.8)	$251.60 ($503.20)
Meridian, MS	80 (160)	0.4 (0.8)	$66.60 ($133.20)
Mobile, AL	90 (180)	0.5 (1.0)	$83.25 ($166.50)
Montgomery, AL	186 (372)	0.9 (1.8)	$171.13 ($342.25)
Natchez, MS	122 (244)	0.6 (1.2)	$112.85 ($225.70)
New Orleans, LA	110 (220)	0.6 (1.2)	$101.75 ($203.50)
Oxford, MS	216 (432)	1.1 (2.2)	$199.80 ($399.60)
Pascagoula, MS	86 (172)	0.4 (0.8)	$79.55 ($159.10)
Starkville, MS	155 (310)	0.8 (1.6)	$143.38 ($286.75)
Tallahassee, FL	300 (600)	1.5 (3.0)	$277.50 ($555.00)
Tampa, FL	525 (1050)	2.6 (5.2)	$485.63 ($971.25)
Vicksburg, MS	119 (238)	0.6 (1.2)	$110.08 ($220.15)
Washington, D.C.	896 (1792)	4.5 (9.0)	$828.80 ($1657.60)

For cities that do not appear, contact Motor Pool, 4435.

Figure 3.17. Continued.

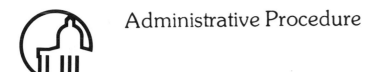

Administrative Procedure

- RETRIEVAL NO. 30041
- PAGE   1 of 11
- ISSUE DATE   September 2, 1986
- ORIGINATOR   Controller
- SUPERSEDES   30023

THE UNIVERSITY OF SOUTHERN MISSISSIPPI

ACCOUNTING SERVICES

SUBJECT: TRAVEL PROCEDURES

Employees of the University are reimbursed for reasonable and necessary expenses incurred while in the performance of approved travel. The following forms are used in the procedure.

Form	Source
Permission to Travel Form (ACC 1)	Printing Center
Travel Voucher (ACC 2)	Printing Center
Remittance Voucher	Financial Affairs

INDEX

Advance payment, registration fees
Approval for travel
Authorization for Travel
Cancellation, Travel Request
Change, Travel Request
Common Carrier
Domestic Travel
Employee Business Expense
Foreign Travel
High Cost Cities
Lodging, shared, spouse, family
Meals, day trips, overnight trips
Motor Pool
Other expenses
Parking
Permission to Travel Form and Instructions
Personal Travel Log
Private Vehicle
Pro Travel
Receipts
Registration fees
Reimbursement Procedure
Rental car
Spouse accompanying
Tips
Tolls
Travel Advance
Travel Voucher and Instructions
University vehicle, credit card

Figure 3.18. Travel procedures.

AUTHORIZATION FOR OFFICIAL UNIVERSITY TRAVEL

Each employee required to travel in performance of official duties and entitled to reimbursement for expenses incurred shall have prior authorization from the department chairman and/or other designated officials. The Permission to Travel Form must be submitted at least two weeks in advance of expected departure date to conferences, conventions, and meetings. In the case of out-of-country travel, the request must be submitted at least 90 days in advance of the requested departure date.

The originating department should be certain that the travel request form is properly completed. The four-part Permission to Travel Form is prepared by the applicant and routed as follows:

A. Domestic Travel:
    (1) Department Chairman
    (2) Dean of College of School or Division Chairman
    (3) Financial Affairs (funds available)

B. Foreign Travel, including Hawaii and Alaska, add:
    (4) Vice President
    (5) President (after obtaining State approval)
    (6) Financial Affairs (for distribution)

When Financial Affairs receives the request for Permission to Travel, it will determine if funds are available. If there is a problem and the request cannot be further processed, it will be returned to the Dean's or Director's Office. If funds are available, Financial Affairs will retain the white and canary copies and return the other copies to the applicant.

Distribution

White - Financial Affairs (for encumbrance)
Canary - Employee (used to obtain travel advance, if needed)
Pink - Employee (to file with travel voucher)
Goldenrod - Departmental file

If a travel advance is requested, the employee will obtain the canary copy from Financial Affairs and take it to the Business Office to obtain cash advance. Money will not be advanced earlier than two weeks prior to the meeting or conference. No cash advance for trips within the State.

The pink copy of the travel request must be attached to travel voucher when it is submitted for payment. The goldenrod copy of the travel request should be maintained in the department's file.

Figure 3.18. Continued.

Required Approvals

The approval requirements for travel are as follows:

A. In-State and Out-of-State Business trips require approval of
   immediate supervisor. No permission to travel form required.
   Categories 1 and 2 on Travel Vouchers.

B. In-State and Out-of-State trips for conferences, conventions,
   associations and meetings require approvals of the Chairman,
   Dean, or Division Chairman and Financial Affairs. Permission
   to Travel Form required. Categories 3 and 4 on Travel Voucher.

C. Travel outside the Continental United States requires the
   approvals in B above, the Vice President, President, Trustees,
   the Executive Director of the Commission of Budget and Accounting
   and the Governor of Mississippi. Category 5 on Travel Voucher.

Changes and Cancellation of Travel Request

An amended Permission to Travel request form must be submitted to change
place or dates of meeting, or to change department account number.

When a Permission to Travel request has been canceled, a copy of the
request with the word "Canceled" written across the face should be sent to
Financial Affairs to release the encumbrance of funds. Funds will remain
encumbered until the travel voucher is paid or until notice is received of
cancellation.

Advance Payment – Conference Registration Fees

To pay registration fees in advance of the conference, these procedures
must be followed:

> The request should be made at least 20 days in advance of the
> start of the conference.

> The request should be made on a Remittance Voucher form with
> both the literature concerning the conference and photocopy
> of the Permission to Travel Form attached.

University Vehicles

To obtain a vehicle from the Motor Pool, the request is made to the
Physical Plant Division as outlined in the University Motor Pool operating
procedures and regulations.

The University of Southern Mississippi uses the State Credit Card for
vehicles assigned to the Motor Pool and USM Gulf Park.

The Motor Pool will charge the account through a Motor Pool Invoice.
The amount charged is based on mileage with a $15.00 per day minimum.
Motor Pool charges should never be reported on a Travel Voucher.

Figure 3.18. Continued.

REIMBURSEMENT OF TRAVEL EXPENSE

GENERAL

Travel Vouchers received in the Financial Affairs Office by 5 P.M. Thursday will be paid the following Thursday, provided there are no problems with the voucher.

Expense Reimbursement

Immediately upon returning from a trip, the traveler should submit a voucher for reimbursement of travel expenses. If not filed within 30 days of the return, any advance received will be deducted from the traveler's pay check for the next full pay period. The first two copies of the Travel Voucher, with required receipts attached, should be completed as outlined in the attachment hereto and submitted to Financial Affairs. For other than business travel, the pink copy of the Permission to Travel must be attached to the Travel Voucher when it is submitted to Financial Affairs for payment. The departmental account number shown on the Permission to Travel will be charged regardless of the department shown on the Travel Voucher. Vouchers submitted with errors other than mathematical errors will be returned. Travel expenses will be reimbursed only for the employee's own expense. One employee cannot submit expense for reimbursement on the same voucher with another person.

If members of the family accompany the University representative, request hotel clerk to note the single room rate on the bill; otherwise, reimbursement will be made for one-half cost of the room. Expenses as a result of unofficial stopovers, side trips, telephone charges, or any other items of a personal nature should not be submitted for reimbursement. Long distance telephone charges must be documented to show place, party called, and purpose of call.

Reimbursement for Meals

Reimbursement for meals will be for actual expenditure (plus tips) at a reasonable amount with the following maximum daily limits for three meals:

In Mississippi	- $18 per day
Out of Mississippi	- $24 per day
High-cost cities (specific)	- $30 per day (receipts required)

Day Trips

No reimbursement is authorized for meals when travel is confined to the vicinity of your home campus. For other travel, reimbursement for meals shall be:

Breakfast - When travel begins before 6 A.M. and extends beyond 8 A.M.
Lunch - When travel begins before 12 P.M. and extends beyond 2 P.M.
Dinner - When travel extends beyond 8 P.M.

No reimbursement is authorized for a dinner meal when the meeting is completed in sufficient time for the traveler to return by 6 P.M.

Figure 3.18. Continued.

Lodging Expenses

Reimbursement will be made for lodging expense incurred in a hotel or motel on the presentation of a paid original bill. When a room is shared with other employees on travel status, reimbursement will be calculated on a pro rata share of the total cost. The other traveler must submit a copy of the lodging receipt indicating that the room was shared. An employee on travel status, if accompanied by spouse who is not an employee on travel status, is entitled to reimbursement at the single room rate. Request the hotel clerk to note the single room rate of the bill.

Normally if the order of business for which the travel is authorized begins after 3 P.M., reimbursement will not be made for lodging prior to the first day of business. If the order of business begins prior to 3 P.M., reimbursement is made for lodging and meals for the preceding day if the lodging is necessary for the traveler to be present prior to the first order of business. Reimbursement is made for lodging the final evening of the trip if the traveler is not able to return home by 9 P.M.

Modes of Transportation

Transportation authorized for official travel include University vehicles (Motor Pool), private vehicles, common carriers, and rental cars.

If travel is by other than the most direct route between points where official University business is conducted, the additional cost must be borne by the traveler. No traveler can claim transportation expense when he is gratuitously transported by another person, or when he is transported by another traveler who is entitled to reimbursement for transportation expense. Private vehicle mileage reimbursement cannot exceed cost of round-trip air coach fare.

Private Vehicles

The employee shall receive the legal rate established by the State of Mississippi for each mile actually and necessarily traveled in the performance of official duties.

The following situations justify the use of private vehicles for travel:

1. When travel is required at such time or to such places that common carrier transportation may not be reasonably available.

2. When one or more persons travel to the same destination in the same car and total mileage claimed does not exceed the total airline tourist fares for transporting the same number of people.

Figure 3.18. Continued.

Common Carriers

Employees are reimbursed for actual airline and train fares. All airline tickets must be purchased from Pro Travel, the official travel agent of the University.

The employee will purchase his own common carrier transportation and claim reimbursement. Employees are <u>not allowed to charge</u> the transportation to the University. Ticket cost reimbursement <u>must</u> be handled through the travel voucher.

Travel by airline shall be at the tourist rate. Certification that tourist accommodations are not available will be necessary when travel is first class.

Rental Cars

Limit the use of rental cars as much as possible. There are times when common carriers, private cars, and University vehicles are not available and rental cars are the only means of transportation. Below are examples:

1. When a destination has been reached by common carrier and several locations in the same vicinity must be visited.

2. When transportation between airport terminal and destination is needed and taxi or limousine service is not fesible or available.

3. When a schedule cannot be met through the use of common carrier.

Before you accept the rental car, examine the vehicle for any prior damage. If prior damage is discovered, it should be reported immediately to the rental agency to prevent improper claims against the University.

At the time you return the rental car, report any accident involving the rental vehicle and file an accident report with the rental agency.

Other Expenses

Registration fees paid by the employee at the conference will be reimbursed on a travel voucher when supported by a paid receipt. The portion of the fees applicable to meals shall be reported as meal expense.

Tips for meals and taxi should be included as part of those charges. Tips reported here include baggage handling tips when arriving and departing a hotel or at airports.

Actual parking fees while away from home, and road and bridge tolls are reported here.

Figure 3.18. Continued.

Receipts

Major expense incurred by an employee while on official travel for the University require receipts. The receipts must be originals and not copies.

Expenses that <u>require</u> original receipts:

1. Lodging
2. Rail, plane, or bus
3. Registration fees
4. Car rental (including gasoline tickets)
5. Telephone expense (only as listed on motel receipt)
6. Gas for University vehicle (see reimbursement procedure)

Expenses that <u>do</u> <u>not</u> require receipts:

1. Meals, including tips (receipt required for any meal if over $25)
2. Mileage of personal vehicle
3. Tips
4. Taxi/Limousine, including tips
5. Parking/Tolls

Reimbursement Procedure

Payment checks for travel expenses are sent to Business Services and applied to the employee travel advance receivables. If reimbursement exceeds advance, Business Services will send a check for the excess to the traveler. If advance exceeds expenses, Business Services will notify the traveler of the amount applied and amount due. Monthly statements are sent also.

Figure 3.18. Continued.

COMPLETING THE PERMISSION TO TRAVEL FORM

a. Date submitted.

b. Employee name, title and social security number.

c. Name of convention, association or meeting. If for normal business travel out-of-state, enter "Business Travel."

d. Enter city and state where meeting is being held.

e. Enter dates of meeting.

f. Enter department name and account number to be charged for the travel.

g. Enter purpose of the meeting.

h. Estimated total cost of attending.

i. Signature and Southern Station Box Number.

j. Required approvals of domestic travel.

k. Additional approvals for travel outside continental United States.

l. Amount of advance when requested.

m. Signature of employee.

n. Date advance received.

o. Completed by Business Services when advance is issued.

p. Completed by Financial Affairs when Permission is approved.

All costs of conventions, associations and meetings are reported annually to the State Peer Committee. This report shows the convention name, place, dates, employee attending and total cost.

Figure 3.18. Continued.

PERMISSION TO TRAVEL

Submit at least two weeks prior to date of proposed trip (90 days prior to foreign travel).

THE UNIVERSITY OF SOUTHERN MISSISSIPPI

a , 19____

Name: **b** _____ Title **b** _____ S.S. No. **b** _____

In compliance with Section 25-3-45 Mississippi Code 1972, request is made for authorization to attend the following convention, association, or meeting:

c _____   **d** _____

Complete Name of Convention, Association or Meeting (Do Not Abbreviate)   Place of Meeting

e _____   **f** _____   **f** _____

Dates of Meeting   Department Name   Department Code

Purpose of convention, association, or meeting (If an advance is needed, but cost of trip will be reimbursed by an outside organization, please explain).

g

Estimated Cost $ **h** _____

I acknowledge that I have read and that I understand the summary of travel policies on the back of this form.

Domestic Travel

1. Chairman _____ **j**

2. Dean or Division Chairman _____ **j**

3. Funds Available—Accounting (5143) **j** _____

Foreign, Hawaii, Alaska Travel

4. Vice President _____ **k**

5. President _____ **k**

i
_____
Signature of Applicant

Southern Station Box No. **i** _____

FOR ACCOUNTING AND BUSINESS OFFICE USE ONLY

ADVANCE (Cannot exceed estimated cost above)

Amount of advance $ **l** _____ Signature **m** _____ Date **n** _____

I hereby certify that the above trip has been properly approved. The amount advanced will be repaid from reimbursement check for travel expenses, and it is expressly understood and agreed that unless this amount is repaid by me before the next full pay period after the date of my return, it may be deducted from my next salary check.

ACCOUNT RECEIVABLE , **o**

Date MMDDYY	F/GL	OBJ.	SOCIAL SEC. NO.	AMOUNT		DR
	1014	1169				4

ENCUMBRANCE **p**

P.O. CONTROL	F/GL	OBJ.	DEPARTMENT	SOCIAL SEC. NO.	AMOUNT		DATE MMDDY

White Copy—Accounting • Canary Copy—Employee (For Advance) • Pink Copy—File with Voucher • Goldenrod Copy—Dept. File Copy

ACC 1 (Revised 7/84)

Figure 3.18. Continued.

COMPLETING THE EMPLOYEE TRAVEL VOUCHER

a. Employee name, social security number and address.

b. Purpose of trip and city and state.

c. Department name and account number to be charged. Must be same as Permission to Travel.

d. Names of others on trip, whether traveling together or not.

e. Date of travel, departure and arrival times.

f. Meals -- Daily meal maximums are:

In Mississippi	$18
Outside Mississippi	$24
Listed high-cost cities	$30

g. Lodging -- Original hotel or motel bill required. If bill shows two persons, indicate single room rate for this room. Do not report charges other than room charges as lodging (telephone, room service, etc.)

h. Travel by personal vehicle -- Indicate if University Motor Pool vehicle was used. If so, do not enter any miles here. If personal vehicle is used, enter departure and arrival location and miles. Enter current approved rate (20¢ mile).

i. Travel by Public Carrier -- Date, city leaving from, destination city, mode and ticket amount. Airline ticket coupon must be attached.

j. Registration fees -- If paid by employee, receipt or copy of program stating fee must be attached.

k. Tips -- Only for baggage handling or valet parking.

l. Taxi/limousine -- Actual taxi fare plus tip or airport limousine charge.

m. Parking/Tolls -- Actual parking charges or road or bridge tolls paid.

n. Car rental -- Receipt required.

o. Check travel category. If category 3, 4 or 5 are checked, approved copy of Permission to Travel form must be attached.

p. If travel advance was received, enter amount and date received.

q. Enter total of all expenses on Travel Voucher.

r. Maximum Reimbursement Allowed -- If chairman approving enters a smaller amount here than the total amount, then the smaller amount will be paid. Some departments have a travel limit on each trip.

s. Signature of employee and account director and dates.

t. For Accounting use only.

Figure 3.18. Continued.

EMPLOYEE TRAVEL VOUCHER

THE UNIVERSITY OF SOUTHERN MISSISSIPPI

IMPORTANT—SEE INSTRUCTIONS ON BACK

Employee	**a**	S.S. No.	**a**

Address To Which Check Should Be Sent	**a**
	a

Purpose and Place of Visit		
b	Dept. **c**	Dept. No. **c**
	Others On Trip **d**	

MEALS AND LODGING

								Total
Date								
Departure Time	AM-PM	AM-PM	AM-PM	AM-PM	AM-PM	AM-PM	AM-PM	
Arrival Time	AM-PM	AM-PM	AM-PM	AM-PM	AM-PM	AM-PM	AM-PM	
Breakfast								
Lunch								
Dinner								
Lodging								

Total Meals and Lodging

TRAVEL BY PERSONAL VEHICLE (Did you use University vehicle? ☐ Yes ☐ No)

Date	From	To	Miles

Total Miles   X Rate   =

TRAVEL BY PUBLIC CARRIER

Date	From	To	Mode	Ticket Amount

Total Travel By Public Carrier

OTHER EXPENSES

Item	Date	Place Where Expense Incurred	Amount
Registration Fees			
Tips (baggage handling)			
Taxi/Limousine			
Parking/Tolls			
Car Rental			

Check Category of Travel (3 Through 5 Require Permission to Travel Form) **o**

1 ☐ Business Trip In-State/No Advance

2 ☐ Business Trip Out-of-State/No Advance

3 ☐ Business Trip Out-of-State/With Advance

4 ☐ Conventions, Conferences, Associations/In-or Out-of-State

5 ☐ Out-of-Country

Travel Advance For This Trip

$ **p** Date **p**

Employee Signature **s** Date **s**

Approved By **s** Date **s**

Total Other Expenses	**q**
Total Expenses	
MAXIMUM REIMBURSEMENT ALLOWED ▶	**r**

Accounting Distribution	F/GL	Object	Department	Liquidation	Expense
Voucher No. **t**					
Voucher Date **t**					
P.O. No. **t**					
Verified By Date **t**					

ACC 2 (4/85)

White Copy—Accounting • Canary Copy—Accounting • Pink Copy—Department • Goldenrod Copy—Employee

Figure 3.18. Continued.

CHAPTER 4
FORMS MANUAL:
I'VE GROWN
ACCUSTOMED TO
YOUR FACE

The forms manual is the easiest module of documentation to prepare. However, unless the organization has a forms specialist or a formal documentation unit, this documentation is seldom started, let alone completed. While forms design can be critical, a poorly designed form will handle the transaction accounting process adequately even if the form is difficult and cumbersome to use.

FUNDAMENTAL RULES

As users of forms and not as specialists in their design, you should be aware of some fundamental rules when developing a new accounting form. Answers are required during the forms development stage to determine form specifications and use.

Purpose

Determine exactly what the form is designed to do. First, determine which unit within the accounting department will be the primary user because the data needed by that unit will generally determine the minimum content of the form. Next, determine whether the form relates to the updating of a master file—such as an employee payroll file, a price file, a vendor description file—or whether it is a dollar or quantity accounting transaction form.

If the form updates a master accounting file such as a table, a price list, or cost accounting detail record, the form can be somewhat informal because the preparer is an accountant familiar with the operation. A transaction form initiated by an outside department needs to be more explicit in its content and preparation.

Use of the Form

Determine the department or unit initiating the form and how the data are developed and entered. The answer determines where the working supply of forms should be stored. Follow the form through the various processing steps and indicate by number or letter which person or unit entered the information in each space on a blank form.

For example, letter each person or function entering data on the form. The foreman would be "A," the superintendent "B," cost accountant "C," and cost ledger bookkeeper "D." An "A" would be placed in each space completed by the shop foreman. Continue this process until every blank space requiring information is filled.

Number of Copies and Distribution

Forms are expensive, particularly if multiple copies are printed. Retention of a copy implies permanent storage and future reference, both expensive operations. Thus there must be a strong reason given when a department or individual insists on retaining a copy, particularly if the copy is retained before it is completed. If information is to be entered manually on a form, the maximum number of copies that may be used is usually four, including the original. This is true whether NCR (no carbon required) paper is used or carbon sheets are interleaved, an even more expensive proposition. Even then, a ball-point pen and heavy pressure are needed. Any form of more than four copies must be typewritten or computer-printed.

Permanent or Interim Document

If the form is to be retained permanently, how will the form be filed and how will it be accessed after filing? The answers determine the type and quantity of future storage and, to some extent, the quality of the paper and the printing. For instance, some photocopies have a very short life, sometimes less than a year. Such forms cannot be retained very long.

Forms Numbering

Prenumbering a form with consecutive numbers *means* control. Printing forms with consecutive numbers is very expensive and should be avoided unless required for reference and control purposes. Numbering during the processing, such as adding a file or reference number, is not as critical. However, the accounting reason for numbering should be determined.

Form Size

Unless absolutely required because of the amount of data needed, an accounting form should not be larger than $8\frac{1}{2} \times 11$ (standard stationery size) or smaller than a 3×5 index card. To avoid extra printing charges, forms smaller than a full size page should be designed to be cut from regular paper stock sizes. Standard file cabinets hold file folders for $8\frac{1}{2} \times 11$ paper. Legal files hold $8\frac{1}{2} \times 14$ paper.

Oversize pages are difficult to file and require more storage space, legal-size files, or special file storage. Very small forms, if retained, also require special filing cabinets. Small forms which are attached to other papers tend to become separated in the filing process.

Data Entry Forms

Entering data from a form to other media can be done manually, through a user-department terminal, or by a remote data entry operation for input into a computerized system. In all cases, the form should be designed so the needed items are selected in a logical sequence. If the reader's eyes have to jump all over the form to pick up the information for transcription or data entry operations, the form itself is causing severe mechanical friction. This problem leads to fatigue, transcription errors, and, in some cases, loss of data. Figure 4.1 illustrates an accounting input document that is difficult to use because of the location of the various data fields.

If the document is fairly simple, one solution is to add a section that summarizes the information in the proper sequence for the data entry operation. Figure 4.2 shows the same information as Figure 4.1 with such a section added. In this real situation, the data entry error rate fell from 5 percent to almost zero.

Manual or Typewritten Entry

If entries are to be typed on the form, all spacing from top to bottom should be in multiples of one-sixth inch, standard vertical typewriter spacing. If entries are to be handwritten, vertical spacing should be one-quarter or one-third inch or multiples thereof. Because most typing is done with elite print of 12 characters to the inch, a grid chart with both horizontal and vertical lines spaced at intervals of one-sixth inch is very useful in designing an internal form or preparing a rough draft of a form for subsequent printing. Vertical spacing is for typewriter use and horizontal spacing permits two characters to each square of one-sixth inch. Grid paper of six squares to the inch both vertically and horizontally is usually available from office supply stores.

THE FORMS SURVEY

The next step in preparing a forms manual is to complete a forms survey. Figure 4.3 shows a form survey worksheet that simplifies the information-gathering process. The survey is generally limited to forms initiated or processed by the accounting department such as:

Purchase order
Remittance voucher (authority to pay an invoice which usually does not require a purchase order)
Checks
Receipt forms
Employment authorization forms
Employment termination forms
Time reporting forms
Payroll deduction authorization forms
Travel expense reimbursement forms
Budget forms
Accounts receivable forms

PERMISSION TO TRAVEL

UNIVERSITY OF SOUTHERN MISSISSIPPI
Hattiesburg, Mississippi 39401

Submit at least two weeks prior to date of proposed trip.

(1) _____, 19____

TO: President

FROM: _____ Title _____ S. S. No. _____

In compliance with Section 25-3-45 Mississippi Code 1972, request is made for authorization to attend the following convention, association, or meeting:

_____ _____
Complete Name of Convention, Association or Meeting (Do Not Abbreviate)   Place of Meeting

_____ _____
Dates of Meeting   Departmental Name   Departmental Code

Purpose of convention, association, or meeting

Estimated Cost $ _____

I acknowledge that I have read and that I understand the summary of travel policies on the back of this form.

Signature of Applicant _____

Southern Station Box No. _____

1. Chairman _____

2. Dean of College or School
   or Division Chairman _____

3. Vice President _____

4. Funds Available—Accounting _____

5. President _____

FOR ACCOUNTING AND BUSINESS OFFICE USE ONLY

S. S. No	Encumbered Control No.	P. O. Date
(4)		
F/GL OBJ.	DEPT./S. S. NO.	AMOUNT
(2) → (3)		(5)

Amount of advance $ _____

I hereby certify that the above trip has been properly approved. The amount advanced will be repaid from reimbursement check for travel expenses, and it is expressly understood and agreed that unless this amount is repaid by me before the next full pay period after the date of my return, it may be deducted from my next salary check.

Signature _____

Date _____

White Copy—Accounting • Canary Copy—Employee (For Advance) • Pink Copy—File with Voucher • Goldenrod Copy—Dept. File Copy

103

ACC. 1 (Revised 7/81)

Figure 4.1. An accounting input document that is poorly designed for data entry.

PERMISSION TO TRAVEL

Submit at least two weeks prior to date of proposed trip (90 days prior to foreign travel).

THE UNIVERSITY OF SOUTHERN MISSISSIPPI

_____ , 19_____

Name: _____ Title _____ S.S. No. _____

In compliance with Section 25-3-45 Mississippi Code 1972, request is made for authorization to attend the following convention, association, or meeting:

_____   _____

Complete Name of Convention, Association or Meeting (Do Not Abbreviate)   Place of Meeting

_____   _____   _____

Dates of Meeting   Department Name   Department Code

Purpose of convention, association, or meeting (If an advance is needed, but cost of trip will be reimbursed by an outside organization, please explain).

Domestic Travel

Estimated Cost $ _____

I acknowledge that I have read and that I understand the summary of travel policies on the back of this form.

1. Chairman _____

2. Dean or Division Chairman _____

3. Funds Available—Accounting (5143) _____

Foreign, Hawaii, Alaska Travel

4. Vice President _____

_____

Signature of Applicant

Southern Station Box No. _____

5. President _____

_____   _____

FOR ACCOUNTING AND BUSINESS OFFICE USE ONLY

ADVANCE (Cannot exceed estimated cost above)

Amount of advance $ _____ Signature _____ Date _____

I hereby certify that the above trip has been properly approved. The amount advanced will be repaid from reimbursement check for travel expenses, and it is expressly understood and agreed that unless this amount is repaid by me before the next full pay period after the date of my return, it may be deducted from my next salary check.

ACCOUNT RECEIVABLE

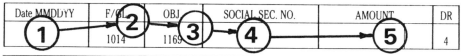

Date MMDDYY	F/GL	OBJ	SOCIAL SEC. NO.	AMOUNT	DR
	1014	1169			4

ENCUMBRANCE

P.O. CONTROL	F/GL	OBJ.	DEPARTMENT	SOCIAL SEC. NO.	AMOUNT		DATE MMDDY

White Copy—Accounting   •   Canary Copy—Employee (For Advance)   •   Pink Copy—File with Voucher   •   Goldenrod Copy—Dept. File Copy

ACC 1 (Revised 7/84)

Figure 4.2. An accounting input document designed for efficient data entry.

104

FORM SURVEY   Survey No. _____

Name of Form _____

Form No. _____ Date of Last Revision _____

Copies and destination or use. Number of parts _____
Copy No.   Color   Destination or Use

   1   _____   _____

   2   _____   _____

   3   _____   _____

   4   _____   _____

   5   _____   _____

Is the form prenumbered?   ____ Yes   ____ No

Source of supply:

   ____   Purchased. Name of printer, if known _____

   ____   Own Print Shop

   ____   From another department? Which? _____

   ____   Other. Describe _____

If retained in Accounting, how is form filed? _____

Estimated quantity used per month _____

Originating Department _____

How is Form completed: ____   Handwritten
                          ____   Typewriter
                          ____   Computer output (Invoice, check, etc.)
                          ____   Terminal device or Personal Computer
                          ____   Other _____

Remarks: _____

_____

_____

                                       Information
Prepared by _____ Date _____ Provided by _____

Attach original or copy of Form

Figure 4.3. Form survey worksheet.

Stores issues forms (inventory)

Sales forms

Petty cash forms

The form survey can be handled by various employees who are familiar with specific forms or may be done on a consulting basis by one or two experienced people discussing the form with the person most familiar with its use. If a large number of forms are to be surveyed, the consultant method is more efficient.

In either case, the requested information is entered on the form survey and an actual form or a copy of it is attached. The survey forms should be numbered so they can be accounted for later when the forms manual is written. The survey form is completed as follows:

1. If a general survey of existing forms is being made, enter a generated survey number such as "Payroll 1" or "Accounts Payable 3."

2. Enter the actual name of the form, the form number, and last revision date, if any.

3. Enter the number of copies, the color of each copy (if colors are used), and the destination or use of each copy.

4. Indicate if the form is prenumbered. The control aspects of prenumbering should be described in the remarks section.

5. Indicate the source of supply of the form.

6. If a copy is retained in the accounting department, describe the method of filing, such as alphabetically by vendor, numerically by voucher number, attached to another controlled form, in folders by month, and so on.

7. If available, obtain an estimate of the quantity used per month or per year to show the relative importance of the form in the overall operation.

8. Enter the name of the department that enters the first data on the form. In most cases, the accounting department completes a form. Purchasing initiates purchase orders, Personnel provides completed employment or termination forms, and any department in the organization could initiate a nonpurchase order to pay a vendor.

9. Indicate the normal method of preparation, such as handwriting, typing, stamping, stickers, and so on.

10. Enter the name of the person preparing the survey form and the date prepared. If the information was provided by an employee, also indicate the name of that person in case additional information is needed later.

If possible, a copy of a processed form should be obtained to show what information is entered by the various users.

In a small accounting operation, the controller or chief accountant could probably describe adequately all the forms used in the operation. In a very large organization, a state government for example, the use of a form for collecting forms data is mandatory.

ASSEMBLING THE FORMS MANUAL

Now that the mechanics are out of the way, we can begin to assemble the Forms Manual. The sections of this module describe the physical characteristics of the form, show the form itself, and describe briefly and clearly the information to be entered in each field of the form. Also shown are the names of the persons, units or departments responsible for completing each field or section of the form. Most forms require three pages.

Page 1. Physical description of the form (see Figure 4.4).
   A. Name of form (the name printed on the form).
   B. Form number.
   C. Date of last revision.
   D. Number of parts, color of each part if colors are used to identify copies, and destination or use of each part.
   E. Department supplying form. The name of the department responsible for storing the blank supply of forms. This informs other users where a supply of blank forms may be obtained.
   F. Printing source. Name of vendor who printed the form. The source may be a captive, in-house printing center or it may be an office photocopier form.
   G. Purpose of the form. Purpose does not mean a description of the procedure to complete the form, but the uses of the form. Examples would be to "request payment of items not requiring a vendor invoice, such as payments for subscriptions, dues, casual labor, tax payments, periodic contract payments, and so forth." Repetitive problems with the form such as confusion with another similar form should be explained here.
   H. Distribution of the copies. Distribution may be to a designated person, unit, department, or outside organization. Distribution information can describe how the form is delivered or provided and may indicate its primary use by each recipient.

Page 2. The second page is titled "COMPLETING THE (NAME OF FORM)." To complete the description, it is necessary to enter sequential numbers or letters in each area of the form requiring data in the order the data is entered. This sequence is vital as it permits separating the entries into groups of sequential users.

   Once the original form has a number or letter in each field a sequential description can be written. The first line would indicate the person or department completing each of the fields in order. This is followed by the field numbers or letters and the descriptions of permitted or required content. A simple form would be described as follows:

COMPLETING THE MULTIPLE VENDOR-PAYEE ATTACHMENT

The form is completed entirely by the department.
   A. Name of department.
   B. Account number of department.
   C. Telephone number of preparer.
   D. Date the form is submitted.
   E. Vendor code number, if known. For an individual, vendor code is the Social Security number.
   F. Vendor or payee name and address, if needed. The form provides for 12 vendors.
   G. Amount to be paid to each person such as $50.00.
   H. Total payments on this page. Each page should be separately totaled and the summary remittance voucher will show the page totals and the grand total to be paid.
   I. Page number as Page 1 of 5, 2 of 5, and so on.
       Note that the word *enter* is implied in each section. In this illustration, if something had to be added by another department or by Accounting, the next line after Item I would be the name of the person or unit responsible for that item beginning with J.

FORM DESCRIPTION

NAME OF FORM _____

FORM NO. _____ DATE OF LAST REVISION _____

COPY NO.   COLOR   DESTINATION OR USE

  1   _____   _____

  2   _____   _____

  3   _____   _____

  4   _____   _____

  5   _____   _____

IS THE FORM PRENUMBERED? ____ YES ____ NO

DEPARTMENT SUPPLYING FORM:

PRINTING SOURCE:

PURPOSE:

DISTRIBUTION OF THE COPIES:

Figure 4.4. Form for physical description of a form.

Page 3. Copy of the actual form with the sequential numbers or letters added. These reference numbers or letters should be in bold print so they are not confused with the form itself. Press-on letters or numbers can be purchased by the sheet in almost any size or type style. Characters of $\frac{1}{8}''$ or $\frac{3}{16}''$ are satisfactory. A simpler method is to draw quarter-inch circles in the center of each field of the form, using a good black pen and a plastic template containing circles of the desired size. The numbers or letters are then typed in the circles.

The 3-page system works best if the description page is odd-numbered (1, 3, 5, etc.), and the completion page and form are on facing pages (pages 2 and 3, 4 and 5, etc.). The completion page is on the left side and the form on the right side. If the form can be reduced and still retain its clarity, pages 2 and 3 can be placed side-by-side and reduced to fit one full page. See Figures 4.5, 4.6, and 4.7 at the end of the chapter.

TWO-SIDED FORMS

Although two-sided forms present problems because of the tendency not to complete the back of the form, they are described exactly as shown for the front of the form with two pages added to provide instructions on how to complete the back, followed by a photocopy of the back of the form with all spaces lettered for reference. The form documentation would consist of the following five pages:

1. Physical description of the form.
2. Completing the front of the form.
3. Front of actual form.
4. Completing the back of the form.
5. Back of actual form.

CONCLUSION

This forms manual may be maintained as a separate manual or may be included in the general accounting manual. The information about those forms processed or handled by users outside of the accounting operation will be included in the user manual described in Chapter 7.

The quickest way to study an accounting operation is to review accounting forms in detail to determine if they are easy to use, provide adequate information, are approved properly, and are easy to record and summarize. Forms are also an integral part of the internal control of the using operations.

FORM DESCRIPTION

NAME OF FORM ____Multiple-Invoice Voucher_____

FORM NO. ___ACC 11_____ DATE OF LAST REVISION ____1-83_____

COPY NO.   COLOR   DESTINATION OR USE

   1   __White__   ____Accounting_____

   2   __Canary__   ____Vendor_____

   3   __Pink___   ____Department_____

   4   _____   _____

   5   _____   _____

IS THE FORM PRENUMBERED? ____ YES __X__ NO

DEPARTMENT SUPPLYING FORM: Accounting

PRINTING SOURCE: Printing Center

PURPOSE:

Used by those departments who handle their own large-volume purchasing such
as the Bookstore, Library and Food Services. It is also used by the
Athletic Department for required medical examination fees and by Accounting
Services to process partial payments or payments on standing purchase
orders for the Physical Plant operations.

The form is identical to the Remittance Voucher form ACC 14 except for the
description area.

Supporting documents are to be attached to the accounting copy of the form.

DISTRIBUTION OF THE COPIES:

Accounting - Permanent accounts payable file.

Vendor - Mailed with check.

Department - Retains and compares to next monthly Budget Report.

Figure 4.5. Physical description of a form.

COMPLETING THE MULTIPLE-INVOICE VOUCHER

Department enters:

A. Department name.
B. Account number.
C. Telephone number of preparer.
D. Name and address of vendor.
E. Description of each invoice to be paid.

    1. Purchase order number assigned to the purchase.
    2. Vendor invoice number.
    3. Invoice date.
    4. Receiving report number.
    5. Total dollar amount of the invoice.
    6. Dollar amount of cash discount permitted by vendor.

F. Amount to be paid. Attach supporting document, if any.
G. Total to be paid on this voucher.
H. Signature of person requesting payment and date signed.
I. Approval signature and date. Payments to individuals require two approval signatures if an invoice is not available.
J. General Ledger Code, Object Code and Department to be charged. If Department is not entered, the charge will be made to the account shown at the top of the form.
K. Amount to be charged to this account. Form provides distribution for up to eight accounts.

Financial Affairs enters:

L. Vendor code number.
M. Voucher number.
N. Voucher date.
O. Purchase Order Number, if any.
P. Name of person processing the voucher and date processed.
Q. Name of person reviewing or verifying information.
R. Preprinted number of special check used to pay voucher.
S. Special handling required or enclosure to be mailed with check.
T. Amount of encumbrance to be liquidated, if any.

Figure 4.6. Completing the multiple-invoice voucher.

MULTIPLE-INVOICE VOUCHER
UNIVERSITY OF SOUTHERN MISSISSIPPI
HATTIESBURG, MISSISSIPPI 39406-5143

DEPT NAME	**A**
ACCT NO	**B**
TEL NO	**C**

VENDOR _____**D**_____

VENDOR CODE
L

PURCHASE ORDER NUMBER	INVOICE NUMBER	INVOICE DATE	RECEIVING REPORT NUMBER	INVOICE PRICE	LESS DISCOUNT	NET PRICE
E1	**E2**	**E3**	**E4**	**E5**	**E6**	**F**

REQUESTED BY	DATE	APPROVED BY	DATE	TOTAL	
H		**I**			**G**

ACCOUNTING USE	GL	OBJECT	DEPARTMENT	LIQUIDATION	EXPENDITURE
VOUCHER NUMBER **M**		**J**		**T**	**K**
VOUCHER DATE **N**					
PURCHASE ORDER NUMBER **O**					
PROCESSED BY DATE **P**					
VERIFIED BY: **Q**	SPECIAL CHECK NO. **R**	ACCOUNTING USE **S**			

ACC. 11 (REV. 1-83)   WHITE—ACCOUNTING   CANARY—VENDOR   PINK—DEPARTMENT

Figure 4.7. Multiple-invoice voucher.

DEPARTMENTAL DEPOSIT TICKET

A. FORM NO. AND NAME: ACC 35 - DEPARTMENTAL DEPOSIT TICKET

B. NO. OF PARTS: 2 LAST REVISION DATE: 4/1983

C. SOURCE OF SUPPLY: Cashier

D. PURPOSE: To describe the account number, account name, source of funds and amount of cash or checks in sufficient detail to provide supporting documentation to a cash deposit with the University Cashier.

When the cash (and/or checks) and the Departmental Deposit Ticket are brought to the Cashier (Forrest County Hall), the depositor will receive an official prenumbered Cash Receipt form. The second copy of the Deposit Ticket (with the official receipt number entered thereon) and a copy of the receipt will be returned to the depositor. These forms should be held in the department making the deposit.

E. DISTRIBUTION OF COMPLETED FORM: Original held by Cashier and filed with receipt copy. Copy returned to person making the deposit.

Figure 4.8. Description of the departmental deposit ticket.

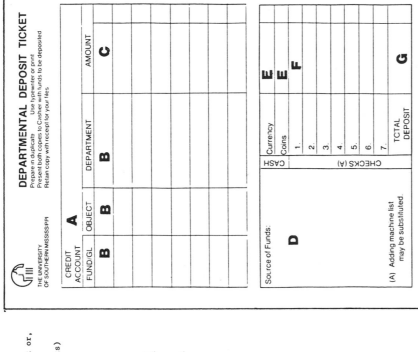

COMPLETING THE DEPARTMENTAL DEPOSIT TICKET

A. Enter the name of the account to be credited. May be an income account or, if permitted, an expenditure account.

B. Enter the Fund-General Ledger Code (4 digits), the object code (4 digits) and, if required, the department account number (7 or 10 digits).

C. Enter the amount to be credited to the account entered.

D. Describe the source of the funds.

E. Enter the amount of currency and coins being deposited.

F. Enter the checks individually unless there is a large number of checks, in which case an adding machine list is attached and "See List" entered on check line 1.

G. Total the cash and checks being deposited. This amount must agree with total in account distribution section.

H. Enter name of depositor, campus telephone number, and date deposited.

I. Bring both copies of Ticket and the cash and checks to the University Cashier.

To insure proper account coding for research accounts (Fund 30), checks received from a granting agency are to be routed through the Grants and Contracts unit of Financial Affairs.

Figure 4.9. Completing the departmental deposit ticket.

CHAPTER 5
YEAR-END MANUAL:
GOOD FISCAL EXERCISE

When accountants neatly divided the life of a business into 12-month units they created a significant problem at the end of the fiscal year. The year-end closing, one to three months long, requires concentrated efforts by several people to correct, summarize, analyze, schedule, and report the year's activity. Much of the work is required to insure that the statements of financial condition and results of operations are accurate and, more importantly, can be presented to management, stockholders, and the public clearly and succinctly.

Many organizations and all exchange-listed companies are assisted in the closing by independent auditors who require information to enable them to attest to the fairness and consistency of the reported results. Independent auditors are expensive, with rates ranging from $20 to more than a $100 an hour, depending on the level of expertise offered. Even so, many chief financial officers and controllers tend to rely on their own ability and memory to complete the closing without error and on time.

There is no need for them to do so, particularly when a simple year-end closing manual can be prepared long before the fiscal year ends. This relatively simple manual lists in fairly extensive detail the jobs to be done by the company's staff to insure the accounting records are complete and accurate, all special year-end requirements are handled adequately, and schedules needed by the auditors and tax accountants are prepared in sufficient detail.

The year-end assignment manual needs to be prepared completely only once and then updated annually. A simple layout would include columns for:

Assigned completion date

Task or item

Person assigned to

Date completed

Hours to complete (optional)

The preferred sequence of the manual seems to be in major account number order of assets, liabilities, equity, income, expense, financial statements and schedules, and special tax return schedules. At the end of this chapter is the complete year-end manual used at the University of Southern Mississippi for the fiscal year 1985–1986 (Figure 5.1).

The manual should be issued one or two months before the fiscal year-end to every person who is listed in the assignment column. One person in the organization should be assigned to receive reconcilements, analysis worksheets, trial balances of subsidiary ledgers, and other required memos or schedules. The logical person for this assignment is the controller. The transmittal letter should state that all papers submitted show the name of the account or accounts included in the workpaper, the year-end date, the name of the person who prepared the worksheet, and the date completed.

The rest of this chapter will be devoted to listing major account names and typical internal assignments such as reconcile, schedule, calculate, compare, and so on. To show typical completion dates, the fiscal year-end is December 31, 1986. The last item for each account will be "Suggested working days to completion date," followed by a number. Using this number as a guide, it will be comparatively simple to determine assigned completion dates for the first year-end assignments manual. The manual should state that all assignments are due at the close of the assigned completion date.

ASSETS

Assets should be fairly stated, generally at realizable amounts. Several assets require additional information for reporting purposes. Examples are the allowance for uncollectible amounts for accounts receivable; market value for investments; valuation method for inventories; and basis of valuation for property, plant, and equipment.

The related working papers should show the basis and, when required, how the amounts were calculated.

Cash. Prepare reconcilement of December 31 balance per bank to the balance per books for each account. Show origination date and description of each reconciling item. Prepare necessary journal entries and adjust the reconcilements.

Count cash and cash items on January 5 for in-transit deposit. (Offices closed Friday, January 2.)

Suggested working days to completion date: 15.

Petty Cash and Change Funds. Prepare a summary of all petty cash and change funds as of December 31. Totals must agree with general ledger. Prepare positive confirmations asking for verification of amount and custodian as of 12/31.

Suggested working days to completion date: 10.

Investments. Prepare list of all securities on hand at 12/31 by location held such as vault, broker, bank. Use full names and show face amount or number of shares and date of acquisition. Determine cost and market values. Calculate accrued interest receivable.

Suggested working days to completion date: 5.

Accounts Receivable—Trade. Obtain aged trial balances and reconcile to general ledger. Calculate possible allowance for uncollectible accounts and obtain approval of Controller. Adjust allowance to calculated amount. Write off any unlocated differences.

Suggested working days to completion date: 15.

Other Receivables. Prepare schedule of other miscellaneous receivables and reconcile to general ledger. Comment on collectibility if material.

Suggested working days to completion date: 10.

Inventories. Prepare a summary of raw material, in process, and finished inventories. Prepare proof of proper receiving and shipping cutoffs. Explain significant variations from the prior year.

Reconcile inventories from physical inventory date to year-end. Physical dates in 1986 were November 30 for main plant and October 31 for Western and Southern Branches.

Test the cost of the large quantity current models by comparing total unit cost per unit to current sales less 12 percent cost to sell and normal profit margin for each product type.

Test significant raw material costs by comparison to January 1987 commitments.

Prepare schedule of raw materials which are slow-moving and possibly obsolete. Discuss the amount to be written off with Controller.

Suggested working days to completion date: 15.

Deferred Charges. Prepare a list of all deferred charges. Show calculations and, if necessary, confirm values such as cash surrender value of life insurance. Determine that related liabilities are recorded.

Suggested working days to completion date: 10.

Property, Plant, and Equipment. Prepare schedule of assets and related allowances for depreciation for inclusion in audit report. Reconcile allowance additions to total depreciation expense. Analyze construction projects and equipment additions in process and attach copies of all invoices relating thereto in excess of $5000. Trace disposals to capital gain and loss schedule or to expense if items were scrapped or abandoned.

Suggested working days to completion date: 20.

LIABILITIES AND STOCKHOLDERS' EQUITY

Liabilities are shown at the amount to be paid in the subsequent period. Overstatement, rather than understatement, is the rule for liabilities. When in doubt, record the liability.

Accounts Payable. Determine that all items paid through December 31 are not shown on accounts payable list. Invoices paid through January 15 should be in accounts payable. Any items not paid will be listed and a copy of the supporting data (invoices, receiving reports, etc.) prepared for the auditors.

Maintain a list of any items over $1000 paid until January 31, which items are not included in accounts payable.

Suggested working days to completion date: 12.

Accrued Payroll. Calculate accrued payroll at December 31, including incentive bonuses and other special payroll payments. Record expense in normal manner and reverse in 1987.

Suggested working days to completion date: Immediately after first payroll in 1987.

Other Accrued Expenses. Review accruals for payroll taxes, payroll deductions payable, interest expense on short-term borrowings, and long-term debt. Determine unpaid cost of audit and legal services through December 31 and record.

Suggested working days to completion date: 12.

Federal and State Income Taxes Payable. This schedule is prepared with the auditors. The worksheet shows the prior year's provision for years still open for tax review and the current year's estimated liability. If income taxes are payable in several states, a worksheet is prepared showing the basis for taxes in each state.

Suggested working days to completion date: 25 to 30.

Long-Term Debt. Verify recorded accuracy of long-term debt and calculate portion due within one year.

Suggested working days to completion date: 5.

Contingent Liabilities and Commitments. Legal Department will prepare schedule of any outstanding litigation and possible loss.

Purchasing Department will prepare a schedule of material purchase commitments entered into prior to December 31 and ascertain if any market losses may be incurred.

Suggested working days to completion date: 15.

Stockholders' Equity. Bring permanent file of all stockholders' equity accounts up to date. Determine employee stock option balances.

Suggested working days to completion date: 10.

INCOME ACCOUNTS

Revenues. Prepare a schedule of all revenues and compare amounts to 1985 revenues. Comment on significant differences. Determine sales cutoff was accurate. Prepare a memorandum on new revenue accounts. Also prepare schedule of revenues by product line for inclusion in the annual report.

Suggested working days to completion date: 15.

EXPENSES

Expenses may be by branch or division. Each expense total should be compared to the prior year's expenses and unusual variances reviewed and explained. Several expense items are directly related to asset or liability accounts and the worksheets for related accounts should be prepared at one time and shown on one schedule. Examples of related accounts are depreciation and the allowances therefor, bad debt expense and the allowance for uncollectible accounts, investment income and investments, interest expense and the liabilities for short-term and long-term debt, and gain and loss on sale of capital assets and the reduction in property, plant, and equipment accounts.

Cost of Goods Sold. Prepare schedule of cost of goods sold. Review calculation of direct overhead costs and compare to rates used in inventories. Comment on unusual variances.

Suggested working days to completion date: 15.

Payroll. Prepare a schedule of all payrolls and reconcile within $10,000 to payroll expense.

Suggested working days to completion date: 10.

Repairs and maintenance. Prepare a schedule of all repair and maintenance accounts for the auditors. List individual charges over $1,000. Attach copies of invoices supporting the charges listed.

Suggested working days to completion date: 15.

Bad Debt Expense. Prepare a list of all accounts written off during the year and attach copies of journal vouchers approving the write-offs. Note specifically any addition to the allowance for uncollectible accounts. The Company is on an actual write-off basis for federal income taxes and this amount is not deductible.

Suggested working days to completion date: 10.

Fringe Benefit Expenses. As part of the gross payroll schedule, list the total of all fringe benefit expenses, compare amounts to prior year as a percentage of direct payroll costs, and explain any unusual variances. Fringe benefits include the company portion of FICA, pension plan contribution, health and life insurance premiums, supplemental unemployment benefits paid and accrued, and so on.

Suggested working days to completion date: 15.

Travel and Entertainment. Prepare a schedule for the auditors of the total travel and entertainment costs of the 10 highest-paid executives.

Suggested working days to completion date: 20.

Provision for Income Taxes. Prepare a schedule of current year's provisions, payments, refunds, assessments paid, and so forth. The provisions less payments should equal the liability for income taxes at year-end.

Suggested working days to completion date: 25.

OTHER INCOME AND EXPENSE

Many companies and organizations record nonrecurring income and expense items or items not related to normal operations in a separate section of the chart of accounts. Because these items are either unusual or nonrecurring, all of the accounts should be analyzed to determine if they are in the proper reporting category. Examples are:

Other Income

Investment income

Interest income

Tax refunds

Proceeds from litigation

Other Expense

Interest expense

Unusual tax assessments and payments

Losses from litigation

Extraordinary losses from prior years

Each account would be listed and assigned to a specific accountant.

FINANCIAL STATEMENTS

The statements of financial position, operations, and changes in working capital are completed at the end of the fiscal closing. They may be prepared in cooperation with the independent auditors. Nevertheless, someone should be assigned to complete these statements. Included therein are the *Notes to Financial Statements* and these should also be assigned.

Suggested working days to completion date: Final closing.

SCHEDULES

Several detailed schedules are usually required, either for inclusion in the published financial report or in internal financial reports distributed to internal management for study and future reference. Not-for-profit institutions, particularly colleges and universities, prepare extensive detailed schedules of the various fund operations, plant investments, details of cash and investments, income details, and details of notes and bonds payable.

Each schedule required as part of the year-end closing should be listed, assigned to a specific accountant, and given a specific date to be completed. In some instances, these schedules are needed to prepare the major financial statements.

SUMMARY

The year-end assignment list, or manual, is a powerful tool to foster consistency and order in the closing procedures. Once developed, maintenance is relatively easy. Much of the manual can be developed during the preliminary discussions with the independent auditors. The internal auditors should be involved because of their direct participation in the closing and their cooperation with the external auditors.

While most assignments will be to the accounting staff, other individuals and departments can be assigned tasks. Other departments involved in closing the books for the fiscal year may be purchasing, legal, public relations, data processing for special data reports, vice-presidents for review and approval, and others.

Figure 5.1 that follows contains the transmittal letter and the complete 1985–1986 year-end assignments for the University of Southern Mississippi. Only minor changes were made to the 1984–1985 list. The assignments are generally listed in balance-sheet order, income and expense order, and in financial statement and schedule order.

UNIVERSITY OF SOUTHERN MISSISSIPPI

INTER-OFFICE CORRESPONDENCE

May 9, 1986

TO: Thomas G. Estes, Jr.
       Ed Champney
       Hugh West
       Jacky Fortenberry
       Sam Clinton
       Cliff Sturdivant
       Bill Rayner
       Linda McFall
       Elsie Peel
       Bill Fron
       Gwen Richardson

FROM: Harry L. Brown

RE: 1986 Closing Assignments

Here is the 1985-86 Year End Assignments list showing specific assignments for the major accounts and activities. Reconcilements, analysis worksheets, trial balances of subsidiary ledgers, and similar items are to be submitted to Ed Champney or me for final review and approval. These working papers are retained in Accounting Services for the State auditors.

All papers submitted should show the name of the account, the date June 30, 1986, the date actually completed and the name of the person who prepared the worksheet. If tracing totals to the General Ledger is required, indicate that the comparison was made.

Please see me if you anticipate any major delay in completing a task or if you have any questions on the information required.

The first closing (issued to Department Heads) should be distributed about July 21, the second closing very early in August, and the third and last closing no later than August 15. The 1986 Financial Report should be printed and distributed by Labor Day.

HLB/lb

Figure 5.1.

ASSIGNED COMPLETION DATE	ITEM	ASSIGNED TO
	CASH (XXII)	
	Cash balances for all bank accounts are summarized in the subsidiary ledger. Bank balances should exclude any investments (certificates of deposit). Activity through June 30 on the California Bank (AFSA Data Corp) should be recorded prior to reconcilement.	
7/25	Provide a reconciliation of the June 30, 1986 balance per bank to the balance per books for each account. Important points to consider are: a. Show origination date and complete description of each reconciling item. b. Prepare any journal entry corrections or adjustments necessary and correct reconcilement for these entries. c. Checks printed Thursday, June 26 are to be included as outstanding checks.	B. Hrdlica
7/10	Provide a summary of all petty cash and change funds as of June 30, 1986. (XX12) Totals must agree with general ledger accounts 1012 and 2012 - Cash in Offices. Prepare positive confirmations asking for verification of amount and custodian as of 6-30.	E. Peel
7/1	Count reserve cash in Business Office and Athletics on July 1.	G. Richardson
7/10	POOLED CASH INVESTMENTS (1011-0002) Prepare a detailed list of short-term investments held at 6/30/86, showing: Name of investment, including bank Date purchased Face amount (cost) Interest rate Total accrued interest (Date of purchase to June 30). Prepare entry to record accrued interest receivable, debiting Prepaid Expense in General Fund.	S. Clinton

NOTE: All Reports are due at close of assigned completion date.

Figure 5.1. Continued.

ASSIGNED COMPLETION DATE	ITEM	ASSIGNED TO
8/1	**OTHER INVESTMENTS** List Plant Fund investments held by trustee and reconcile amount to General Ledger. Obtain market value at 6/30/86. Prepare Investment Schedule for financial report. Use Wall Street Journal, July 1 issue for market prices.	H. Brown
7/19	**ACCOUNTS RECEIVABLE** (XX14) Prepare or obtain detailed trial balances of each account receivable control and balance to general ledger. For each account balance, provide a general aging, particularly items over 90 days old to assist in determining collectibility. Write off any unlocated differences.	S. Clinton
	Prepare schedule of other miscellaneous receivables (not computerized) and reconcile to general ledger. Comment on collectibility.	D. Wilberding
	For restricted fund receivables, determine amounts of accrued but unearned income and process an adjustment to eliminate these amounts. (Special computer program)	J. Fortenberry
	General Fund - receivables from State of Mississippi. Reconcile uncollected amount to General Ledger. Show date received in subsequent year.	E. Champney
	Plant Fund - State Building Commission allotments receivable, as shown by 6/30/86 report is reconciled to appropriate unexpended appropriation accounts.	L. McFall
7/29	**DEFERRED INCOME** Prepare detailed account analysis by income code. Attach copy of supporting document for each item over $500. Continuing Education items should be related to projects ending after June 30. Review Board and Room and Athletic Ticket Sales amounts for reasonableness. Compare to 1985 amounts.	

NOTE: All Reports are due at close of assigned completion date.

Figure 5.1. Continued.

ASSIGNED COMPLETION DATE	ITEM	ASSIGNED TO
7/25	ALLOWANCE FOR POSSIBLE RECEIVABLE LOSSES	
	The allowance for possible receivable losses should be calculated as follows:	E. Champney H. Brown
	If account collection is very doubtful, reserve 100%.	
	A percentage of other accounts should be considered for eventual default.	
	Summarize the allowance required. Computed allowance to to be approved by Dr. Estes.	E. Champney H. Brown
8/1	STUDENT LOANS RECEIVABLE	
	Provide a reconciliation of the June 30 NDSL subsidiary ledger to the general ledger total.	S. Clinton
8/1	Provide an aged listing of all other loan programs as of June 30, 1985. The listing to show name, aging category and loan balance.	
8/1	Summarize loans by aging category (NDSL and other) and evaluate reserve for possible losses. Consider following percentages:	

	% Judged Uncollectible
Payments delinquent 0-6 months	5%
Payments delinquent 7-12 months	25%
Payments delinquent 13-18 months	50%
Payments delinquent over 18 months	75%

NOTE: All Reports are due at close of assigned completion date.

Figure 5.1. Continued.

ASSIGNED COMPLETION DATE	ITEM	ASSIGNED TO
7/16	**INVENTORIES** Provide a summary of 6/30/86 inventories by area. Explain significant variations from the prior year. A memo on the basis used for costing the inventories should be part of the Analysis. Work in Process should be transferred from Auxiliary to General Fund and shown as prepaid expense. Each inventory to be supported by detailed listings showing items, costs, extensions.	E. Champney G. Richardson
7/25	**DEFFERED EXPENSE** (PREPAID) Summarize prepaid expense and accrued income receivable and explain significant variations from the prior year. Deferred expense includes summer session salaries (offset by deferred tuition income), continuing education start-up costs for courses after June 30, 1986, prepaid workers compensation premium, work in process (list of open work orders required) and so forth.	

	Summer Session Salaries
	    Interest Income
	    Continuing Education Costs
	    Workers Compensation
	    Work in Process
		E. Champney
		S. Clinton
		E. Peel
		E. Champney
		L. McFall

7/16	Prepare list of Work in Process job orders (no., expended to June 30, account no. to be charged when completed). Set up other than Physical Plant jobs in deferred expenses, expense all other to Physical Plant O & M. (Special Reports and Maintenance) List all encumbrances on work in process jobs (Auxiliary true encumbrances) and transfer in total to General Fund encumbrances at June 30 (worksheet only). Eliminate all Work in Process encumbrances (total job costs) in General Fund Physical Plant accounts.	L. McFall

NOTE: All Reports are due at close of assigned completion date.

Figure 5.1. Continued.

ASSIGNED COMPLETION DATE	ITEM	ASSIGNED TO
8/9	PHYSICAL PLANT ASSETS	
	Reconcile lists of assets to the General Ledger (Land, Buildings, Improvements, Equipment).	E. Champney
		H. Brown
	Determine source of equipment additions during year as follows:	B. Rayner
	1. Total from other funds (General, Auxiliary, Designated, Restricted)	
	2. Total from Unexpended Appropriations - Plant Fund	L. McFall
	Review each unexpended appropriation account and Renewals and Replacements and separate by account the expensed amounts (repairs and maintenance) and the expenditures to be transferred to Construction in Progress (capitalized).	L. McFall
	Determine estimated cost to complete each project to be capitalized. Describe source of these funds if other than funds already on hand.	L. McFall
	Summarize physical plant assets by category.	H. Brown
7/16	VOUCHERS PAYABLE	
	Vouchers received and processed through Monday, June 23, will be paid by checks dated June 26. Vouchers received and processed through Thursday, July 10 will be set up as Vouchers Payable. The detailed list of vouchers payable will show vendor, vendor invoice number and amount. Maintain copies of vouchers supporting this list.	L. McFall
8/12	Items received after July 10 applicable to 1985-86 are to be listed for possible entry, if material.	
	TRAVEL	
	Travel vouchers received through July 10 will be included in payables if the travel was prior to July 1.	
	Prepare reversal entry for all items recorded as 1985-86 payables but paid in 1986-87.	

NOTE: All Reports are due at close of assigned completion date.

Figure 5.1. Continued.

ASSIGNED COMPLETION DATE	ITEM	ASSIGNED TO
7/20	**ACCRUED PAYROLL** Record entire payroll of June 30 pay date in June. The payroll of July 9 is accrued and 1/10 of July 9 payroll for June 30 work. Prepare Journal entry charging appropriate expenditure accounts (General, Designated and Auxiliary Funds only) and setting up accrual. Work study included in Restricted Fund.	E. Champney
	Prepare list of 9-month faculty checks dated prior to June 30, but on hand on that date. Adding machine tape is sufficient.	E. Champney
7/16	**PAYROLL WITHHELD AMOUNTS** Prepare worksheet on each type of withheld amounts (taxes, retirement, insurance, etc.) and reconcile to General Ledger accrual amounts. Show date payment was made to outside agency. All amounts should be detailed by payroll so they can be traced thereto.	V. Reeves
7/16	**OTHER ACCRUALS** Prepare worksheet on any other accruals, notes payable and reconcile to general ledger.	E. Champney
7/16	**DEPOSITS - HOUSING** Prepare lists or adding machine tapes of deposits held. If not refundable, prepare adjusting entry. Reconcile to general ledger account.	R. Kivetz
7/10	**DEFERRED INCOME - FEES** Calculate summer session fees to be deferred at June 30. Compare to 1985 deferred amount and explain unusual differences.	E. Champney
7/10	**UNEARNED BOARD AND ROOM** Calculate portion of Board and Room to be deferred to 1986-87. Obtain housing occupancy at July 1, 1986 to determine if reasonable.	E. Champney
7/10	**UNEARNED ATHLETIC TICKET INCOME** Prepare worksheet on athletic tickets sold for games subsequent to June 30, 1986. Trace to cash receipts.	E. Champney

NOTE: All Reports are due at close of assigned completion date.

Figure 5.1. Continued.

ASSIGNED COMPLETION DATE	ITEM	ASSIGNED TO
7/16	DEFERRED INCOME - CONTINUING EDUCATION Analyze deferred income of Continuing Education to determine that amounts relate to projects finishing after June 30, 1986. If set up by Journal Entry, prepare reversal entry for July 1986.	E. Peel
7/24	RESERVES - PLANT FUND Schedule all activity in Plant Fund Reserves (Renewals and Replacements and Indebtedness) showing source of funds, expenditures, investment activity and balances. Reconcile amounts to Trustee reports and to general ledger.	H. Brown
7/10	Prepare an adding machine tape of the student deposit accounts at the close of business June 30. Put name of account on all non-student accounts. Put date of last transaction if prior to January 1, 1986.	C. Sturdivant
	INCOME AND EXPENSE	
8/1	Indirect cost recovery Prepare schedule showing indirect costs charged to Restricted Fund accounts and amounts recorded as income to General and Designated Funds. The charge and income totals must agree. Determine that indirect costs earned to June 30 are recorded in 1985-86.	J. Fortenberry
8/15	University Portion of State Retirement Determine amounts paid to and due to the State Retirement System for the fiscal year (amounts based on 1985-86 payrolls). This amount will be included in a footnote to financial statements.	E. Peel
7/16	Student fees Determine amount of student tuition and fees allocated directly to Auxiliary (portion of the regular tuition charge).	E. Champney
7/22	Transfers To and From Prepare a detailed schedule of every transfer between funds showing account and Fund transferred from and account transferred to.	E. Peel

NOTE: All Reports are due at close of assigned completion date.

Figure 5.1. Continued.

ASSIGNED COMPLETION DATE	ITEM	ASSIGNED TO
7/22	Investment Income - Pooled Cash Summarize investment income earned, including year-end accrual. Prepare worksheet showing spread of this income to the Natchez Building Fund, and to the General, Auxiliary, Endowment and Plant Funds at 6/30/86.	H. Brown
8/1	Financial Aid For each federal aid program, provide a detailed listing showing student name, social security number and amount of grant or loan paid during 1985-86. The totals are to be reconciled to General Ledger amounts and to the Fiscal Operations Report.	W. Fron J. Fortenberry
8/20	Provide a copy of the Fiscal Operations Report for 1985-86.	W. Fron J. Fortenberry
8/9	Run special vacation accrual report as of 6/30 on 240-hour basis, using 1986-87 salary rates.	H. Brown
7/22	ENCUMBRANCES After 1985-86 Cash Disbursement vouchers are recorded and encumbrances liquidated, review encumbrance listing with particular emphasis on current encumbrances of last 90 days over $1,000 and all encumbrances more than 90 days old to determine if they are valid. Eliminate encumbrances for contractual services to be performed in the subsequent year such as rental payments, repairs, contractual teaching fees, and so forth.	L. McFall
7/31	Review travel encumbrances (Permission to Travel Forms). If trip is to be made after June 30, 1986, liquidate the encumbrance. Trips beginning in June and ending in July will be recorded as 1985-86 expenditures if Travel Report is received; otherwise, left in encumbrances. All 90 series encumbrances (Work in Process) for Operation and Maintenance of Plant will be liquidated and set up on July 1 (other than O & M accounts to be shown as encumbrances at year end). Adjust encumbrance amounts as necessary. Auxiliary Enterprises Fund encumbrances on Work in Process are moved to General Fund in total on trial balance only.	

NOTE: All Reports are due at close of assigned completion date.

Figure 5.1. Continued.

ASSIGNED COMPLETION DATE	ITEM	ASSIGNED TO
8/1	**BUDGETS** Provide a general summary of the approved initial budget to final financial statements. Explain any unusual differences.	H. West
7/31	**PRIOR YEAR ENCUMBRANCES** After first closing, run special program to move total expenditures in "Prior Year Encumbrances" in General Fund to appropriate expenditure classes within each account. When completed, the "Prior Year Encumbrances" balances and expenditures should be zero.	R. Scott L. McFall
8/15	**FINANCIAL STATEMENTS** Balance Sheets - Champney and Brown Revenues, Expenditures, Transfers - Current Fund - Champney and Brown Changes in Fund Balances - Champney and Brown Details General Fund Revenues - Champney Current Funds Expenditures - Brown (special program) General Fund Expenditures - Champney Designated Fund - Fortenberry Auxiliary Enterprises Fund - Champney Restricted Fund - Fortenberry Loan Fund - Clinton Endowment Fund - Brown Plant Fund - Unexpended - McFall Reserves for Renewals and Replacement - Brown Reserve for Indebtedness - Brown	

NOTE: All Reports are due at close of assigned completion date.

Figure 5.1. Continued.

ASSIGNED COMPLETION DATE	ITEM	ASSIGNED TO
8/15	FINANCIAL STATEMENTS (continued)	
	Agency - Peel	
	State Building Commission Allotment Receivable - McFall	
	Bonds Payable - Brown	
	Land Inventory - Brown and McFall	
	Buildings - McFall	
	Department Equipment - Rayner	
	Improvements other than Buildings - McFall	
	Construction in Progress - McFall	
	Transfers - Peel	
	Investments - Brown	
	Cash and Temporary Investments - Champney	

NOTE: All Reports are due at close of assigned completion date.

Figure 5.1. Continued.

CHAPTER 6
DATA PROCESSING
MANUAL:
PUT YOUR RIGHT
DATA OUT

When accounting systems began to be processed by computer systems, it became necessary to develop methods for accountants to communicate with computer programmers and data processors. Until very recently, most computer processing of accounting data was handled at a remote site, whether down the hall, in another part of the building, or across the city. Most of it still is, although smaller operations are beginning to process accounting on PCs or minicomputers at the accounting location.

When accounting documents are processed by others, a three-way line of communication must be developed and used. The three parties are the accounting department, the systems and analysis staff which is responsible for developing the computer methods and programming, and the computer operating staff which processes the documents on a daily basis. In a perfect situation, the programmers do not need to be accountants; the accountants do not need to understand programming; and the computer operators do not need to understand either accounting or programming.

How then, do these professional staffs communicate? The only way presently known is through adequate, written documentation prepared when a new system is operational, and updated when an approved change is made to the original system. This documentation, fairly standardized in centralized data processing, consists of several forms of communication.

1. A batch or job control card prepared by the accountant to inform the operator which program should be run and the current specifications of that program such as program number, "as of" date, sorting sequence, and account or transaction selection criteria.

2. Input record transaction layouts prepared by the programming staff to show others the data entry format of the transaction. These layouts may be terminal input screens used by the accounting staff to enter input directly to a computer file.

3. A description of each output report processed by the operating system, the number of copies printed and the distribution, the general purpose of the report, and its final retention or disposition.

4. Data dictionaries and standard tables used by the computer systems but maintained by accountants. When tables are used in this manner, the systems are said to be table-driven.

5. A complete description of each field in the master file record used in the system.

JOB CONTROL CARD

The job control card is the principal means of communicating between the accountant and the computer operations staff. It tells data processing operations what job is to be run or processed, what special specifications are to be used in the procedure, the date or dates to be used for calculation or printing, and other similar data programmed into the system. The job control card is designed and documented during the systems development stage although it may be redesigned and explained in more detail in the user's general accounting manual or data processing manual. Figures 6.1 and 6.2 show the two most common layouts for job control cards.

SYSTEM CONTROL RECORD MAINTENANCE

CARD TYPE	Process Date			Inpt	Period Indicators					Activity Gen No	Create SCR
					Mo	Qtr	Yr	FY	Int		
ACC02-SPEC											

1   11   17 19   21 22 23 24 25   28   30

Field	Description
PROCESS DATE	Enter the report date, MMDDYY for this maintenance process. Any input batches with dates _after_ this one will be suspended for processing in a future cycle.
INPT	Enter "NO" if Data Base Maintnenace is to be run without input transactions; e.g., for periodic maintenance only.
PERIOD INDICATORS	These are set to control periodic maintenance as follows:

MO -- enter the number of the month being started;
     e.g., "02" to end January and start February.
QTR - enter the number of the quarter being started;
     e.g., "1" to end the 4th quarter and start the
     1st.
YR -- enter "1" to start a new calendar year.
FY -- enter "1" to start a new fiscal year.
INT - enter "X" to initialize all indicators so no
     periodic maintenance takes place. In this
     case, all other indicators must be blank.

The remaining two fields are only completed in the event a restart is necessary and/or program sequence checking is purposefully being bypassed.

ACTIVITY GEN NO	If a change to the current activity generation number is required, the desired value is entered in this field.
CREATE SCR	This field must contain "SCR" if the file is being created.

Revised 4/15/84

Figure 6.1. Job control card to initiate computer processing of a specific program.

SYSTEM CONTROL RECORD MAINTENANCE

Field	Pos.	Data	Description
Card Type	(1-10)	ACC02-SPEC	
Process Date	(11-16)	_ _ _ _ _ _	Enter the report date, MMDDYY. Any input batches with dates after this one will be suspended for processing in a future cycle.
Input	(17-18)	_ _	Enter "NO" if Data Base Maintenance is to be run without input transactions; e.g., for periodic maintenance only.
Period Indicators: Month	(19-20)	_ _	Enter the number of the month being started; e.g., "02" to end January and start February.
Quarter	(21)	_	Enter the number of the quarter being started; e.g., "1" to end the 4th quarter and start the 1st.
Year	(22)	_	Enter "1" to start a new calendar year.
Fiscal Year	(23)	_	Enter "1" to start a new fiscal year.
Initialize	(24)	_	Enter "X" to initialize all indicators so no periodic maintenance takes place. In this case, all other indicators must be blank.

The remaining two fields are only completed in the event a restart is necessary and/or program sequence checking is purposely being bypassed.

Activity Gen No	(25-27)	_ _ _	If a change to the current activity generation number is required, the desired value is entered in this field.
Create SCR	(28-30)	_ _ _	This field must contain "SCR" if the file is being created.

Figure 6.2. A common layout for a job control card.

INPUT TRANSACTION FORMATS

Input transaction data entry layouts are discussed in Chapter 2 because these records are closely related to transaction coding and common transaction forms and procedures. It is not uncommon to have the exact input data entry layout on the accounting form itself, making the data entry operation much simpler and with fewer errors.

Input transaction formats can be video display terminal (VDT) screens. To use them, the accountant calls up the accounting menu. Once the menu is on the screen, the new record format can be selected by a single letter or number. When the screen has the new record format, the operator enters the appropriate data on each line. When completed, a single stroke will move the data to the master account file. Figure 6.3 is an input screen layout to add a master record to a chart of accounts.

OUTPUT REPORTS

Comprehensive accounting systems purchased as a total package from an independent software company are usually documented quite well, particularly in the computer output report sections because the reports are what the developers of the systems are selling. However, systems developed internally by the company's own systems staff are more inclined to emphasize input systems and controls. Also, new reports added to a system after installation tend not to be very well defined or explained. When seeing a computer-prepared report for the first time, the first question is, "What does this report do?" and the second, "How do I understand what it says?" Considering that a major accounting system produces from a few dozen to more than 100 different reports, the explanations would take considerable effort and time of several employees, each of whom would be familiar with different reports.

Standardizing Output Report Descriptions

The solution is to develop a standard method of defining a single report that would inform the reader of the purpose of the report, its frequency and distribution, the order in which the data elements are printed, its retention, and a description of each repetitive data item in the report itself. Most computer-generated reports can be completely defined and documented with three pages: (1) report description, (2) report contents, and (3) a copy of the report itself with each data item numbered for reference.

NEW ACCOUNT SCREEN

```
┌────────────────────────────────────────────────────────────┐
│                                                              │
│   ACCOUNT NUMBER (7 or 10)        :                          │
│   (01) DEPARTMENT NAME            :                          │
│   (02) EXPENDITURE NAME           :                          │
│   (03) BOX NUMBER                 :                          │
│   (04) HIERARCHY CODE             :                          │
│   (05) CONTRACT/GRANT #           :                          │
│   (06) BEGINNING DATE MMDDYY      :                          │
│   (07) ENDING DATE MMDDYY         :                          │
│   (08) FIRST BILLING DATE MMDDYY  :                          │
│   (09) BILLING CYCLE (01-12)      :                          │
│   (10) BILLING CODE 1 OR 2        :                          │
│                                                              │
│                                                              │
│   *** ENTER NEXT DEPT CODE OR STOP ***                       │
│                                                              │
│                                                              │
└────────────────────────────────────────────────────────────┘
```

Note:

01   Department Name limited to 30 characters.

04   Hierarchy Code may be left blank.

09   Billing cycle indicates number of months between billings.
      01 = monthly, 03 = quarterly, 06 = semiannually, 12 = annually.

10   1 = Fixed Price, 2 = Cost Reimbursement

Figure 6.3. Input screen layout.

Report Description Form

The report description form has been developed solely to describe in detail the general attributes of a single computer report (see Figure 6.4). The form is completed as follows:

Report Title. Enter the exact name of the report as printed in the heading thereof.

Number. Enter the number of the report, if any.

Type. Enter the general class or type of report such as edit, table maintenance, control and audit, controller's report, informational and reference, cash, and so on.

Frequency. The frequency of the report is entered, such as daily, weekly, monthly, quarterly, annually, on demand, or when changes are made to the underlying data.

Sequence. Enter the sequence of the line items in the report. Typical sequences are alphabetical, Social Security number, transaction type, purchase order or invoice number, date, as processed, and so forth.

Report Produced by Program. Enter the program number that printed this report, usually shown on the report itself in most data processing systems.

Number of Copies and Distribution. Enter the name of the department or unit to which each copy or the report was sent.

Retention and Disposition. A sentence or two on the retention of the report and the final disposition of the report are entered here. Both retention and disposition are highly variable. Typical retention cycles might be until a new report is produced, 30 days until a new accounting period is started, permanent, until year-end audit is completed, or even more specific, such as one year from date of filing report.

Purpose. The specific purpose and use of this report are entered in this section. If several purposes are served, they can be listed in numerical order. Usual purposes of accounting reports are to provide an audit listing or changes, provide control over data entry accuracy and editing, provide a reference list, provide a special calculation for additional reporting, and so on. Almost anything can be written in this section to provide more help to the user of the report, particularly the first-time user such as a new employee or an outside auditor.

Procedure. This area is completed by the accountant to describe very briefly the procedure accomplished by this particular report. Reference may be made here to unusual input forms and procedures used to initiate or complete the report.

Report Contents Form

The report contents form is tied directly to a copy of the actual computer report to describe each item on the report itself. The individual sections or items on the report

```
                    FINANCIAL ACCOUNTING SYSTEM
                       REPORT DESCRIPTION


     REPORT TITLE _____NUMBER _____

     TYPE _____

     FREQUENCY _____

     SEQUENCE _____

     NUMBER OF COPIES AND DISTRIBUTION - REPORT PRODUCED BY PROGRAM _____

     1.

     2.

     3.

     4.

     5.

     6.

     _____
     RETENTION AND DISPOSITION:




     _____
     PURPOSE:







     _____
     PROCEDURE:
```

Figure 6.4. A report description form.

are numbered consecutively and these numbers are used as line numbers on the report contents form (see Figure 6.5). This form is completed as follows:

Report Title. Enter the exact name shown as a heading on the computer report and on the report description form that precedes this page in the output report section of the data processing manual.

Report No. Enter the report number printed on the computer output report.

Ref. This is a preprinted list of consecutive numbers used to reference the definitions to the related report. Second sheets are numbered 21 to 40. Very few computer-generated reports contain more than 40 separate data fields or items.

Chars. Enter the maximum number of characters capable of being printed in this data field.

Field Definition. A free-form description of each data field on the report from the heading to the final control total or ending indicator. The meaning of the field or the method of calculation may be described if meaningful to the user of the report. Almost every report contents field description area would describe the report number, title, date processed, consecutive page number printed, and any other heading information shown on the report. The number of characters is not shown on those lines which are printed as headings directly from a computer program.

Report Index

An index of all reports is needed to facilitate looking up a specific report description, contents, and layout. Most reports are numbered for reference purposes by the programmer. The report numbers form a logical sequence. However, if some reports are not numbered, the programmers should be requested to number them. If that is not possible, consider the use of assigned retrieval numbers as discussed in Chapter 3. If the report titles are quite descriptive, report numbers may not be needed. The output report section of the data processing manual, when complete, contains the index followed by three pages for each report included therein: report description, report contents, and a copy of the report with the data fields numbered. For convenience, the reports should be reduced to a standard page size.

THE DATA DICTIONARY

A data dictionary is usually provided in a computerized accounting system with a data base. The data dictionary is a list of all data fields and related codes used in the system. The basic presentation is almost identical to the standard account definitions illustrated in Chapter 2 but is usually much more detailed. When the dictionary is

FINANCIAL ACCOUNTING SYSTEM

REPORT CONTENTS

REPORT TITLE _____   REPORT NO. _____

REF.	CHARS.	FIELD DEFINITION
1		
2		
3		
4		
5		
6		
7		
8		
9		
10		
11		
12		
13		
14		
15		
16		
17		
18		
19		
20		

Figure 6.5. A report contents form.

processed through a computer program, the definitions are compared by field number to the actual computer file definitions in the programs and the file information is brought over to the dictionary. For example, the definition of *number of federal withholding exemptions* can be completed in one or two sentences. When the accounting file is accessed, the name of the field in the computer program, the number of characters in the field, and the permissible codes will be selected and printed. Figure 6.6 is an example of three fields from a data base dictionary used in a large, computerized personnel and payroll system. While the voluminous systems documentation manuals of the payroll system would not be included in the general accounting manual, the data base dictionary would be included because of its detailed definitions of the codes used in the accounting process.

COMPUTER SYSTEMS TABLES

Today, many accounting systems use tables to define frequently used parts of the system. In fact, these computerized systems are generally referred to as table-driven. There may be several tables in a large system. Following are descriptions of tables provided in a large payroll system.

Parameter Table. This table sets minimum and maximum amounts for certain calculations or specific accounts.

Gross-To-Net Table. Sets the priority of calculating taxes and employee deductions. It also specifies which deductions will be taken from either the first or second payroll in the month. Account distributions of deductions withheld are also shown in this table.

Job Class Table. Defines the title of each position in the payroll system, the minimum and maximum rate for each job, and the equal employment opportunity classification codes.

System Calendar Table. Shows payroll closing dates and pay dates for each payroll.

Data Element Table. Describes each field in the employee data base record. The table shows the element number and name, data type, length, number of decimal positions, starting location in the record, and all permitted variable editing specifications.

Message Table. Shows the text of every error message generated by the program during processing and the degree of seriousness of each message.

Accrual Table. Lists the formula for calculating vacation and sick pay hours earned.

Earnings Table. Lists every type of earnings that may be paid, the elements used to accumulate the amounts, and the program routine that handles the calculations.

Department Table. Contains the account number and full name and address of every department coded into the accounting system.

0124-1   EMPLOYEE TYPE

DEFINITION: A CODE USED TO INDICATE THE INDIVIDUAL'S PRIMARY
PERSONNEL CLASSIFICATION.

USE(S):   PERSONNEL REPORTING: EEO-6 REPORTING

CODING: 1 - EXECUTIVE/ADMINISTRATIVE/MANAGERIAL
2 - FACULTY
3 - PROFESSIONAL NON-FACULTY
4 - SECRETARIAL/CLERICAL
5 - TECHNICAL/PARAPROFESSIONAL
6 - SKILLED CRAFTS
7 - SERVICE MAINTENANCE
8 - STUDENT

0125-2   FEDERAL TAX MARITAL STATUS

DEFINITION: THE MARITAL STATUS THE EMPLOYEE DECLARES ON THE W-4
FORM FOR COMPUTATION OF THE FEDERAL WITHHOLDING TAX.   WIDOWED,
DIVORCED, HEAD OF HOUSEHOLD, AND LEGALLY SEPARATED PERSONS ARE
CONSIDERED SINGLE.   IF LEFT BLANK, THIS ELEMENT DEFAULTS TO
SINGLE.

USE(S):   FEDERAL WITHHOLDING TAX COMPUTATION DURING PAYROLL
CALCULATION.

CODING: BLANK - SINGLE
S - SINGLE OR MARRIED WITHHOLDING AT THE HIGHER
SINGLE RATE
M - MARRIED

0126-3   FEDERAL TAX ALLOWANCES/FEDERAL REGULAR ALLOWANCES

DEFINITIONS: IF THE STANDARD SYSTEM IS USED TO CALCULATE TAXES,
THIS DATA ELEMENT INDICATES THE TOTAL NUMBER OF ALLOWANCES AN
EMPLOYEE HAS CLAIMED ON HIS OR HER W-4 FORM FOR FEDERAL WITH-
HOLDING TAX PURPOSES.

USE(S):   COMPUTATION OF FEDERAL WITHHOLDING TAX DURING PAYROLL
CALCULATION

CODING: 00-50 - NUMBER OF ALLOWANCES
98 - SPECIAL EXEMPTION CLAIMED (MUST BE FILED
ANNUALLY ON OR BEFORE APRIL 30)
99 - EXEMPT FROM FEDERAL TAXES

Figure 6.6. Sample fields from a data element dictionary.

DATA ELEMENT AND CK DIGIT	ELEMENT NAME	LEGAL F/M	DATA TYPE	LENGTH EXT	LENGTH INT	DEC PNT	REQD DATA	START-P EXT	START-P INT	STORE MODE	VARIABLE SPECS.	HIST FLAG
0122-9	SPCL STATUS DT	YES	N	04	04				105	CHAR	DATE	HST
0123-0	PART/FULL TIME	YES	AN	01	01		1		109	CHAR	VALUE: F VALUE: P	HST
0124-1	EMPLOYEE TYPE	YES	N	01	01		1		110	CHAR	RANGE: 1-8	HST
0125-2	FED TX MAR STAT	YES	AN	01	01		2		111	CHAR	VALUE: M VALUE: S	
0126-3	FED EXEMPTIONS	YES	N	02	02				112	CHAR	RANGE: 00-50 RANGE: 98-99	
0127-4	ST TAX MAR STAT	YES	AN	01	01				114	CHAR	VALUE: S VALUE: M	
0128-5	STATE EXEMPTNS	YES	N	02	02				115	CHAR		
0129-6	FICA ELIGIBLE	YES	AN	01	01				117	CHAR	VALUE: N VALUE: S	
0130-4	RETIREMENT PLAN	YES	AN	01	01				118	CHAR	VALUE: Y VALUE: N	HST
0131-5	RETRMT PLN DATE	YES	N	06	06				119	CHAR	DATE	
0132-6	MARITAL STATUS	YES	AN	01	01				145	CHAR	VALUE: S VALUE: M VALUE: D VALUE: L VALUE: W	

Figure 6.7. Sample data element table information.

Tax Table. Defines the parameters for income tax calculations.

The tables in total may be quite large, 200 pages or more, and are usually maintained as separate reference documentation. However, the general accounting manual should include the table names, brief descriptions of the contents of the tables, and the general use of the tables in the accounting system. Figures 6.7 through 6.10 are four examples of the table information to be included in the data processing manual.

```
AIMS 007/PP0100                    PAYROLL/PERSONNEL SYSTEM                    PAGE NO. 0001
                                   CONTROL FILE MAINTENANCE                    RUN DATE 4/25/86
                                          BANK TABLE


    TRANSIT NO    MEDIA     BANK NAME           ADDRESS            CITY         STATE      ZIP


    065300486     TAPE      1ST MISSISSIPPI NAT  301 2ND AVENUE    HATTIESBURG   MS       39401

    065300499     REPORT    CITIZENS BANK        601 MAIN STREET   HATTIESBURG   MS       39401

    065301100     REPORT    DEPOSIT GUARANTY     500 MAIN STREET   HATTIESBURG   MS       39401

    065302808     REPORT    BANK OF HATTIESBURG  1300 HARDY STREET HATTIESBURG   MS       39401

    065302950     REPORT    SOUTH MISS BANK      40TH AVE UNIV MALL HATTIESBURG  MS       39401

    265370957     REPORT    FIRST MAGNOLIA S&L   PO BOX 8150       HATTIESBURG   MS       39401

    265370960     REPORT    FIRST GUARANTY S&L   300 HARDY STREET  HATTIESBURG   MS       39401

    265370986     REPORT    PINE BELT S&L        700 HARDY STREET  HATTIESBURG   MS       39401

    265371040     REPORT    UNIFIRST S&L         110 EAST FRONT ST HATTIESBURG   MS       39401
```

Figure 6.8. Sample bank table information.

MASTER FILE RECORD DESCRIPTIONS

Another section of the Data Processing Manual is one on master file record layouts. Three types of record layout forms are in use. They are:

1. 80-column card layout.
2. Standard record layout forms, similar to card layout forms but containing 100 character spaces per line and several lines on the page.
3. A vertical data record layout which describes each field, shows whether the input is numeric or alphanumeric, the number of characters in each field, and the actual codes permitted in a field (see Figure 6.11).

The first two methods are generally used by data processing specialists because they provide a quick overview of the record. Space limitations of these layouts limit the descriptive information that can be shown. The third method was developed for users to describe each field in the record and the special codes pertaining thereto. It may also provide volume statistics and other information for each record layout described.

```
AIMS 008/FP0100              PAYROLL/PERSONNEL SYSTEM              PAGE NO. 0005

                            CONTROL FILE MAINTENANCE              RUN DATE 4/25/86

                                  MESSAGE TABLE 8
```

MSG. ID.	MESSAGE TEXT	REFERENCED	SEVERITY
01-001	PARAMETERS TABLE: INVALID PARAMETER NUMBER	NO	FATAL ERROR
01-002	PARAMETERS TABLE: INVALID PARAMETER VALUE	NO	FATAL ERROR
01-003	INVALID TABLE NUMBER	NO	FATAL ERROR
01-005	PARAMETERS TABLE: DESCRIPTION MUST BE PRESENT	NO	FATAL ERROR
01-018	LEAVE ACCRUALS: INVALID LEAVE TYPE	NO	FATAL ERROR
01-019	LEAVE ACCRUALS: YEARS OF SERVICE MUST BE SEQUENTIAL:		
	LOW TO HIGH	YES	SERIOUS ERROR
01-020	LEAVE ACCRUALS: LEAVE PLAN HAS NO DATA ELMT ENTRY	YES	FATAL ERROR
01-021	LEAVE ACCRUALS: BALANCE ELEMENT NONNUMERIC OR INVALID	YES	FATAL ERROR
01-022	LEAVE ACCRUALS: ADD'L ACCUMALTOR NONNUMERIC OR INVALID	YES	FATAL ERROR
01-023	LEAVE ACCRUALS: PAY CYCLE INVALID	YES	FATAL ERROR
01-024	LEAVE ACCRUALS: MAXIMUM ACCRUAL HOURS NONNUMERIC	YES	FATAL ERROR
01-025	LEAVE ACCRUALS: ADD MATCHES EXISTING TABLE ENTRY	YES	FATAL ERROR
01-026	LEAVE ACCRUALS: YEARS OF SERVICE/HOURS NONNUMERIC	YES	FATAL ERROR
01-027	LEAVE ACCRUALS: MISSING BALANCE ELEMENT	YES	SERIOUS ERROR
01-028	ACTION CODE IS "CHANGE" BUT RECORD DOES NOT EXIST	NO	FATAL ERROR
01-029	ACTION CODE IS "DELETE" BUT RECORD DOES NOT EXIST	NO	FATAL ERROR
01-030	ACTION CODE IS NOT, "ADD," "DELETE," OR "CHANGE	NO	FATAL ERROR
01-031	SYSTEM CALENDAR: YEAR, MONTH, OR DAY IS NONNUMERIC	NO	FATAL ERROR
01-032	SYSTEM CALENDAR: CENTURY NOT "19"	NO	FATAL ERROR
01-040	A GROSS-TO-NET SEGMENT HAS BEEN INITIALIZED	NO	INFORMATIONAL
01-042	DATA ELEMENT TABLE: INVALID SEGMENT NUMBER	NO	FATAL ERROR
01-043	DATA ELEMENT TABLE: INVALID INTERNAL START POSITION	NO	FATAL ERROR

Figure 6.9. Sample message table information.

Purpose of Record Layouts

While the record layout formats are referred to infrequently by the accounting staff, they may be useful in determining data input errors and correction methods to be used. Such layouts are needed when a change in the system is contemplated or

AIMS 011/PP0100   PAYROLL/PERSONNEL SYSTEM   PAGE NO. 0012
CONTROL FILE MAINTENANCE   RUN DATE 4/25/86
DEPARTMENT TABLE 11

UNIT NO	LOC CD	UNIT NAME/ADDRESS		REPORT GROUPS (1) (2) (3)	ORG LVL 1 2
01		INSTRUCTION	INSTRUCTION HATTIESBURG MS 39406		
011		GENERAL ACADEMIC	GEN ACADEMIC HATTIESBURG MS 39406		
01103		COLLEGE OF LIBERAL ARTS	LIBERAL ARTS HATTIESBURG MS 39406		
0110301-000		AEROSPACE STUDIES	AEROSPACE STDY HATTIESBURG MS 39406		
0110327-000		SCHOOL OF COMMUNICATION SOUTHERN STATION BOX 5158	SCH OF COMM HATTIESBURG MS 39406		
0110331-000		CRIMINAL JUSTICE SOUTHERN STATION BOX 5127	CRIMINAL JUST HATTIESBURG MS 39406		
0110333-000		DEBATING SOUTHERN STATION BOX 5131	DEBATING HATTIESBURG MS 39406		
0110334-000		DIVISION OF COMMUNICATION SOUTHERN STATION BOX 5158	DIV-COMMUNIC HATTIESBURG MS 39406		
0110339-000		ENGLISH SOUTHERN STATION BOX 5037	ENGLISH HATTIESBURG MS 39406		
0110339-107		PILOT GRAD TEACH ASST TRAIN SOUTHERN STATION BOX 5037	HATTIESBURG MS 39406		
0110339-108		SOUTH MISS WRITING PROJECT SOUTHERN STATION BOX 5037	SO MS WRITING HATTIESBURG MS 39406		
0110339-206		RESIDENCIES FOR WRITERS SOUTHERN STATION BOX 5144	RES FOR WRITERS HATTIESBURG MS 39406		
0110343-000		FOREIGN LANGUAGES SOUTHERN STATION BOX 5038	FOREIGN LANG HATTIESBURG MS 39406		
0110345-000		GEOGRAPHY AND AREA DEVELOPMENT SOUTHERN STATION BOX 5051	GEOGRAPHY HATTIESBURG MS 39406		

Figure 6.10. Sample department table information.

DATA SHEET

RECORD _____

_____

SEQUENCE _____

REFERENCE TO EXHIBIT _____

INPUT ☐

OUTPUT ☐

VOLUME	FREQUENCY

RECORD DESCRIPTION		NUMBER OF CHARACTERS	ALPHA/ NUMERIC
FIELD NO.	FIELD DEFINITION		

Figure 6.11. Vertical data record layout.

under study. It is sometimes surprising to the accountant with limited knowledge of data processing that a significant portion of the master file record is never printed for review. Examples are imbedded codes used to trigger some action or calculation, accumulator fields for storing historical information, codes to facilitate editing of the incoming transactions, and fields used to retain statistical information.

A good example of a nonprinted field is a field in every checking account file in every bank in the country. This field is a 2- or 3-digit numeric field called *number of times overdrawn*. Every time there is a nonsufficient funds check, this field is increased by one. As long as this field remains very small, say up to three or four, no action is taken. However, if this number grows larger, the computer will report the overdraw and the number in this field. The bank manager then decides whether to cover the check and notify the issuer to come in to cover it, or to return the check to the depositor and charge the account for the inconvenience.

A second example would be the dollar credit limit in most accounts receivable records and in all credit card operations. This field is used to check that the total amount due from the customer does not exceed the authorized limit. As long as the balance is lower than the credit limit, no action is taken. When the balance does exceed the limit, a computer warning that the credit limit has been exceeded by Customer X will be printed for human action. The report may or may not print the credit limit amount.

Electronic data processing (EDP) auditing techniques make extensive use of the master file record layouts to develop computer audit procedures.

SUMMARY

The data processing manual is a compilation of the data input processing formats, output report descriptions, control records for initiating processing, data dictionaries, and tables used in processing accounting data. It is important that this documentation be written in plain English for the accountants and not in computerese or data processing jargon. The items in this manual should be indexed and the index included in the general accounting manual to inform the users of that manual that these informative documents are available.

Changes in the documentation described are usually generated by maintenance computer programs on a demand or request basis. When an item is updated, the replaced documentation is deleted from the existing manuals. Data processing documentation for the accountants is seldom released to outsiders and the only existing copies are kept in accounting and data processing documentation files. Auditors planning to process accounting files with special audit programs would use the existing copies of the documentation for their planning.

The figures that follow include two complete report descriptions with report contents and the actual reports (Figures 6.12 and 6.13), and four report descriptions only to show how they are used (Figures 6.14 through 6.17).

REPORT TITLE <u>Reference Table Maintenance Listing</u> NUMBER <u>GL-E01</u>

TYPE <u>Table Maintenance Edit</u>

FREQUENCY <u>When additions, deletions or changes are entered.</u>

SEQUENCE <u>Table, Reference Number Within Table</u>

NUMBER OF COPIES AND DISTRIBUTION - REPORT PRODUCED BY PROGRAM <u>GL1965</u>

1. Accounting Control

2. Data Processing

3.

4.

5.

6.

RETENTION AND DISPOSITION: Filed until a new reference table is produced. Table can be produced on request.

PURPOSE:

1. Provides audit listing of changes for manual review.
2. Provides control over changes to reference table items.
3. Provides additional reference in conjunction with the reference table listing.

PROCEDURE: Table additions, deletions, and changes are entered on table maintenance forms, processed and printed on the reference table maintenance listing for verification. Deleted entries remain in table until end of fiscal year.

Figure 6.12. Sample reference table report description, report contents, and actual report.

FINANCIAL ACCOUNTING SYSTEM

REPORT CONTENTS

REPORT TITLE Reference Table Maintenance Listing

REPORT NO. GL-E01

REF.	CHARS.	FIELD DEFINITION
1	6	Report Number
2	–	Title of Report and Date Processed
3	–	Consecutive Page Number of Report
4	3	Transaction Type or Table Code
5	4	Transaction Type or Table Name
6	–	Letters Indicate Beginning of Each Field and 80-Column Record
7	80	Contents of Record Before Change (Old) and After Change (New)
8	3	Error Message Number (See Message Table for Definition)
9	1	Severity of Message Defined in Message Table
10	20	Short Error Message
11	2	Number of Transactions Listed (New Records)
12	2	Number of Transactions Listed (New Records) With Errors
13		
14		
15		
16		
17		
18		
19		
20		

Figure 6.12. Continued.

154

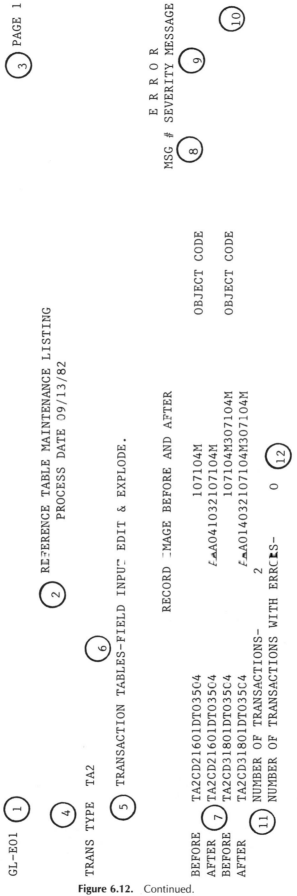

GL-E01 ①

③ PAGE 1

④ TRANS TYPE   TA2

② REFERENCE TABLE MAINTENANCE LISTING
PROCESS DATE 09/13/82

⑤ TRANSACTION TABLES-FIELD INPUT EDIT & EXPLODE.   ⑥

RECORD IMAGE BEFORE AND AFTER

                                                        ERROR
                                                MSG # SEVERITY MESSAGE
                                                 ⑧   ⑨   ⑩

BEFORE TA2CD21601DTO35C4   107104M   OBJECT CODE
AFTER ⑦ TA2CD21601DTO35C4   EⱯA04103Z107104M
BEFORE TA2CD31801DTO35C4   107104M307104M   OBJECT CODE
AFTER   TA2CD31801DTO35C4   EⱯA01403Z107104M307104M

     NUMBER OF TRANSACTIONS-   2
 ⑪ NUMBER OF TRANSACTIONS WITH ERRORS-   0 ⑫

Figure 6.12. Continued.

155

REPORT TITLE Batch Error Report   NUMBER   GL-E02

TYPE   Transaction Edit

FREQUENCY   Daily or when transaction batches are entered for processing.

SEQUENCE   Same as transaction entries. Only records with errors printed.

NUMBER OF COPIES AND DISTRIBUTION - REPORT PRODUCED BY PROGRAM _____

1. Accounting control

2.

3.

4.

5.

6.

RETENTION AND DISPOSITION: Held until batch appears on Batch Transaction
List GL-E03.

PURPOSE:

1. Provides link between input transaction batch and batch transaction
    list of accepted batches.
2. Provides information to correct transaction errors determined by edit
    and validation routines.
3. Error messages are defined in message tables.

PROCEDURE: Editing and validating routines are performed against each
transaction and errors are identified for correction. Batch total is
compared to generated batch totals for differences. When errors are
corrected, the batch details will be printed on the Batch Transaction
List GL-E03.

Figure 6.13. Sample batch error report description, report contents, and actual report.

FINANCIAL ACCOUNTING SYSTEM

REPORT CONTENTS

REPORT TITLE		Batch Error Report	REPORT NO. GL-E02
REF.	CHARS.	FIELD DEFINITION	
1	6	Report number	
2	–	Title of Report and date processed	
3	–	Consecutive page number of report	
4	–	Batch number	
5	–	Type of transactions in batch	
6	80	Batch header card information (?)	
7	4	Generated consecutive number	
8	80	Transaction input image without editing	
9	3	Error message number (see message table for definition)	
10	1	Severity of message (define 1, 2, 3, 4, etc.)	
11	20	Short error message	
12	–	Number of transactions in batch card	
13	–	Number of transactions read	
14	9	Dollar amount in batch card	
15	9	Dollar amount of transactions read	
16	?	Number of transactions with errors (not number of errors)	
17	–	End of report balance total message	
18			
19			
20			

Figure 6.13. Continued.

```
GL-E02  ①                        BATCH ERROR REPORT  ②              PAGE 1  ③
                                 PROCESS DATE 03/03/81

BATCH NO:  ABCDE02  ④                    CASH DISB  ⑤

         12345678901234567890123456789012345678901234567890
         CASH DISBURSEMENT  ⑥                                  00000580

                              TRANSACTION                              E R R O R
MIS                           INPUT IMAGE                      MSG #  SEVERITY  MESSAGE
REF                                                             ⑨       ⑩         ⑪
          ⑧
0001  CDO             CO1000000200005
0002  CD11234567890123456781234  000000040001V02  810303CAPS  ABCDE0200000900   103    2    INVALID LEDGER CODE
0003  CD11234567890123456781234  000000040001V02  810303CAPS  ABCDE0200000950   101    2    INVALID ACTIVITY
  ⑦                                                                              102    2    INVALID FUND CODE
                                                                                 103    2    INVALID LEDGER CODE

0004  CD11234567890123456781234  000000040001V02  810303CAPS  ABCDE0200000950   103    2    INVALID LEDGER CODE
                                                                                 101    2    INVALID ACTIVITY
                                                                                 102    2    INVALID FUND CODE
                                                                                 103    2    INVALID LEDGER CODE

0005  CD11234567890123456781234  000000040001V02  810303CAPS  ABCDE0200000950   102    2    INVALID FUND CODE
                                                                                 103    2    INVALID LEDGER CODE

0006  CD11234567890123456781234  000000040001V02  810303CAPS  ABCDE0200000950   104    2    INVALID OBJECT CODE
                                                                                 101    2    INVALID ACTIVITY

                              NO. OF TRANS          AMOUNT
                               ⑫  5   ⑬              ⑭
BATCH TOTAL                        5             2,000.05
COMPUTER TOTAL                     5             2,000.05  ⑮

NUMBER OF TRANSACTIONS WITH ERRORS:    4   ⑯

                    ********  ⑰  BATCH IN BALANCE  ********
```

Figure 6.13. Continued.

FINANCIAL ACCOUNTING SYSTEM
REPORT DESCRIPTION

REPORT TITLE Daily Departmental Free Balance Report   NUMBER   GL-D01

TYPE   Informational and Reference

FREQUENCY   After posting transactions in GL-E06

SEQUENCE   Fund - Account Number - Major Object Class

NUMBER OF COPIES AND DISTRIBUTION - REPORT PRODUCED BY PROGRAM

1. Budget Office

2. Accounts Payable

3. Purchasing

4. Contracts and Grants

5.

6.

RETENTION AND DISPOSITION: Retained until next report of daily balances
is received, then old report destroyed.

PURPOSE:

1. Provides departmental available balances for controlling encumbrances
   and to answer department inquiries.

2. Provides information for budget analysis of problem accounts.

PROCEDURE: Summarized revenues, expenditures, encumbrances and budgets by
department to produce available balances (35, 40, 45, 50). Totals agree
with General Ledger control totals in GL-D02.

Figure 6.14. Sample report description.

FINANCIAL ACCOUNTING SYSTEM
REPORT DESCRIPTION

REPORT TITLE <u>General Ledger Balances - 18 Digit</u>   NUMBER <u>GL-D02</u>

TYPE <u> Informational and Reference</u>

FREQUENCY <u> Each time general ledger file is updated</u>

SEQUENCE <u>   Fund - Account Number</u>

NUMBER OF COPIES AND DISTRIBUTION - REPORT PRODUCED BY PROGRAM <u>   </u>

1.   Accounting Control

2.   Director of Accounting

3.

4.

5.

6.

RETENTION AND DISPOSITION: Retained until a current report is received,
then destroyed.

PURPOSE:

Provides summarizing information at the 18-digit account level on the
financial position of the institution.

PROCEDURE: At the completion of a posting cycle, the summary totals of
transaction and the beginning balances are combined to produce the current
balance of each balance sheet account.

Figure 6.15. Sample report description.

FINANCIAL ACCOUNTING SYSTEM
REPORT DESCRIPTION

REPORT TITLE <u>General Ledger Balances - 8 Digit</u>   NUMBER <u>GL-D03</u>

TYPE <u>Informational and Reference</u>

FREQUENCY <u>When D01 and D02 are produced.</u>

SEQUENCE <u>8-digit Account Number (Fund - General Ledger-Primary Object)</u>

NUMBER OF COPIES AND DISTRIBUTION - REPORT PRODUCED BY PROGRAM <u>   </u>

1. Accounting Control

2. Director of Accounting

3.

4.

5.

6.

RETENTION AND DISPOSITION: Retained until a current report is received, then destroyed.

PURPOSE:

Provides summary information after last posting cycle on 8-digit account level.

PROCEDURE: At the completion of a posting cycle, the beginning balance, current month's activity to date, and current balance are reported at the 8-digit account level.

Figure 6.16. Sample report description.

FINANCIAL ACCOUNTING SYSTEM
REPORT DESCRIPTION

REPORT TITLE ___Bank Balances Report_____ NUMBER ___GL-D04____

TYPE ___Informational_____

FREQUENCY ___Each time transaction cycle is completed_____

SEQUENCE ___General Ledger Bank Number_____

NUMBER OF COPIES AND DISTRIBUTION - REPORT PRODUCED BY PROGRAM _____

1. Accounting Control - Bank Reconcilement Clerk

2. Director Investments (Bursar)

3.

4.

5.

6.

_____
RETENTION AND DISPOSITION: Retained until a current report is received,
then destroyed.

_____
PURPOSE:

Reports the cash balance in each bank available for investment and
forecast of cash needs.

_____
PROCEDURE: Daily cash receipts and disbursements which have been posted
to the accounting transaction journal are summarized by bank.

Figure 6.17. Sample report description.

CHAPTER 7
USER MANUAL:
GROUP ACCOUNTING
THERAPY

I t's time now for mergers and conglomerates. For that is exactly what the user manual is, a conglomeration of documentation originally prepared for internal accounting use and management. Many, if not most, of the transactions received in accounting for reviewing, recording, summarizing, and reporting are initiated in other departments. These departments are both the suppliers and the users of accounting.

As suppliers of accounting, the various departments provide the data that become the input to accounting systems to produce accounting information when processed. As users, they receive from accounting the information needed to make other decisions such as reduce staff, hire additional people, reduce scrap, increase purchases, travel less, reduce or increase maintenance, increase facilities, and so forth.

Following are some of the actions initiated at the user level.

Complete the annual budget form for operations.

Approve hiring an applicant for employment.

Terminate an employee for cause.

Requisition a commodity or service through the purchasing operation.

Request payment for a commodity or service not requiring a purchase order.

Request service or supplies from another department.

Prepare a charge slip for a customer.

Deposit cash or checks with the company cashier.

Prepare or approve time reports of employees.

Authorize deductions from payroll.

Provide material and production counts for the cost accounting and inventory systems.

Complete material receiving reports.

Compile shipping information for customer billings.

Request permission to travel and complete travel expense reports for reimbursements.

There certainly are more, but those are enough for starters. Every one of the actions listed results in one or more pieces of paper received in accounting as a transaction input document.

There are also accounting documents or reports sent to the user departments by accounting in a routine manner. These items may include:

Monthly statements of department operations and comparisons to budgets or targets.

Charge slips from other departments for supplies or services provided such as special maintenance.

Corrections in the original documents supplied to accounting.

Production reports, cost summaries, and scrap reports.

Payroll checks for distribution.

NEED FOR THE USER MANUAL

There is, then, a steady stream of accounting documents flowing between user departments and accounting operations. These documents usually are reports providing information or forms requiring some action to be taken and recorded. The problem is, many of these reports and forms are designed or prepared by accountants, but are used by people who are not accountants. Thus the need for a user manual. As stated in Chapter 1, this manual for users is an internal working manual and serves little purpose for employee or customer relations. It is a *training manual* for new line and staff supervisors and for the employees who are using the reports and forms. It is a *reference manual* when a rare or unusual event occurs. It is an *infor-*

mation manual to inform the users of company policies and procedures and how to complete accounting forms.

STARTING THE MANUAL

If you have a policy/procedure statement system in place, start by reviewing each statement and ask if officers, department supervisors or chairpeople, functional units or individual employees are involved in receiving data, forms, or reports from accounting. If yes, then mark that statement for possible inclusion in the user manual. Then review each accounting form and ask if information is initiated or processed by an outside user before the form reaches accounting. If so, that form should be selected for the manual.

If the P/PS system and forms manual are not in place, then review the list of actions at the beginning of this chapter and list those in use at your operation. Continue beyond these lists and identify other forms or actions the nonaccounting employee may be involved with. Either way, you now have a list of potential accounting policies, procedures, or forms that may be included in the user manual.

Before going much further, make a rough list of the potential distribution of such a manual. Is it every senior officer and department chairperson or supervisor? Is it just selected departments? Could it be all employees above a certain classification level? All professionals in a professional service organization? Or just one copy to each branch office? This list could range from a few dozen locations or persons to a hundred or more.

If the list is extremely diverse, you may elect to issue different manuals to different users. For example, there could be a factory or shop department user manual that includes only policies and procedures that affect those operations. The factory manual may cover only hourly payroll procedures and forms, and the travel policies and cash and accounts receivable sections may be deleted. A special section on inventory control forms may be included in this manual.

Likewise, the manual for branch operations may be expanded to cover special problems such as procedures for shipping goods from the home office and receiving them at the branch. There may also be special provisions for transmitting data and for automatic deposit of payroll checks of branch employees. The procedure for handling and reporting branch deposits of cash would be included here but nowhere else.

The third separate manual may be the administrative department accounting manual. This manual may cover special reports prepared by the sales department, forms for reporting customer credit ratings, or special reports covering research and development located only at the primary office of the company.

This list also helps to determine the level of detail to be provided and possibly the style of the manual. One other consideration might be the number of recurring input document errors or the number of inquiries received daily or weekly from employees initiating the addition of information to the accounting forms at their respective locations. Steadily recurring errors on input documents is a positive sign that a user manual is needed.

OUTLINING THE USER MANUAL

The next logical step is to outline the manual, generally by accounting function such as payroll, accounts payable, cashier, accounts receivable, production, and so forth. A sentence outline should provide enough information to select the various policy and procedure documents and write explanations or rewrite existing form instructions or other information. The outline should look like the one in Figure 7.1.

Putting the user manual together is now a matter of selecting the available documentation, adding or deleting information where needed, preparing an index, and printing and publishing the manual. Unlike a book, the index or contents should be on the cover where it is immediately available. Each topic, instruction sheet, and form should be indexed by name and page number. The user manual is usually between 50 and 100 pages. Any larger manual tends not to be used.

ACCOUNTING CODES MANUAL

Many accounting functions today are heavily computerized. In such systems, shorthand codes are developed to trigger actions, to change information, and to reduce the size of computer files. If a form included in the user manual has a few codes, they should be included in the instructions for completing the form or on the form itself. Examples are *P* and *F* for part-time and full-time employee status, or *E* or *N* for exempt or nonexempt overtime status. Some fields may have 10 or 15 codes and the employee filling in the form would have little knowledge of the codes or their meanings. In some organizations there even may be codes for units of measure.

If there are several lengthy code structures and the codes are not shown on the form, then an accounting codes manual may be issued as part of the user department accounting manual. One such manual would be issued to each user department. The codes would be indexed by form number and line number or line description.

REVISING AND ADDING MATERIAL

Study the materials brought together for the user manual. Some policy/procedures statements may be quite long, with extensive introductions and copies of laws and regulations. If adequate as originally printed, use them as is. If not, prepare a condensed version for the user manual, stripping out material of little interest to the departmental user.

Likewise, the forms manual discussed in Chapter 4 suggests a 3-page layout consisting of a page of logistics about the form, a page on completing the form, and the form itself. For the user manual, the first page probably should be replaced with a description and purpose of the form, the situations that the form covers, the distribution of copies of the form, and the filing and retention requirements.

OUTLINE -- USER DEPARTMENT ACCOUNTING MANUAL   Date

L. O. GRANT ORGANIZATION, INC.

I. Listing of accounting employees by function, internal
    mailing address, and phone number

II. Completing payroll forms
 A. New hire
 B. Transfer
 C. Termination
 D. Time reporting, including vacation and sick time

III. Requisitioning purchases or paying non-purchase items
 A. Requisition Order
 B. Remittance Voucher
 C. Receiving report handling
 D. Discrepancy in receiving
 E. Returning merchandise
 F. Requesting services and supplies from another
  department

IV. Processing shipping and receivable documents
 A. Shipping and freight billing
 B. Back-order reporting
 C. Discrepancy reporting

V. Reporting production information
 A. Raw material and supply usage
 B. Finished production counts

VI. Travel policy and reports

VII. Departmental budgeting
 A. Preparing initial budget
 B. Budget revisions
 C. Checking the monthly accounting report

VIII. Depositing cash and checks
 A. Departmental Deposit Ticket
 B. Official Company Receipt
 C. Reporting branch deposits to main office

IX. Accounting transaction codes
 A. Department and branch codes
 B. Income codes
 C. Expense codes

Figure 7.1. Outline of user manual.

PRINTING AND PUBLISHING

The manual may be printed on both sides of the paper but printing on only one side is recommended. Printing on one side leaves the back of the preceding page available for user notes, additions, deletions, and changes until a new manual is published. Use standard white paper and provide an index and date of issue on the cover. After collating, the manual should be held together with a single staple in the upper left corner unless placed in a three-ring binder.

Another suggestion, if the manual is to be issued to department supervisors and chairpersons, is to provide a second copy of the manual marked *Office Copy* or *Secretary's Copy,* for most accounting documents prepared at remote locations will be done by the secretary or clerk in the department under the direction of the supervisor. It will be the clerk or secretary who will be calling the accounting department for assistance with a problem.

Distribute the manual to the selected recipients through the normal delivery system used in the company. The first time the user manual is distributed, a cover letter explaining its purpose and use would be helpful.

UPDATING THE USER MANUAL

Periodically updating parts of the user manual by issuing corrected insert sheets is not generally recommended. Users tend not to delete superseded pages or add new pages to a previously published manual. One way of notifying such users of changes is through interoffice correspondence to the original holders of the manuals. The *From* section would be the accounting department, the *Subject* section would indicate the specific page and item to be changed, such as *Addition to Branch Codes, Page 54 of User Department Accounting Manual.*

The first paragraph can explain the addition or change in some detail. The second paragraph would specifically state that the following addition should be made to Page 54, Section B, item 12, as follows:

12. San Antonio, Branch 26, Manager: Alex Bell

In most cases, the reader will update the manual in writing.

The user manual probably should be updated in total and published annually, unless significant additions or changes have made the current version almost unusable before then. More information on updating techniques is covered in Chapter 11.

Figures 7.2 through 7.13, which complete this chapter, show portions of a typical user department accounting procedures manual. The amount of information included is directly proportional to the departmental employee involvement in preparing and coding accounting transaction forms.

USER DEPARTMENT ACCOUNTING PROCEDURES

UNIVERSITY OF SOUTHERN MISSISSIPPI

May 1986

Figure 7.2. Cover of typical user manual.

ORGANIZATION OF FINANCIAL AFFAIRS DIVISION

Telephone

FINANCIAL AFFAIRS - 201 FORREST COUNTY HALL   BOX 5143

Harry L. Brown, Director   4084

Edward H. Champney, Assistant Director   4101
  New account initiation
  Monthly Budget Reports
  Payroll

Linda McFall, Manager of Disbursements   4098
  Vendor Payments
  Interdepartmental Invoices
  Travel Vouchers

Jacky Fortenberry, Manager of Restricted Funds   5086
  Restricted accounts control
  Designated accounts
  Federal financial reports

Hugh West, Manager of Budgets   4091
  Annual Budget
  Budget revisions

Lucia Burt, Department Secretary - Information   4084

BUSINESS SERVICES - 101 FORREST COUNTY HALL - BOX 5133

Sam Clinton, Manager of Business Services   4137
  Bank relations
  Registration cash control
  Investments

Clif Sturdivant, University Cashier   4137
  Cashier
  Travel advances

Mary Schlottman, Manager of Accounts Receivable   4141
  Accounts receivable - student, staff, others
  Student loans receivable

Charlie McMillin, Department Secretary - Information   4137

PROPERTY ACCOUNTING - EURE BUILDING - BOX 5086

William Rayner, Manager of Property Accounting   4440
  Physical plant records
  Equipment control - transfers, additions, disposals

Figure 7.3. Organization list for user manual.

OVERVIEW - FINANCIAL AFFAIRS

The general accounting system is designed to produce revenue report details, a monthly budget report for each operating department or project, and a general ledger for accounting control and financial reporting. Several accounting subsystems are related to the main accounting system.

1. Budget
2. Accounts payable and travel
3. Payroll
4. Cashier receipting system
5. Bank reconcilements
6. Accounts receivable
7. Investments
8. Tuition and fee system
9. Student deposit system
10. Work-in-process (Physical Plant)
11. Financial Aid system
12. Inventory and billing systems

Every transaction charged to a department account or credited to income is supported by a report, form or other document, as follows:

Initial Budget

Budget Revision

Vendor Payments
    Requisition
    Purchase Order
    Remittance Voucher

Payroll
    PSO 10 - New Hire
    PSO 11 - Termination
    Single Payment Voucher
    Time and Attendance Report
    Student Employment and Termination

Travel
    Permission to Travel
    Travel Voucher
    Motor Pool Invoice
    Aircraft Use Invoice

Interdepartment Invoices

Revenues and Receipts
    Departmental Deposit Ticket
    University Receipt
    Accounts Receivable Worksheet

Other
    Petty Cash
    Refund Authorizations

Figure 7.4. User manual overview of Financial Affairs.

EXAMPLE OF BUDGET REPORT

Every operating department receives a financial report at the end of
each month. This report provides the current status of the budgeted
funds for the department and contains the following information:

A. Account number.

B. Month of report.

C. Name of account.

D. Address to which report is sent.

E. Voucher - A 6-digit number which identifies the source of the
    transactions. The first digit identifies the system that
    generated the transaction.

    1. Cash disbursement voucher
    2. Encumbrance
    3. Payroll (3 + month, day, year)
    8. Cash receipt (8 + working day of year). Actual receipt number
       is recorded in the Description column.
    9. Journal Voucher

F. P/O No. The purchase order number, if one has been issued.

G. Object Description. Description of the transaction or vendor
    name.

H. G. L. Obj. General Ledger Code (4 digits) and specific Object
    Code (4 digits) to which the transaction was charged or credited.

I. Encumbrance. Amount committed to an expenditure for which payment
    has not been made. When item is paid, the encumbrance is
    liquidated (removed) and the actual expenditure amount recorded in
    "Expenditure" column.

J. Expenditure. The actual amount of the expenditure being charged
    to this account. The expenditure may be more or less than the
    encumbrance, depending on freight paid, quantity discount, special
    discount, error, and so forth.

K. Budget. Amount allocated to each expenditure category such as
    Salary, Wage, Travel, and so forth.

L. Free Balance. The amount of the budgeted funds that has not been
    spent or committed. Free Balance = Budget less Expenditures and
    Encumbrances. If overexpended, the balance will have a minus
    sign. Free balances in Salary, Fringe Benefits and Prior Year
    Expense categories cannot be reallocated to other budget categories.

Figure 7.5. User manual example of budget report.

BUDGET REPORT FOR DEPT 0618099 ENDING 12/31/85

C DIRECTOR SPECIAL SERVICE **A** **B** P. O. BOX 4852 **D**

VOUCHER (E)	P/O NO. (F)	OBJECT DESCRIPT (G)	G.L. OBJ. (H)	ENCUMBRANCE (I)	EXPENDITURE (J)	BUDGET (K)	FREE BALANCE (L)
PRIOR YEAR EXPENSE							
113737	22012	DATA GENERAL CO	1041 4157	1,525.00	0.00	1,525.00	0.00 BEGINNING BALANCE
113737	22012	DATA GENERAL CO	1051 4157	1,100.00-	1,100.00	0.00	
TOTAL PRIOR YEAR EXPENSE				425.00	1,100.00	1,525.00	0.00 ENDING BALANCE ✗
SALARY							
311302		SALARY	1040 1000	32,000.00	16,000.00	48,000.00	0.00 BEGINNING BALANCE
311302		SALARY	1050 1000	4,000.00-	4,000.00	0.00	
TOTAL SALARY				28,000.00	20,000.00	48,000.00	0.00 ENDING BALANCE ✗
WAGE							
311172		WAGE	1040 2000	0.00	50.00	500.00	450.00 BEGINNING BALANCE
311032		WORK STUDY CHGS	1040 2860	0.00	90.00	0.00	
				0.00	10.00	0.00	
TOTAL WAGE				0.00	150.00	500.00	350.00 ENDING BALANCE ✗
FRINGE BENEFITS							
990621		RETIREMENT	1040 3011	0.00	3,000.00	8,000.00	5,000.00 BEGINNING BALANCE
990621		SOCIAL SECURITY	1040 3012	0.00	357.00	0.00	
990621		WORKMAN COMP	1040 3013	0.00	50.00	0.00	
990621		HEALTH INS	1040 3014	0.00	7.00	0.00	
990621		LIFE INS	1040 3015	0.00	57.60	0.00	
				0.00	18.00	0.00	
TOTAL FRINGE BENEFITS				0.00	3,489.60	8,000.00	4,510.40 ENDING BALANCE ✗
TRAVEL							
111983		SMITH, AL	1040 4039	150.00	810.00	2,000.00	1,040.00 BEGINNING BALANCE
290605	95358	0095358	1050 4061	0.00	160.00	0.00	
				200.00	0.00	0.00	
TOTAL TRAVEL				350.00	970.00	2,000.00	680.00 ENDING BALANCE ✗
CONTRACTUAL SERVICES							
990523		POSTAGE	1040 4111	200.00	1,700.00	3,500.00	1,600.00 BEGINNING BALANCE
990630		WATS CHARGES	1040 4113	0.00	10.00	0.00	
114850	8902	ENGINEERING CO	1040 4131	0.00	120.00	0.00	
114850	8902	ENGINEERING CO	1040 4131	200.00-	160.00	0.00	
TOTAL CONTRACTUAL SERVICES				0.00	1,990.00	3,500.00	1,510.00 ENDING BALANCE ✗
COMMODITIES							
990628		STORES ISSUES	1040 4242	300.00	1,200.00	3,000.00	1,500.00 BEGINNING BALANCE
111985	9035	FISHER SCIENT	1040 4231	0.00	20.00	0.00	
111985	9035	FISHER SCIENT	1050 4231	0.00	400.00	0.00	
				300.00-	0.00	0.00	
TOTAL COMMODITIES				0.00	1,620.00	3,000.00	1,380.00 ENDING BALANCE ✗

Figure 7.6. User manual budget report.

REVENUE AND EXPENDITURE CODING

Coding consists of 8, 15, or 18 digits:

    1 - 4   Fund and General Ledger
    5 - 8   Revenue or Expenditure Object Codes
    9 - 18   A 7 or 10-digit Account Number

Fund and General Ledger Codes:	Revenue	Expenditure
General Fund	1035	1040
Auxiliary Enterprises Fund	2035	2040
Designated Fund	2535	2540
Restricted Fund	3035	3040
Loan Fund	4035	4040
Endowment Fund	5035	5040
Plant Fund - Unexpended	6035	6040
Replacements	6135	6140
Indebtedness	6235	6240
Agency Fund	7035	7040

Object Codes:

    See Appendix A for Revenue Codes.
    See Appendix B for Expenditure Codes.

Account Numbers:

General Fund	OXXXXXX (A)
Auxiliary Enterprises Fund	11XXXXX
Designated Fund	2XXXXXX XXX
Restricted Fund	OXXXXXX XXX
Loan Fund	15XXXXX
Endowment Fund	16XXXXX
Plant Fund	17XXXXX
Agency Fund	18XXXXX

(A) Account number not required for General Fund revenue codes.

Figure 7.7. Explanation of revenue and expenditure coding for users.

STUDENT EMPLOYMENT

1. Students employed must be full-time students (12 hours undergraduate, 9 hours graduate). The employing department ascertains eligibility for work-study or regular wages and course load prior to the student working any hours.

2. A student employee may not work more than 20 hours per week. However, when school is not in session, a full-time student may be employed for up to 40 hours per week.

3. A student receiving a stipend in the form of a fellowship, scholarship, assistantships, or federal grant compensation may not work in a wage position at the same time.

4. High school students or college students not attending USM are paid at the minimum wage rate and are hired through Personnel Services.

5. Students can work on only one University account during a payroll period (no split wage charges).

6. Student employment forms must be processed by the Student Employment Office prior to the students' employment. Graduate Fellowships and Assistantships are approved by the Graduate Dean before being processed by the Student Employment Office.

7. Rates of pay are:

Wage students with no aid	$3.10 hour
College work study or application for federal aid	$3.35 hour
Graduate work study assistantships:	
Masters	$5.00 hour
Doctoral	$6.00 hour

8. The pay rate for students on Restricted Fund accounts must conform to the budget approved by the Office of Research and Sponsored Programs.

9. Any exceptions to the guidelines for student employment will be considered by the Student Employment Office. Any memo request for a change in status should be submitted with the SEF 1 form. All exceptions are subject to approval by the Director of Student Employment.

Figure 7.8. Procedures for employing students.

ANNUAL BUDGET

When the General and Auxiliary Enterprises annual budgets are printed and approved, each Department receives a copy of the Department Budget.

This report shows:

1. Department Name and Account number
2. Employee name and title (salary personnel only)
3. Employee Level (except academic personnel)
4. FTE (Full time equivalent such as 1.00, .50, .15)
5. No. of months (contract), usually 9 or 12
6. Prior year budget for this position
7. Increase or decrease
8. Current budget for this position
9. Total Salaries of all salary positions
10. Total Wages
11. Total Fringe Benefits
12. Total Travel and Subsistence
13. Total Contractual Services
14. Total Commodities
15. Total Equipment, if any
16. Total Budget for this department

The above totals (Items 9 through 15) are recorded on the Monthly Budget Report.

This report is the only record of contractual salaries issued to the Department Chairman. Any subsequent changes in salary positions requires a personnel change form (hire, terminate, change of name, title, FTE, months, salary or level). See Payroll Section.

TRANSFERRING FUNDS TO ANOTHER ACCOUNT

Transferring funds from a General Fund account to another account in a different Fund requires two steps:

1. Prepare a budget revision to set up a budget amount in the Subsidies, Loans, and Grants category.

2. Prepare an Interdepartmental Invoice or memo requesting that the budget category "Subsidies, Loans and Grants" be charged (transfer out) and the account receiving the subsidy be credited (transfer in).

Figure 7.9. Explanation of annual budget.

UNIVERSITY OF SOUTHERN MISSISSIPPI
CURRENT EDUCATIONAL AND GENERAL AND AUXILIARY ENTERPRISES FUNDS
DETAIL OF EXPENDITURES BY DEPARTMENTS AND OBJECTS

DEPARTMENT NAME TITLE	LEVEL	FTE	NO OF MOS	REVISED BUDGET 1984-1985	INCREASE DECREASE	BUDGET 1985-1986
0110801 SPECIAL PROJECTS						
1 (Name) Professor & Director		1.00	12.0	48,000	4,000	52,000
2 (Name) Assistant Professor to Professor		1.00	9.0	30,000	13,000	43,000
3 (Name) Assistant Professor		1.00	9.0	NEW	33,000	33,000
4 (Name) Instructor		1.00	9.0	23,000	3,000	26,000
5 (Name) Instructor & Supervisor		1.00	12.0	26,100	2,900	29,000
6 (Name) Instructor (See Philosophy)		.50	12.0	9,750	1,250	11,000
SALARIES				127,000	67,000	194,000
WAGES				8,680	1,680-	7,000
FRINGE BENEFITS				14,340	22,460	36,800
TRAVEL AND SUBSISTENCE				2,500	500	3,000
CONTRACTUAL SERVICES				15,200	1,200-	14,000
COMMODITIES				7,000	2,400	9,400
EQUIPMENT				8,398	8,398-	0
TOTAL				183,118	81,082	264,200

Figure 7.10. Example of annual departmental budget.

COMPLETING THE TIME AND ATTENDANCE REPORT

Preprinted by Payroll

A. Department name and campus address and "Biweekly" and "Hourly".

B. Pay Period Ending (Sunday).

C. (see below for completing the form).

D. Control letter (Do not enter if an employee is added to the report.

E. Employee name and social security number.

F. "TX" indicates positive time reporting.

G. Earnings type. Preprinted shows REG (regular) or WSR (College Work Study). If employee is to be paid for a Holiday, enter "HOL". Do not submit holiday pay if employee is not eligible. Only Permanent employees are eligible (excludes students and Temporary classes).

H. Hourly rate of pay.

I. Job Class number.

J. Fund, General Ledger, Object and Account Number to be charged for gross pay and related fringe benefit costs.

Completing the form

C. Enter "X" if employee is to be paid any amount.

G. If earnings is not REG (regular) or WSR (work study) draw a line through preprinted type and enter 3-character type (see top of form for Earnings Type).

L1. Enter hours worked for earnings type shown.

M2. If two earnings type for this payroll,
L2. enter Type in section M2 and hours in L2.
M3. If three earnings type, enter type and hours
L3. in M3 and L3.

H. If employee worked no hours this pay period or is no longer working in this department, put a line through Rate of Pay.

Adding an employee

Complete C, E, F, G, L1, H, I, J

Totaling and Distribution

N., O., P. Add all hours in this column and enter page totals in N, O and P as applicable.

Q. Add rates of pay in H of employees being paid and enter total here.

R. Signature of individual responsible for authorizing the pay.

Figure 7.11. Completing the Time and Attendance Report.

UNIVERSITY OF SOUTHERN MISSISSIPPI

Time and Attendance Report

POSITIVE TIME REPORTING:
PLACE AN "X" IN ALL LINES
TO BE PAID.

EXCEPTION TIME REPORTING:
PLACE AN "X" IN ALL LINES
WITH CHANGES.

MAIL TO:

A

PAGE NO:

SCHEDULE:

SCK: MAJOR MEDICAL LEAVE
VAC: PERSONAL LEAVE
HOL: HOLIDAY

REG: REGULAR HOURS
WSR: WORKSTUDY
OTP: OVERTIME 1.5

PAY PERIOD ENDING

EARNINGS TYPE

EMPLOYEE NAME:

X	CTL	EMPLOYEE ID	TRAN CODE	EARN TYPE	TIME	EARN TYPE	TIME	EARN TYPE	TIME	RATE OF PAY	JOB NO.	JOB CLASS	FD/GL	OBJ	ACCOUNT NUMBER
6	1	9 10 11	18 20 21	25 26	28 29	33 34	36 37	41 42	48 49	50	55 56	59 60	63 64	80

B 12 B 17

C D E F G L₁ M₂ L₂ M₃ L₃ H I J J J

CONTROL TOTALS → N O P Q

I HEREBY CERTIFY THAT THE TIME REPORTED
ABOVE IS A TRUE STATEMENT OF HOURS WORK-
ED BY THESE STUDENTS/PERSONNEL

R

Figure 7.12. Time and Attendance Report form.

ACCOUNTS PAYABLE

The Accounts Payable unit of Financial Affairs is responsible for auditing the supporting documents and preparing disbursement checks for all of the legally-incurred obligations for materials and services other than payroll. Documents processed herein include:

Vendor Invoices
Purchase Orders
Receiving Reports
Travel Vouchers
Permissions to Travel
Contract Payments on leases, bonds and notes payable
Interdepartmental Invoices
Utility Bills
Miscellaneous payments for contractual services (non-employees)

Encumbering

An encumbrance is an obligation of funds for a specific purpose. The encumbrance system assists department chairmen in maintaining control of funds for which they are responsible. Encumbrances insure the necessary funds are available when payment is required.

The Accounts Payable unit encumbers funds as follows:

1. All Purchase Orders over $50 are encumbered except "Confirmation of Goods Received" and "Send Check With Order" purchases.

2. Estimated travel costs are encumbered from Permission to Travel forms.

3. Work-in-Process Orders are encumbered after receiving properly approved documents from Physical Plant.

4. Indirect Costs on contract and grant projects are encumbered in total at the inception of the project.

5. Items not covered by the above rules can be encumbered by notifying the Director of Financial Affairs in writing, giving details and amount to be encumbered.

Encumbrances of other than regular Purchase Orders require the assignment of a special 5-digit number as follows:

91XXX - Work-in-Process Orders
95XXX - Travel
96XXX - Travel
97XXX - Travel
98XXX - Travel
99XXX - Miscellaneous

Figure 7.13. Accounts payable procedures.

A. FORM NO. AND NAME: PUR 001 - REQUISITION

B. NO. OF PARTS: 2   LAST REVISION DATE: July 1981

C. SOURCE OF SUPPLY: Purchasing Department - 301 Forrest County Hall

D. PURPOSE: When supplies or equipment items are needed, the Department completes a Requisition form (PUR 001). The original copy is sent to the Purchasing Department and the canary copy is retained by the requisitioning department for later comparison to the Purchase Order. When the Purchase Order is prepared by Purchasing, one copy is sent to the requisitioning department.

The Department Chairman is to determine that funds are available in the budget when supplies, equipment or contractual services are ordered.

Supplies available from the Bookstore, Physical Plant Stores, Science Stores and Printing and Supply Services must be purchased from those sources.

Purchase Orders over $50 are encumbered. The P.O. and the Requisition are the only information received by the Department. The Vendor invoice is received by Accounts payable and paid if the transaction is completed. When paid, the account is charged and the encumbrance removed.

E. DISTRIBUTION OF COMPLETED FORM: Original white copy to Purchasing, Department canary copy held in preparing Department's file until Purchase Order is received.

Figure 7.14.   Description of Purchase Requisition form.

COMPLETING THE REQUISITION

A. Date – Date the requisition is prepared.

B. Purchase Order No. – To be filled in by Purchasing except when requesting a P.O. # in advance. If so, enter the P.O. # before sending requisition to Purchasing.

C. Name of Account to be Charged – The official name of the account to be charged must agree with the Department Code Number.

D. Deliver to – Building – Room – For the Receiving Department to deliver items to correct location.

E. Required Delivery Date – Date items are needed.

F. To be Used for – Reason for purchasing.

G. Name and Address of Vendors Suggested – Complete name and address of the company or companies which can furnish the item or service.

H. Quantity, Description, Estimated Unit Price – This area described what is wanted. It is very important to show complete and detailed information here. Questions concerning Bid procedures and Quotation procedures should be directed to Purchasing.

I. Charge Code No. – The General Ledger Code depends on the department code.

DEPARTMENT CODES	FUND	G. L. CODE
01XXXXX - 09XXXXX	General	1040
11XXXXX	Auxiliary Enterprises	2040
21XXXXXXXX-29XXXXXXXX	Designated	2540
01XXXXXXXX-09XXXXXXXX	Restricted	3040
15XXXXX	Loan	4040
171XXXX-176XXXX	Plant-Unexpended	6040
178XXXX	Plant R&R	6140
179XXX	Plant-Debt	6240
18XXXXX	Agency	7040

See object code listing for appropriate code.

J. Signatures – Must be signed by the person who has the Budgetary authority.

K. Name and Phone Number – For obtaining additional information, if needed.

Figure 7.15. Completing the Requisition form.

REMITTANCE VOUCHER

A. FORM NO. AND NAME: ACC 14   REMITTANCE VOUCHER

B. NO. OF PARTS: 3   LAST REVISION DATE: 1-83

C. SOURCE OF SUPPLY: Financial Affairs, 201 Forrest County Hall

D. PURPOSE: The Remittance Voucher is used for disbursements that normally do not require a Purchase Order or a receiving report for goods received. Examples are:

Seminar and conference registration fees for employees
Honorariums to non-employees
Speaker's fee
Travel expense reimbursement for non-employees (recruiting, speakers, professional fees and so forth)
Stipends
Agency accounts
Items on contract (leases, land purchases, entertainment groups, Cablevision, etc)
Legal, audit and other professional fees
Payroll taxes and amounts withheld for payment to others
Insurance
Postage (Post Office only)
Advertising
Utilities
Telephone
Freight when shipper is USM
Band and music awards (not trophies or plaques)
Registration workers
Officials - Athletic and Intramural Departments
Sales Tax
Refunds - housing deposits and Continuing Education fees

The form is used as a cover document for form ACC 14A - Multiple Vendor-Payee Attachment.

E. DISTRIBUTION OF COMPLETED FORM:
1. White - Accounts Payable unit with supporting documents
2. Canary - Accounts Payable unit. Enclosed with check to vendor if necessary
3. Pink - Held by issuing Department for comparison to Monthly Budget Report.

Figure 7.16. Description of Remittance Voucher form.

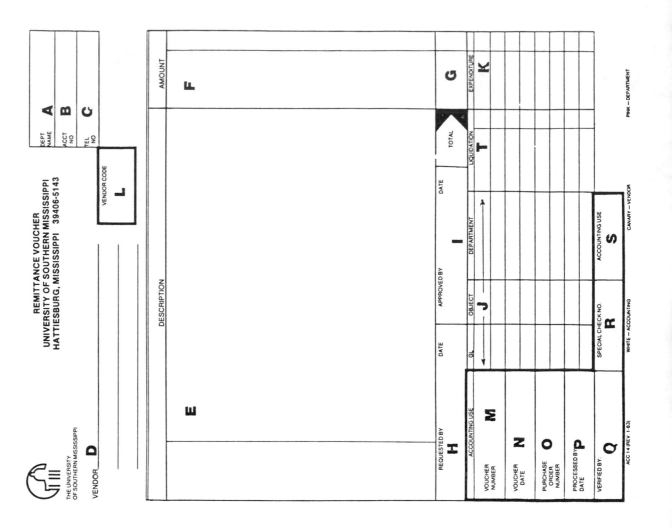

COMPLETING THE REMITTANCE VOUCHER

Department enters:

A. Department name.
B. Account number.
C. Telephone number of preparer.
D. Name and address of vendor. If used as a cover form for the Multiple Vendor-Payee Attachment, etner "See Attached Forms". Social Security number must be supplied for payment to individuals.
E. Description of charge to be paid, including name of registrant(s) at a seminar or conference, purpose of payment and so forth. If registration form, document or letter is to be sent with check, indicate that enclosure is attached.
F. Amount to be paid. Attach supporting document, if any.
G. Total to be paid on this voucher.
H. Signature of person requesting payment and date signed.
I. Approval signature and date. Payments to individuals require two approval signature if an invoice is not available.
J. General Ledger Code, Object Code and Department to be charged. If Department is not entered, the charge will be made to the account shown at top of the form.
K. Amount to be charged to this account. Form provides distribution for up to eight accounts.

Financial Affairs enters:

L. Vendor code number.
M. Voucher number.
N. Voucher date.
O. Purchase Order Number, if any.
P. Name of person processing the voucher and date processed.
Q. Name of person reviewing or verifying information.
R. Preprinted number of special check used to pay voucher.
S. Special handling required or enclosure to be mailed with check.
T. Amount of encumbrance to be liquidated, if any.

Figure 7.17. Completing the Remittance Voucher form.

TRAVEL EXPENSE

Employees of the University are reimbursed for reasonable and necessary expenses incurred during approved travel. Note maximums for mileage and meals.

Authorization. Travel requires approval of Department Chairman or designated official. Permission to Travel form must be submitted at least two weeks in advance of departure date to conferences, conventions and professional meetings. Request for out-of-country travel must be submitted 90 days in advance. Permission to Travel form is not required for business trips.

The 4-part request form is prepared by the applicant and routed as follows:

> Domestic travel (48 contiguous states)
> 1. Department Chairman
> 2. Dean or Division Director
> 3. Accounting department for funds availability and encumbering
>
> Foreign travel
> 4. Vice President
> 5. President

Accounting retains white copy and canary copy. Pink copy is returned to employee, and goldenrod copy is for department files. If employee needs travel advance for out-of-pocket costs, Accounting will provide canary copy. The American Express card should be used for airline tickets and lodging. No advance is permitted for in-state travel.

Change or Cancellation of Travel Request. An amended Permission to Travel must be submitted to change place or date of meeting, accounting distribution or cancellation of meeting.

Advance Payment of Conference Registration Fees. To pay registration fees in advance of conference, the request should be made at least 20 days in advance of conference date on a Remittance Voucher. Literature concerning the conference and fee amount and a photocopy of Permission to Travel must be attached to the voucher.

University Motor Pool Vehicle. See the University Motor Pool "Operating Procedures and Regulations" Handbook. The account number will be charged to the department through a Motor Pool Invoice. Motor Pool charges are never reported on a Travel Voucher.

Reimbursement of Travel Expense. Immediately upon returning from a trip, the traveler should submit a Travel Voucher for reimbursement. The first two copies with required receipts attached are submitted to Financial

Figure 7.18. User manual travel expense procedures.

Affairs. For other than business travel, the pink copy of the Permission to Travel is also attached. Travel Vouchers received by 5 p.m. Thursday will be paid the following Thursday. All Travel Vouchers require independent approval. The Department retains the third copy and the employee retains the last copy for his or her records.

Lodging. If more than one person is indicated on the logdging bill, the single rate of the room should be shown; otherwise, reimbursement will be made at 50% of the room charge.

Lodging reimbursement will be made for the final evening of the trip if the traveler is not able to return home by 9 p.m. Original lodging bill required.

Meals. Reimbursement for meals will be for actual expenditure, plus tips, at a reasonable amount with the following maximum daily limits for three meals:

In Mississippi	$18 per day
Out of Mississippi	$24 per day
High-cost cities (specific)	$30 per day (receipts required)

Mileage. Mileage for personal vehicle is reimbursed at 20 cents per mile for the most direct route. Private vehicle mileage reimbursement cannot exceed cost of round-trip air coach fare to the named destination.

Public Carrier. Airline tickets must be purchased from Pro Travel, the official USM travel agency. Certification that coach rate was not available is necessary when travel is first class. Ticket coupon is required to document flight cost.

Registration Fees. Fees are reimbursed on a travel voucher when supported by a paid receipt, unless paid on a Remittance Voucher prior to conference date.

Tips. Tips for meals and taxi should be included as part of those charges. Tips reported here include baggage-handling tips when arriving and departing a hotel or at airports and should not exceed $1.00 per bag.

Taxi and Limousine. Actual charges, including tip, are reimbursable.

Parking and Tolls. Actual parking charges and road and bridge tolls are reimbursable if using personal vehicle, Motor Pool vehicle, or rental car.

Car Rental. Actual cost of car rental is reimbursable. Receipt required.

Figure 7.18. Continued.

A. FORM NO. AND NAME: EMPLOYEE TRAVEL VOUCHER

B. NO. OF PARTS: 4   LAST REVISION DATE: 4/85

C. SOURCE OF SUPPLY: Printing Services

D. PURPOSE: To reimburse employee for all approved travel. It is also used
                for group travel (students and employee) if one employee is paying
                for meals and lodging for several travelers.

                Two approval signatures are required for travel reimbursement.

                IMPORTANT: It is important that Department retain the Pink copy
                as a record of employee travel as reported in the Monthly Budget
                Report. The employee should retain the Goldenrod so he or she
                has a copy of the reimbursed costs.

                Vouchers with errors or missing documentation will be returned
                to the employee for correction.

                Vouchers received in Financial Affairs by 5:00 p.m. Thursday
                will be paid the following Thursday.

E. DISTRIBUTION OF COMPLETED FORM:
    White - Accounting with required receipts
    Canary - Accounting
    Pink - Department
    Goldenrod - Employee

Figure 7.19. Description of Employee Travel Voucher.

COMPLETING THE EMPLOYEE TRAVEL VOUCHER

a. Employee name, social security number and address.

b. Purpose of trip and city and state.

c. Department name and account number to be charged. Must be same as Permission to Travel.

d. Names of others on trip, whether traveling together or not.

e. Date of travel, departure time on first day and arrival time last day traveling.

f. Meals -- Daily meal maximums are:
   In Mississippi $18
   Outside of Mississippi $24
   Listed high - cost cities $30   (receipts required)

g. Lodging -- Original hotel or motel bill required. If bill shows two persons, indicate single room rate for this room. Do not report charges other than room charges as lodging (telephone, room service, valet, etc.).

h. Travel by personal vehicle -- Indicate if University Motor Pool vehicle was used. If so, do not enter any miles here. If personal vehicle is used, enter departure and arrival location and miles. Round trip can be entered as "Hattiesburg to Jackson and return -- 190." Enter current approved rate (20¢ mile).

i. Travel by Public Carrier -- Date, location leaving from (city), destination city, whether by air, bus, or train and ticket amount. Airline ticket coupon must be attached.

j. Registration fees -- If paid by employee, receipt or copy of program stating fee must be attached.

k. Tips -- Only for baggage handling or valet parking. Meal tips are part of meal cost.

l. Taxi/limousine -- Actual taxi fare plus tip or airport limousine charge.

m. Parking/Tolls -- Actual parking charges or road or bridge tolls paid.

n. Car rental -- Receipt required.

o. Check travel category. If category 3, 4 or 5 are checked, approved copy of Permission to Travel form must be attached.

p. If travel advance was received, enter amount and date received.

q. Enter total of all expenses on Travel Voucher.

r. Maximum Reimbursement Allowed -- If chairman approving enters a smaller amount here than the total amount, then the smaller amount will be paid. Some departments have a travel limit on each trip.

s. Signature of employee and date signed. Signature of account director and date. No employee can approve his or her own travel.

t. For Accounting use only.

Figure 7.20. Completing the Employee Travel Voucher form.

A. FORM NO. AND NAME: ACC 20 - PETTY CASH VOUCHER

B. NO. OF PARTS: 1   LAST REVISION DATE: 4/86

C. SOURCE OF SUPPLY: Financial Affairs

D. PURPOSE: Used to obtain cash for emergency purchases under $50.

If the department has a petty cash fund, disbursements are
accumulated until the fund is nearly depleted. The receipts
and one copy of this form are brought to Financial Affairs.
A cash ticket is written for the amount of the expenditures
and the Business Office will issue cash or a check for the
amount.

If the department has no fund, the invoice or receipt under
$50 is brought to Financial Affairs with the approved
voucher. The cash ticket can be exchanged for cash at the
Business Office.

E. DISTRIBUTION OF COMPLETED FORM: Held by Financial Affairs and filed
with accounts payable vouchers.

Figure 7.21. Description of Petty Cash Voucher.

PREPARING A PETTY CASH VOUCHER

Complete the form according to the following instructions.

A. Department - Enter the complete account title.

B. Date - Enter the date the voucher is prepared.

C. Date - Enter date of each transaction.

D. Vendor - List the name of the vendor on each transaction.

E. G.L. - Enter general ledger code of each transaction.

F. Object Code - Enter object code of each transaction.

G. Department - Enter the department account number for each transaction.

H. Amount - Enter the total of each transaction.

I. Total - Enter total to be reimbursed.

J. Summarize Information in E, F, G, H.

K. Submitted By - Name of individual to receive the reimbursement.

L. Approved By - The signature of the budgetary authority as listed in the University Chart of Accounts.

M. Verified By - For Accounting use only.

N. Approved By - Approved signature by Accounting Department.

O. Date - Enter the date the voucher is approved by the Accounting Department.

P. Petty Cash Authorization No. - Accounting enters the number of the authorization.

Figure 7.21. Continued.

THE UNIVERSITY OF SOUTHERN MISSISSIPPI

Petty Cash Voucher

DEPARTMENT **A** _____ DATE **B** _____

DATE	VENDOR	G.L.	OBJECT	DEPARTMENT	AMOUNT	
C	**D**	**E**	**F**	**G**	**H**	
				TOTAL	**I**	

DEPARTMENT

SUBMITTED BY **K** _____

APPROVED BY **L** _____

FINANCIAL AFFAIRS

VERIFIED BY **M** _____

APPROVED BY **N** _____

DATE **O** _____

P.C. AUTHORIZATION NO. **P** _____

G.L.	OBJECT	DEPARTMENT	AMOUNT	
J	**J**	**J**	**J**	
		TOTAL	**I**	

ACC 20 4/86

Figure 7.21. Continued.

EXPENDITURE OBJECT CODES - 1

Object Group	Used With Fund/General Ledger	Categories
1000	1040, 2040, 2540, 3040	Salaries
2000	1040, 2040, 2540, 3040	Wages
3000	1040, 2040, 2540, 3040	Fringe Benefits
4000	1040, 2040, 2540, 3040	Travel
5000	1040, 2040, 2540, 3040, 6040	Contractual Services
6000-6499	1040, 2040, 2540, 3040, 6040	Commodities
6500-6900	2040 only	Merchandise for Resale
7100	4040 only	Student Loan Fund
7200	5040 only	Endowment Fund
7300	6240 only	Payment on Indebtedness and Interest-Plant
7400	7040 only	Agency Fund
8100	1040, 2040, 2540, 3040, 6040, 6140	Capital Outlay-Other than Equipment
8200	1040, 2040, 2540, 3040, 6040, 6140	Capital Outlay-Equipment
9000	All funds except 7040	Transfers

Figure 7.22. Expenditure object codes.

EXPENDITURE OBJECT CODES - 2

SALARIES

1100	Executive, Administrative and Managerial
1200	Faculty
1300	Professional Non-faculty
1400	Clerical and Secretarial
1500	Technical and Paraprofessional
1600	Skilled Craft
1700	Service/Maintenance
1800	Students

WAGES

2100	Executive, Administrative and Managerial
2200	Faculty
2300	Professional Non-faculty
2400	Clerical and Secretarial
2500	Technical and Paraprofessional
2600	Skilled Craft
2700	Service/Maintenance
2800	Students

FRINGE BENEFITS

3910	Employees' Retirement Matching
3920	FICA Matching
3930	Workers' Compensation
3940	Health Insurance Contribution
3950	Group Life Insurance
3960	Civil Service
3970	Unemployment Tax
3980	Remission of Fees

Figure 7.22. Continued.

TRAVEL AND SUBSISTENCE--IN-STATE OFFICIAL

4010	Meals and Lodging
4020	Travel in Private Vehicle
4030	Travel in Rented Vehicle
4040	Travel in Public Carrier
4050	Travel in Motor Pool Vehicles
4060	Other Travel Costs

TRAVEL AND SUBSISTENCE--OUT-OF-STATE OFFICIAL

4110	Meals and Lodging
4120	Travel in Private Vehicle
4130	Travel in Rented Vehicle
4140	Travel in Public Carrier
4150	Travel in Motor Pool Vehicle
4160	Other Travel Costs

TRAVEL AND SUBSISTENCE--IN-STATE CONFERENCES

4210	Meals and Lodging
4220	Travel in Private Vehicle
4230	Travel in Rented Vehicle
4240	Travel in Public Carrier
4250	Travel in Motor Pool Vehicle
4260	Other Travel Costs

TRAVEL AND SUBSISTENCE--OUT-OF-STATE CONFERENCES

4310	Meals and Lodging
4320	Travel in Private Vehicle
4330	Travel in Rented Vehicle
4340	Travel in Public Carrier
4350	Travel in Motor Pool Vehicle
4360	Other Travel Costs

TRAVEL AND SUBSISTENCE--GROUP

4510	Meals and Lodging
4520	Travel in Private Vehicle
4530	Travel in Rented Vehicle
4540	Travel in Public Carrier
4550	Travel in Motor Pool Vehicle
4560	Other Travel Costs

Figure 7.22. Continued.

EXPENDITURE OBJECT CODES - 4

CONTRACTUAL SERVICES

GRANTS, SCHOLARSHIPS AND AWARDS

5110	Grants
5120	Fellowships
5130	Scholarships
5140	Awards
5150	Dependency Allowances
5160	Professional Development Fees
5170	Other Institutional Allowances

COMMUNICATIONS AND TRANSPORTATION OF COMMODITIES

5210	Postage and Post Office Charges
5220	Telephone Local Service
5230	Telephone Long Distance
5240	Telephone Installation and Maintenance
5250	Cable TV
5260	Transportation of Things

UTILITIES

5310	Electricity
5320	Heat
5330	Water
5340	Sewage
5350	Garbage Disposal

PUBLIC INFORMATION

5410	Advertising
5420	Publicity and Public Information

RENTS

5510	Rental of Buildings and Floor Space
5520	Rental of Land
5530	Rental of Office Equipment
5540	Rental of EDP and Computer Equipment
5545	Computer Usage Charger
5550	Rental of Farm Equipment
5590	Other Rental

Figure 7.22. Continued.

EXPENDITURE OBJECT CODES - 5

REPAIRS AND MAINTENANCE

5610	Repair and Service Streets and Parking Lots
5620	Repair and Service - Buildings and Grounds
5630	Repair and Service Farm Equipment
5640	Repair and Service Vehicles
5650	Repair and Service Office Equipment
5660	Maintenance Contracts - Equipment
5670	Repair and Service Medical Equipment
5690	Repair and Service Other Equipment

FEES, PROFESSIONAL

5710	Engineering
5720	Architecture
5730	Auditing Fees
5740	Medical
5750	Instructional Services
5760	Legal Fees
5770	Laboratory and Testing Fees
5780	Consultant Expense Reimbursements
5790	Other Professional Fees and Services

OTHER CONTRACTUAL SERVICES

5810	Insurance and Fidelity Bonds
5820	Dues
5830	Laundry, Dry Cleaning and Towel Service
5840	Subscriptions
5850	Payments to Visiting Athletic Teams
5860	Employee Recruitment Costs
5865	Employee Moving
5870	Computer Software Acquisitions
5880	Computer Software Maintenance
5890	Other Contractual Services
5891	Provision for Bad Debts
5892	Cash Over and Short
5895	Accreditation and Review
5910	Indirect Cost Recovery - Federal Government
5920	Indirect Cost Recovery - State Government
5930	Indirect Cost Recovery - Local Government
5940	Indirect Cost Recovery - Private
5995	Refunds and Adjustments

Figure 7.22. Continued.

EXPENDITURE OBJECT CODES - 6

COMMODITIES

MAINTENANCE MATERIALS AND SUPPLIES - BUILDINGS, GROUNDS, IMPROVEMENTS

6010	Land Improvement Supplies
6020	Building Construction Supplies
6030	Paints and Preservatives
6040	Hardware, Plumbing, and Electrical Supplies
6050	Custodial Supplies and Cleaning Agents
6090	Other Maintenance Materials

PRINTING AND OFFICE SUPPLIES

6110	Printing, Binding and Padding
6120	Duplication and Reproduction
6130	Office Supplies and Materials
6140	Purchased Instructional Materials

EQUIPMENT REPAIR PARTS, SUPPLIES AND ACCESSORIES

6210	Fuels
6220	Lubricating Oils and Greases
6230	Tires and Tubes
6240	Repair and Replacement Parts
6250	Shop Supplies
6290	Other Equipment Repair Parts and Supplies

PROFESSIONAL AND SCIENTIFIC SUPPLIES AND MATERIALS

6310	Laboratory and Testing Supplies
6320	Photographic and Reproduction Supplies
6330	Drugs and Chemicals for Medical and Laboratory Use
6390	Other Professional and Scientific Supplies

OTHER SUPPLIES AND MATERIALS

6410	Small Tools
6420	Radio, Television Supplies and Repair Parts
6430	Clothes and Dry Goods for Persons
6440	Food for Persons
6450	Feed for Animals
6460	Seed and Plants
6470	Fertilizer and Chemicals
6480	Food Service Expendable Equipment
6490	Other Supplies and Materials
6495	Equipment Under $300

Figure 7.22. Continued.

MERCHANDISE FOR RESALE

TELEPHONE

   6510   Merchandise for Resale - Telephone
   6519   Merchandise for Resale - Postage

FOOD SERVICES

   6520   Merchandise for Resale - Food
   6522   Merchandise for Resale - Expendables
   6523   Merchandise for Resale - Meats
   6524   Merchandise for Resale - Beverages

BOOKSTORE

   6530   Merchandise for Resale - New Books
   6531   Merchandise for Resale - Used Books
   6532   Merchandise for Resale - Paperbacks
   6533   Merchandise for Resale - Arts and Crafts
   6535   Merchandise for Resale - School Supplies
   6536   Merchandise for Resale - Soft Goods

POWER PLANT

   6550   Merchandise for Resale - Electricity
   6551   Merchandise for Resale - Gas
   6552   Merchandise for Resale - Fuel Oil
   6553   Merchandise for Resale - Water

PHYSICAL PLANT

   6560   Merchandise for Resale - Gasoline and Oil
   6563   Merchandise for Resale - Equipment

PRINTING CENTER

   6570   Paper
   6571   Envelopes
   6572   Typesetting Supplies
   6573   Make-up Stripping Supplies
   6574   Quick Copy Dept Supplies
   6576   Press Room Supplies
   6579   Other Supplies and Materials

GENERAL

   6900   Merchandise for Resale - General

Figure 7.22. Continued.

EXPENDITURE OBJECT CODES - 8

NON-CURRENT FUND CODES

STUDENT LOAN FUND EXPENDITURES

7110	Litigation Expenses
7120	Administration Expenses
7130	Other Collections Expenses
7140	Cost-Prin/Int Cancelled for Teaching Prior 72
7145	Cost-prin/Int Cancelled for Teaching After 72
7150	Cost-Prin/Int Cancelled Military Prior 72
7155	Cost-Prin/Int Cancelled Military After 72
7160	Cost-Prin/Int Cancelled Death
7165	Cost-Prin/Int Cancelled Disability
7170	Cost-Prin/Int Cancelled Bankruptcy
7175	Other Cost or Losses
7180	Prin/Int Cancelled Prior 11/71
7185	Prin/Int Cancelled After 11/71

ENDOWMENT FUND

7210	Distribution to Beneficiary Funds

PAYMENT OF INDEBTEDNESS AND INTEREST - PLANT

7310	Bond Redeemed
7320	Payments on Notes
7330	Interest Payments on Bonds
7340	Interest Payments on Notes
7350	Trustee Fees
7360	Premium paid on Bonds Redeemed
7370	Discount on Bonds Redeemed
7390	Provision for Compensated Absences

AGENCY FUND

7410	Withdrawal from Agency Funds

Figure 7.22. Continued.

EXPENDITURE OBJECT CODES - 9

CAPITAL OUTLAY - OTHER THAN EQUIPMENT

8110	Land
8115	Improvements Other Than Buildings
8120	Payment to Contractors
8130	Buildings
8140	Farm Animals
8150	Historical Articles and Museums
8160	Library Books
8165	Paper Back Binding (Libraries Only)
8170	Periodicals (Libraries Only)
8175	Periodical Binding (Libraries Only)
8180	Films (Libraries Only)
8185	Microforms (Libraries Only)
8189	Audio-Visual Materials (Libraries Only)
8190	Maps (Libraries Only)
8191	Band Uniforms

CAPITAL OUTLAY - EQUIPMENT

8210	Office Machines, Furniture, Fixtures and Equipment
8220	Vehicles
8230	Farm
8240	Medical Equipment
8250	Data Processing Equipment
8260	Radio and Television Equipment
8270	Scientific Equipment
8290	Other Equipment

TRANSFERS OUT

9100	Transfers Out - Mandatory
9200	Transfers Out - Other

Figure 7.22. Continued.

USER DEPARTMENT BUDGET CONTROL SYSTEM

1. Set up three file folders to maintain--

    - Open items not yet recorded
    - Monthly Budget Reports received from Accounting
    - Closed items reported on prior budget reports

2. File all department copies of accounting documents in "Open" file when
    received.

        Payroll Summaries
        Budget Revision - Copy to Department
        Petty Cash - Copy to be retained by Department
        Postage - Special billing from Post Office
        Printing - Priced Job Order (may be more than one object code)
        Purchase Order - Copy to Department (match to Requisition)
        Remittance Voucher - Copy to be retained by Department
        Requisition - Copy to be retained by Department
        Expendable Supplies - Weekly listing and charge slips
        Telephone - Monthly billing from Telecommunications

3. When the Budget Report is received, match items in "Open" file to
    transactions on Report. Mark each item supported by a document and file
    these documents in "Closed" file. Budget Report transactions for which
    there are no documents should be investigated and cleared.

4. Return all unmatched documents to the "Open" file.

5. Lines on Budget Report marked "Ending Balance" are budget group totals.
    "Budget" less "Expenditures" equals "Free balance."

6. File Budget Report in "Department Budget Report" file.

SUGGESTIONS AND COMMENTS

File completed documents by the 4-digit expense code to provide a quick analysis
of the year-to-date items within a specific expenditure code.

Accounting uses an early monthly cutoff of transactions in some areas. Thus, a
transaction originating in the last week of a month may be reported in the
following month.

Figure 7.23. User manual control system.

CHAPTER 8
INFORMATION RELEASE SYSTEM:
YOU LIGHT UP MY LIFE

As stated in Chapter 1, the information release system can be an important part of the employee relations aspect of the accounting and finance operation of the company. It is written in newspaper style to inform the readers about an event or to provide information of interest to the staff. Distribution is usually limited, such as the accounting staff only, but it may also be used to release general information to others in the organization.

Some of the uses of the Information Release (IR) are:

Announce a new addition to the staff.

Announce a termination of an employee by resignation or retirement.

Announce a promotion or title change.

Introduce the independent auditors or a consulting team accounting personnel will be dealing with.

Announce an event or the holiday schedule.

Discuss a minor procedural change or reinforce a recent policy/procedure statement and describe the department's involvement.

Announce any event which may disrupt or otherwise affect normal operations.

Everyone likes and wants to be informed. Employees are no exception. An informed employee is not only happier, he or she tends to be more cooperative with other workers and thus works better as part of the team during stressful times. A knowledgeable employee is a smarter employee. And a professional-looking message is a more convincing message.

INFORMATION RELEASE FORMAT

To make the information readily recognizable, a preprinted *Information Release* form is suggested. It follows the pattern developed for the *Policy/Procedure Statement* with the exception of a place to indicate that a previous release is superseded. The form contains the logo, name of the company, retrieval number, page, issue date, and originator. See Figure 8.1 at the end of this chapter for the description of the information release layout and its preparation.

This informal document should have its own retrieval number series. It is considered to be a throw-away document to be retained by employees at their discretion. However, one person in the department should retain a complete set of all information releases issued, similar to the retention of formal correspondence. It may or may not have a subject title. If the release is distributed within the accounting department, it may be signed informally by the originator.

The opening statement of an IR should emulate newspaper style by answering who, what, where, when, and why. Opening sentences should be direct, such as "Company President Brown stated today that," or "We are pleased to announce," or "Bill Jones, Manager of Disbursements, will be retiring June 30."

Certainly, any information in the information release could be handled by normal interoffice correspondence, intraoffice memos, and even bulletin board messages, but none of these have the impact of the somewhat formal announcements indicated by the IR, particularly if the senior member of the department signs the release. A release always implies a multiple distribution, whereas a letter or memo might get only very limited distribution to one or two people.

Using information releases or some similar information system to keep employees informed about their working world is good management practice, and as Mikey says, "Try it. You'll like it." The rest of this chapter is devoted to examples of typical Information Releases.

NEW EMPLOYEE RELEASE

A new employee release should give the employee's full name, nickname if any, location of residence, marital status, and children. This information forms communication lines with coworkers in the department. A typical new employee announcement might read:

> I am pleased to announce that Karen Jones has joined Accounting as a Supervisor in Accounts Receivable. Karen is married to William Jones and they have two children, Ann, 8, and Mark, 6. They live in Centerville.
>
> Karen will be working with Margaret Smith in Credit Analysis. She was previously employed by RST Corporation. Please join me in welcoming Karen to L.O. Grant.

If Karen is being transferred from another department, the transfer should be mentioned and the welcome changed to welcoming her to this department.

EMPLOYEE RETIREMENT/RESIGNATION

Normally, only "good" terminations are mentioned. Good terminations are resignations for a position with another firm, a transfer to another company location, or retirement.

> William O. Martin, Manager of General Accounting, has informed me that he will be retiring from L.O. Grant after 35 years of service. Bill has been Manager for the past 15 years and has done an outstanding job.
>
> Bill and Martha plan to travel throughout the western states and possibly to Australia.
>
> Please join me in wishing Bill much happiness in his retirement and that he and Martha have many new and interesting journeys.

An example of a release concerning an employee resignation:

> Ronald Smith has resigned from L.O. Grant to become chief financial officer at Fosgroves and Sons. Ron has been Assistant Controller here for the past five years. Prior to that, he was Chief Cost Accountant. He and his wife, Pat, will be moving to Chicago within the next month.
>
> Please join me in wishing Ron much luck and success in his new endeavors.

INTRODUCING OUTSIDERS

The auditors from the firm of Countem & Worry, Certified Public Accountants, will he here for the next six weeks, beginning next Monday. Those assigned to the L.O. Grant audit are:

James Woodhead, Manager
Gwen Peterson, Supervisor
Bill Gunthorpe, Staff Accountant

Please cooperate with them so we may complete this audit efficiently and quickly. They have been told that any requests for special computer reports or extensive trial balances must be in writing to the manager of the unit involved. They are being furnished a list of your names and your area of work.

Please inform me if there are any problems in obtaining the information requested by the auditors.

ANNOUNCING AN EVENT

There may be an occasional event that disrupts the accounting operation. Knowledge about the event and how it is to be handled, in writing, minimizes the problem and diminishes the disruption. Here is an information release concerning new carpet installation.

The carpet installers will be here Friday, Saturday, and Sunday to completely remove all carpeting on our floor and install new carpeting. The office will be closed Friday. Because furniture will be moved in and out of the rooms as they proceed, all the items on your desk must be placed in the desk or in boxes provided.

Place stickers with your employee number and name on your desk, chair, file cabinets, storage boxes, and telephone. Calculators, terminals, and microfiche readers will be brought to the storage area before leaving Thursday night. The items will be placed back in your location after the installers leave Sunday.

Mr. Smith or I will be here during the installation. Our maintenance crew will be here Monday morning to help you place your heavy equipment items in their proper locations.

PROVIDING ADDITIONAL INFORMATION

Because a policy/procedure statement or other announcement of a change may not provide enough detail about how something is to be handled, the information release can be used within the department to expand the information, somewhat as follows.

Policy/Procedure Statement 10068 covered the new travel expense rules and forms. Several questions have arisen in our department concerning responsibility for approving expenses for branch office employees.

Effective immediately, Miss Durksen will review and approve all travel expense reports in accordance with P/PS 10068, and will then submit the summary schedule and the reports to the Accounts Payable Data Control Clerk.

EXTENDED DISTRIBUTION OF INFORMATION RELEASES

The information release is sometimes used to provide information to other departments in the company. It may be to inform employees about an honor or award the company or one of its employees has received, or a reprint of an article in a newspaper or journal. The release may also be used as a transmittal letter for a booklet being distributed to employees, or to explain a new insurance program or change in payroll deductions, and so forth.

SUMMARY

Information releases, even at the department level as illustrated herein, not only document the actions and activities of an important function, but they can be an important part of the solution to the communication problem that exists in many operations. They also provide a brief history of the department's activities.

Several information releases are shown on the following pages to illustrate typical uses of this information system (see Figures 8.2 through 8.16).

Information Release

FINANCIAL AFFAIRS

L. O. GRANT ORGANIZATION, INC.

- RETRIEVAL NO. 20,000
- PAGE 1 of 2
- ISSUE DATE January 5, 1985
- ORIGINATOR Financial Affairs

INFORMATION RELEASES

General Purpose

To communicate current information which will affect, or is directly
related to, the operation of Financial Affairs, a formal system of
Information Releases has been established. The type of information to be
distributed to designated or all employees through this system generally
will consist of:

- introduction of new employees, transfers, promotions and other
  personnel changes.

- proposed rules, regulations or laws issued by government regulating
  agencies or legislatures.

- published pamphlets or documents related to our industry and to
  us in particular.

- other types of information of interest to the staff.

Procedures for issuing an Information Release

Any officer or manager can initiate an Information Release. The attached
request form will be completed and forwarded with the proposed statement
and any supplemental printed material to the Director of Financial Affairs.
The Director will edit and format the proposed statement for publication.
If any changes are made, the final draft will be returned to the originator
for approval. The approved draft will be returned to the Director for
Retrieval No. assignment, printing and distribution. The original copy of
the Information Release and all supporting documents will be maintained in
a permanent file.

Updating Prior Information Releases

Because the contents of any one Information Release will always be self-
explanatory when issued, no Information Release will be used to update a
prior statement. If a subsequent event occurs which changes the meaning or
content of a prior release, a new release may be issued.

Figure 8.1. Information releases.

Format

Information Releases will be printed on this form, corner-stapled and
affixed to any pamphlet or other attachment. Comments on the format
follows:

Retrieval No. -- This consecutive number will be assigned at the time the
  Information Release is issued. A five-digit number will be used,
  beginning with 20,000. Thus, this is the first release. This number
  will be in the upper right hand corner on all pages of the Information
  Release.

Page -- In the form Page 1 of 4. The subsequent pages will be numbered at
  the top right, Page 2 of 4, Page 3 of 4, etc.

Issue Date -- The actual date the Information Release is issued and
  available, in the form January 10, 1985.

Originator -- The name of the person or operating unit originating the
  Information Release such as Sam Jones, General Accounting, Accounts
  Payable, Payroll, Budget, Property Accountability, and so forth.

Title -- The descriptive title will be in caps and will be used for
  indexing. All section headings will be in lower case and underlined.

Format -- Many releases will have an introductory paragraph labeled
  Summary, Background or General Purpose, explaining briefly the contents
  of the Information Release or the problem or reason for the release, and
  any references to additional information. Reference material may be
  attached. However, if the reference material has only limited interest
  or is difficult to acquire or reproduce, only the original Information
  Release will contain the attachments which will be available on request
  (Master copy maintained by Department secretary).

  A distribution list may be shown at the end of the Information Release,
  such as:

      All Employees

      Designated - Used if it relates only to one operating unit.

Retention

The retention of Information Releases is at each employee's discretion.
Releases will not contain policy or administrative procedures and therefore
have no standing as official pronouncements requiring compliance.

Attachment

Request for Information Release

Distribution

All Employees
Officers

209

Figure 8.1. Continued.

REQUEST FOR INFORMATION RELEASE

SUBJECT _____

BRIEF DESCRIPTION _____

_____

_____

ATTACHMENTS   SOURCE

    1. _____   _____

    2. _____   _____

    3. _____   _____

REQUESTED BY _____   DATE _____

                                                 DATE
DIRECTOR APPROVAL _____   RETURNED _____

ORIGINATOR - FINAL APPROVAL _____   DATE _____

SUGGESTED DISTRIBUTION _____

HEADINGS

    RETRIEVAL NO. _____

    PAGES _____

    ISSUE DATE _____

    ORIGINATOR _____

DISTRIBUTION (Person, Group, Department)

    Director   1   _____   _____

    Managers   5   _____   _____

    Vice President   1   _____   _____

    Number of Copies Printed _____

Figure 8.1. Continued.

Information Release

FINANCIAL AFFAIRS

L. O. GRANT ORGANIZATION, INC.

CLASSIFICATION SALARY RATE STRUCTURE

To ensure that equitable salaries are paid throughout the Company the following guidelines will be used:

(1) New employees hired with virtually no related experience will start at the minimum salary for the job level.

(2) The salary structure provides for steps in the rate of pay based on experience. This experience <u>must</u> be job related in a similar type position.

(3) Regardless of the funds available in the departmental budget, starting salary will be governed by the minimum starting rate and years of related experience.

(4) Employees making a lateral move in classification levels will not be considered for a salary adjustment until new budget recommendations are made.

(5) Should an employee be considered for promotion to a higher classification level and due to longevity currently earns more than the minimum rate for the higher level, the salary to be paid will be the next higher rate in the step process.

(6) Regardless of years of related experience and the amount of funds available in the budget, the maximum starting salary for a new employee will be the mid-point in the salary structure.

The final approval authority of all reclassification and rate structure adjustments is the President.

The foregoing procedures were reviewed by the Personnel Classification Committee and approved by the President January 15, 1985.

Figure 8.2. Classification salary rate structure.

Information Release

FINANCIAL AFFAIRS

- RETRIEVAL NO. 20,009
- PAGE   1 of 2
- ISSUE DATE   March 17, 1985
- ORIGINATOR   Harry L. Brown

L. O. GRANT ORGANIZATION, INC.

AUDITS

We have recently completed the general audit for fiscal year 1984 and the biennial equipment and facilities audit. We are pleased that we received a clean opinion on the general audit, meaning that our financial statements are in conformity with generally accepted accounting principles and present fairly the financial position and the results of operations of the Company.

The auditors made several recommendations to improve our accounting and administrative procedures. These recommendations are summarized as follows.

Cash and Temporary Investments

1. Improve handling of special checking accounts.

2. Require all bank reconcilements be done in Accounting, and reconciling items cleared prior to the year-end closing.

3. Establish written policy for the mechanical check signer.

4. Improve investment of idle cash in banks.

Accounts Receivable

1. Maintain a separate employee travel advance receivable account.

2. Improve receivable aging procedures to provide data for allowance provisions.

Inventories

1. Study the feasibility of installing a perpetual inventory system for industrial supplies in Plants 1 and 2.

Accounts Payable and Deferred Revenues

1. Discontinue use of the undistributed income account.

2. Mark paid invoices to prevent reuse.

3. Review disbursements to eliminate the expensing of container deposits and prepayments.

Figure 8.3. Audits.

Payroll

1. Update personnel files to include current authorizations for
   payroll deductions and withholding exemption forms.

Revenues

1. Require cash receipt forms to include adequate detail of the
   source of money received.

2. Develop a standard deposit summary form to accompany cash deposits
   of the local branch offices.

Summary

While many of the suggestions and recommendations are relatively minor, we
will be working during the next few months to eliminate them. In a few
cases, new forms and new procedures will be developed.

Figure 8.3. Continued.

Information Release

FINANCIAL AFFAIRS

L. O. GRANT ORGANIZATION, INC.

- RETRIEVAL NO. 20,012
- PAGE   1 of 1
- ISSUE DATE   April 1, 1985
- ORIGINATOR   Harry L. Brown

RECLASSIFICATIONS AND NEW POSITIONS

Following are the results of our requests for reclassification this fiscal year.

Accounting Services

    Hugh West to Level 15
    Ken Hayman to Level 14
    Elsie Peel to Level 7

Property Accountability

    William Rayner to Level 9
    Geneva Terry to Level 6

Business Services (Name changed from Bursar)

    Sam Clinton to Level 15

While I regret that all the requests were not approved, some progress was made. We also obtained permission to initiate the following new positions.

    Coordinator of Accounts Receivable (11)
    Data Control Clerk – Payroll (6)
    Data Control Clerk – General Accounting (6)

The Manager of Accounts Receivable position will be filled as soon as possible. The data control clerk positions are scheduled to be filled in late 1985.

Figure 8.4. Reclassifications and new positions.

Information Release

FINANCIAL AFFAIRS

L. O. GRANT ORGANIZATION, INC.

FILES IN STORAGE

The following files were taken to the Records Center storage area on May 1, 1985.

File	Period
Cash Disbursement Vouchers	1981/82
Cash Receipts	1981/82
Journal Vouchers	1981/82
Travel Voucher Copies	1981/82
X Receipts (Accounts Receivable)	#1 - 3665
Department Expense Reports -	
12 Month Detail	1979/80, 1980/81
	1981/82, 1982/83
Monthly Cash Receipt Detail	1978/79, 1979/80
	1980/81, 1981/82

Payroll Checks

Deposit Guaranty	40,409 - 76,421	7/80 - 11/81
First Mississippi National Bank	31,328 - 67,577	10/80 - 6/82
First Mississippi National Bank	1 - 5,880	8/81 - 12/81

General Checks

Deposit Guaranty	38,883 - 72,144	10/80 - 6/82

Bank Statements

Payroll First Mississippi National		6/75 - 6/83
Payroll Deposit Guaranty		6/75 - 6/83
Payroll Citizens Bank		6/75 - 6/83
General First Mississippi National		8/75 - 6/83
General Deposit Guaranty		10/76 - 6/83
General Citizens		1/77 - 6/83

Figure 8.5. Files in storage.

◯ LOGO

- RETRIEVAL NO. 20,026
- PAGE   1 of 1
- ISSUE DATE   June 5, 1985
- ORIGINATOR   Harry L. Brown

L. O. GRANT ORGANIZATION, INC.

CARPET INSTALLATION

We should be prepared for the carpet installation. Best estimate to complete the job is two days. Everything will be moved two or more times and, following the installation, some of you will be moved to a different location. Therefore, every separate item will be marked with your number and name (printed) on masking tape and attached as follows:

    Desk - Center of top
    Side extension - Center of top (may be removed and reattached during
       move)
    In-Out Trays - Center of top shelf
    Chairs - On metal supports for back
    File Cabinets - Front of top drawer. (If several, letter them A, B, C
       in addition to number, as 1 Brown A, 1 Brown B)
    Low cabinets, tub files, etc - center of top
    Boxes - Top surface and one end
    Calculators - Top surface. Electric cord removed and placed in desk.
    Typewriters - Top surface.
    Microfiche reader - Top
    Plastic Floor Mat - Back corner

Typewriters and calculators will be taken to the vault. Everything else not in desks will be left on top of desk (trays, boxes, readers). We will ask that the installation be made on Thursday and Friday and, unless there is an emergency, you will be excused from work on those days.

Please do not leave anything valuable in your desk such as watches, money, etc, as the contents may have to be removed and replaced to facilitate moving the equipment out and in.

Number and Name

No.	Name	No.	Name
1.	Brown	12.	Deas
2.	Champney	13.	Peel
3.	West	16.	Brunson
4.	Hayman	17.	Copeland
5.	Martin (Research files)	18.	McCain
6.	Gurney	19.	Slade
7.	Breland	20.	Tisdale
8.	Carter	21.	Freeman
9.	Reeves	22.	Curtin
10.	Wilberding	23.	Pigford
11.	Burt		

All packing and marking will be done the afternoon before the day of installation.

Figure 8.6. Carpet installation.

Information Release

FINANCIAL AFFAIRS

L. O. GRANT ORGANIZATION, INC.

- RETRIEVAL NO. 20,027
-
- PAGE 1 of 1
-
- ISSUE DATE June 30, 1985
-
- ORIGINATOR Financial Affairs

BANK ASSIGNMENTS

Effective July 1, 1985, the following banks are used for the purposes indicated.

    First Mississippi National - General Disbursements

    Trustmark National - Salary Payroll

    Bank of Hattiesburg - Wage Payroll (same)

    Deposit Guaranty National - Deposits

Figure 8.7. Bank assignments.

Information Release

FINANCIAL AFFAIRS

L. O. GRANT ORGANIZATION, INC.

- RETRIEVAL NO. 20,028
- PAGE   1 of 1
- ISSUE DATE   July 5, 1985
- ORIGINATOR   Harry L. Brown

NEW TELEPHONE NUMBERS

Under our new Dimension telephone system, each employee has his or her own number. However, the department number, 4084, is assigned to Lucia. If unanswered, the call rotates to four other phones, as follows:

    4084   Lucia Burt
    4087   Linda Slade
    4086   Olivia Pigford
    4096   Mildred Freeman
    4088   Betty Breland

It is suggested by Jim Winstead, Telecommunications, that the individual phone numbers not be given out to callers except by the person assigned to that number.

New phone numbers are assigned as follows:

    4084   Lucia Burt
    4085   Ann Copeland
    4086   Olivia Pigford
    4087   Linda Slade
    4088   Betty Breland
    4089   Vivian Reeves
    4090   Betty Brunson, Madelon Deas
    4091   Hugh West
    4092   Dot Wilberding
    4093   Floy Tisdale, Mary Lou McCain
    4094   Elsie Peel
    4095   Carmen Curtin
    4096   Mildred Freeman
    4097   Katherine Carter
    4098   Ken Hayman
    4099   Teresa Martin
    4100   Anita Gurney
    4101   Ed Champney
    4102   Harry Brown

Figure 8.8. New telephone numbers.

Information Release

FINANCIAL AFFAIRS

L. O. GRANT ORGANIZATION, INC.

- RETRIEVAL NO. 20,031
- PAGE   1 of 1
- ISSUE DATE   August 6, 1985
- ORIGINATOR   Harry L. Brown

JOB TITLE CHANGES

We have received permission to change certain job titles. Effective September 1, 1985, the following titles will be used.

Ed Champney	Assistant Director
Hugh West	Manager - Budgets
Kenneth Hayman	Manager - Disbursements
Teresa Martin	Manager - Contract Accounting
Betty Breland	Accounting Supervisor
Katherine Carter	Accounting Supervisor
Vivian Reeves	Payroll Supervisor
Dorothy Wilberding	Senior Accounting Specialist
Elsie Peel	Accounting Supervisor
Mary Schlottman	Manager - Accounts Receivable
William Rayner	Manager - Property Accounting
Geneva Terry	Property Clerk - Senior

The name of the Property Accountability department is changed to Property Accounting.

The following classification level changes have been approved.

William Rayner	To Level 10
Linda Slade	To Level 6

Figure 8.9. Job title changes.

Information Release

FINANCIAL AFFAIRS

L. O. GRANT ORGANIZATION, INC.

- RETRIEVAL NO. 20,033
- PAGE 1 of 1
- ISSUE DATE August 19, 1985
- ORIGINATOR Accounts Payable

TRAVEL REPORTING PROBLEMS

We have been receiving many calls and complaints about the present rules for travel expense reporting, particularly the maximum meal allowances.

We are operating under the following rules.

1. Travel expenses are reported only on the official Travel Voucher (ACC 2 7/81).

2. The travel regulations do not relate to entertainment costs, food for employees or recruiting expenses.

3. If receipts are required, they must be provided.

4. The maximum meal allowances are mandatory for employee <u>and</u> group travel.

Generally, travel expenses relate to trips away from home for a day or longer. A dinner at a professional society meeting with no travel required is considered Food for Persons (6440) and should be submitted on a Remittance Voucher. If on a Travel Voucher, the amount should be clearly marked as food for persons (no dollar limitation).

Likewise, entertainment such as a dinner is also food for persons. However, the name of the person(s), place, date and business purpose, discussion or benefit to the Company must be disclosed.

All travel costs for staff recruitment, including a local dinner, are charged to object 5860, Employee Recruitment Costs. If the expense is in connection with a professional service such as legal, architectural or general consulting, then object series 5710-5790, Fees, Professional, is used.

Requests for reimbursement of Food for Persons, Employee Recruitment Costs and Professional Fees should be submitted on a Remittance Voucher. If a Travel Voucher is used, the items should be clearly marked as other than Travel.

We all should be familiar with Company regulations and our releases covering travel policies. If you are not sure of your answer to an employee inquiry, obtain clarification from the Manager of Disbursements or the Director.

Distribution: Financial Affairs only

Figure 8.10. Travel reporting problems.

Information Release

FINANCIAL AFFAIRS

L. O. GRANT ORGANIZATION, INC.

- RETRIEVAL NO. 20,038
-
- PAGE   1 of 1
-
- ISSUE DATE   September 6, 1985
-
- ORIGINATOR   Harry L. Brown

OBSOLETE FORM

All departments are asked to please discontinue using the Permission to Travel form dated 7/81. The new form ACC 1 (Revised 7/85) can be obtained from Printing and Supply Services.

All of the present stock of the superseded form dated 7/81 should be discarded.

One copy of this Release is being sent to each Box Number. Please furnish this information to other departments using the same Box Number.

Figure 8.11. Obsolete form.

Information Release

FINANCIAL AFFAIRS

L. O. GRANT ORGANIZATION, INC.

- RETRIEVAL NO. 20,039
- PAGE 1 of 1
- ISSUE DATE September 20, 1985
- ORIGINATOR Harry L. Brown

STAFF ADDITIONS

I am pleased to announce the following additions to the Financial Affairs staff.

Mary Ross, Data Control Clerk, has a Bachelor's and Master's degrees in Home Economics from USM and is working towards an accounting degree. She lives in the Hattiesburg area with her husband, Raymond, and their three girls, Annette, Margaret and Sylvia. Mary's former employer was the Internal Revenue Service here in Hattiesburg.

Mary will be dividing her efforts between our budget operations and the wage payroll operation.

Jacky Fortenberry, Cost Analyst, graduated from Oak Grove High School and has an accounting degree from the University of Mississippi. Her husband, Larry, is a pharmacist at Methodist Hospital and they have two girls, Jessi, 4, and Laura, 10 months old.

Jacky will be involved in calculating indirect costs for government contracts, a function that will require studies of the use of Company-wide research facilities and equipment.

Jimmie "Pinkie" Matthews, Accounting Clerk, is a native of Hattiesburg. Pinkie has a Special Education degree and is working on a Master's degree in the same field. She has a daughter, Paige, age 5.

Pinkie will divide her time among bank reconcilements for General Accounting, accounts payable check distribution and various assignments in Contract Accounting.

Please join me in welcoming Mary, Jacky and Pinkie to Financial Affairs.

Figure 8.12. Staff additions.

222

Information Release

FINANCIAL AFFAIRS

L. O. GRANT ORGANIZATION, INC.

- RETRIEVAL NO. 20,051
- PAGE 1 of 1
- ISSUE DATE November 29, 1985
- ORIGINATOR Financial Affairs

AUDITORS

We are beginning the independent annual audit for the fiscal year 1985.
The following auditors will be here at various times beginning December 5:

    Steve Duncan
    John Young
    Brent Ballard

In addition, the following audit representatives of the federal
government's Department of Defense may visit here occasionally.

    Jeff Lordlaw
    Brian Rooney

Please cooperate fully with the auditors in providing any financial
information they may require. All requests for special reports or other
significant data will be coordinated by Ed Champney, Linda McFall, and
Jacky Fortenberry.

The auditors will be located in the Internal Auditor's office, Room 317,
telephone 4130.

We hope to have completion of the audit field work by March 1, 1986.

Figure 8.13. Auditors.

Information Release

FINANCIAL AFFAIRS

LOGO

- RETRIEVAL NO.   20,052
- PAGE   1 of 2
- ISSUE DATE   December 2, 1985
- ORIGINATOR   Personnel

L. O. GRANT ORGANIZATION, INC.

EMPLOYMENT INTERVIEWING

We will be employing several new people over the next several months and many of you will be involved in the interview process. There are several characteristics you should be looking for during the interview. These are:

1. Responsiveness
2. Relevance of previous work experiences
3. Skill and competence
4. Leadership
5. Stability
6. Level of accomplishment

These elements cannot be approached directly. The line of inquiry suggested below may provide insight into the abovementioned categories.

An interviewer should make use of a variety of questions and recognize the value of comments made by the applicant during the conversation. A good interviewer is a good listener. Please work closely with the Personnel Department regarding the hiring of a new employee so we may select the best qualified applicant for each position to be filled.

Following is a suggested outline for the pre-employment interview.

A. Introduction

   Greeting
   Small talk to put applicant at ease
   Lead questions to move discussion into main sequence of the interview.

B. Work Experience

   Descriptions of positions held
   Military assignments in the Armed Forces or service in a particular
     branch
   Inquire about:
     Things done best
     Things liked best
     Things liked less well
     Major accomplishments
     Level of earnings
     Reasons for changing jobs
     What applicant is looking for in a job

Figure 8.14. Employment interviewing.

C. Education

      High School
      College
      Specialized training
      Inquire about:
        Best subjects and subjects done less well
        Level of grades and special achievements
        Relation of education to career

D. Special Interests and Hobbies (Optional)

E. Job Description

      Job responsibilities and requirements
      Hours of work
      Background information on our Company

F. Summary

      Answer questions from applicant
      Course of action to be taken

Unlawful pre-employment questions

A. Applicant's maiden name

B. Birthplace of applicant

C. Age of applicant or date of birth

D. Inquiry into applicant's religious denomination, religious
      affiliations, church, parish, pastor or religious holidays observed.

E. Inquiry about applicant's height or weight

F. Inquiry into marital status or children of applicant

G. Whether Miss or Mrs. or any inquiry regarding sex

H. Inquiry into applicant's:

      Lineage
      Ancestry
      National origin
      Descent
      Parentage
      Nationality

I. Inquiry regarding arrests

J. Inquiry into an applicant's general military experience

K. Inquiry into clubs, societies and lodges to which applicant belongs

Figure 8.14. Continued.

```
 /  /  /
/  /  /  /        INFORMATION RELEASE
|__|  |__|  |__|
|            |
|  H E C  |                                   · RETRIEVAL NO. 12,054
|            |                                 ·
|__|__  |__|__|                                · PAGE        1 of 2
|  |  |  |  |  |                               ·
                                               · ISSUE DATE  December 1, 1992
HAEUSSLER ENTERPRISES COMPANY                  ·
                                               · ORIGINATOR  P.B. Haeussler
```

DEALING WITH THE NEWS MEDIA

It is very important that the Company establish good relations with people employed by newspapers, magazines, radio and television, and other communications media. The best means of developing such a relationship is by providing honest and helpful information to the media in an atmosphere of mutual respect and candor. When a company is not successful in establishing good media relations or clear lines of information, the result is often inaccurate news stories.

With this in mind, employees are urged to keep the Director of Public Relations fully and promptly informed about events, incidents and developments in which there is a current or potential public interest. In the event of controversy, as well as in routine matters, it is the Director's responsibility to work with those most directly involved to coordinate the release of news items, respond to inquiries from the news media, and to offer counsel as requested or required.

While Public Relations distributes news releases and responds to the majority of media queries, other members of the staff sometimes receive press queries directly. If the person receiving such a query is comfortable or has experience in dealing with the media, that person should feel free to respond directly if the request pertains to a matter for which he of she has direct responsibility. If the person feels uncomfortable dealing with the media, the reporter may be referred to Public Relations.

Public Relations, in fact, prefers that staff persons be spokespersons and that the reporter speak to the person responsible for and with the most knowledge of the area or subject under discussion. However, help is available from Public Relations to those who desire it. If you do answer a media query, it is helpful to inform the Director of Public Relations immediately (or before answering, if there is time).

In responding to media questions, you may find the following recommendations helpful:

1. First, get the reporter's name and the publication or station for which he or she works. Then, if you feel the request for information is reasonable, give the media person your full cooperation. If you feel the request is unreasonable, politely inform the reporter of your feeling and terminate the conversation.

2. In answering questions, be fair, friendly, and factual.

3. Normally, you are expected to comment only on matters within your area of expertise. Sometimes, however, a reporter may ask you to comment on a subject outside your area of expertise. If you do not wish to comment, do not hesitate to tell the reporter so. Refer the reporter to Public Relations if a reporter's questions can best be answered by other persons within the Company.

Figure 8.15. Dealing with the news media.

4. Some reporters may ask you to comment on a controversial issue with the promise that, if you so wish, your name will not be used. Unless you know the reporter, it is not usually wise to do so. (When in doubt, you may call Public Relations for advice.)

5. When you give a personal opinion on any subject, make certain that the reporter understands that you are speaking for yourself, not for your colleagues, the company officers, or the Company.

6. Do not assume that you will see the reporter's story before it is published or broadcast. The reporter is under no obligation to show copy. If scientific or technical data are involved, you might suggest that the reporter check his or her story back with you for accuracy.

7. When an interview is for broadcast, remember that people in radio and television news usually can report only the barest essentials of a story. They are looking for succinct answers to one or two questions. It is best to avoid time-consuming details, rambling explanations and complicated answers.

8. Most reporters dislike material which is "off-the-record" because they may later receive the "off-the-record" information from another source. If for some reason, however, you feel that you must make remarks "off-the-record," do so according to the following standards of journalistic ethics:

   A. Preface each "off-the-record" statement by saying, "The following material if off-the-record." Wait for the reporter to acknowledge acceptance of the "off-the-record" remarks.

   B. Indicate clearly when the reporter is "on-the-record" again.

   C. Don't say belatedly, "The material I have just given you is off-the record."

9. Sarcasm is a dangerous tool to use with the media. A sarcastic comment won't look nearly so good in black and white tomorrow as it sounded when you said it today.

10. It's unlikely your comments will be quoted fully. Excerpts will be pulled out. Plan your comments accordingly so that single sentences and phrases can often stand alone. And don't be too disappointed if your comment is boiled down to two lines of print.

If these recommendations are to be effective, the Director of Public Relations needs to be fully informed on developments in which the media have an interest. Preferably, this should be done before a reporter calls for the information. By discussing the matter in advance, especially when the story is highly controversial, a spokesperson can be designated or a statement can be prepared to be used in responding to queries.

The proper and prompt handling of media queries, whether directly or through Public Relations, helps create goodwill, encourages reporters to seek information from official sources and, above all, assures accurate and balanced news stories.

Figure 8.15. Continued.

/ / /
⊔ ⊔ ⊔
H E C
ⅲ ⅲ
HAEUSSLER ENTERPRISES COMPANY

INFORMATION RELEASE

· RETRIEVAL NO. 231
·
· PAGE   1 of 1
·
· ISSUE DATE November 1, 1992
·
· ORIGINATOR H. L. Brown

PREPARING VISUALS FOR SPEECH OR PRESENTATION

Visuals can enhance or damage a speech or presentation. Visuals, whether overhead transparencies or slides for large audiences, or easel charts for small audiences, should be simple and directly related to the topic.

The presenter should know the type of audience, approximately how many will be in audience, and the basic idea or point of the presentation. Availability of the equipment may be a limiting factor.

In any case, visuals should be carefully prepared. Some rules to remember:

- No more than seven words per line and seven lines per
    visual. Think horizontal.
- Limit each visual to one point or comparison.
- Be sure of titles and all spelling.
- Provide a mental challenge to the viewers.

To develop a good visual, the presenter should evaluate what will be on the screen or easel. In the following scales, those things desirable in a visual are listed on the left side. They degrade into those adjectives listed on the right side. The presenter should evaluate the developing visuals by filling in a box on each line that best describes that visual. Too many checks to the right may indicate the visual should be redrawn or even eliminated.

GENERAL — Good ... Poor

GENERAL					
Pleasant					Unpleasant
Valuable					Worthless
Important					Unimportant
Interesting					Boring

STYLISTIC					
Exciting					Dull
Fresh					Stale
Easy					Difficult
Neat					Messy
Colorful					Colorless

POTENCY					
Bold					Timid
Powerful					Weak
Loud					Soft

ACTIVITY					
Tense					Relaxed
Active					Passive
Modern					Antique

Figure 8.16. Preparing visuals for speech or presentation.

CHAPTER 9
COMPUTER HARDWARE
AND SOFTWARE
STUDIES:
IT'S BEEN A LONG,
LONG TIME

As time goes by, it is certain that computers will age and computer programs will need to be improved or replaced. This chapter discusses the documentation related to acquiring new or replacement computer hardware and software needed in today's complex accounting operations.

Specific hardware and related components will not be endorsed, recommended, or selected. Nor will specific program packages for accounting operations be recommended. This chapter does, rather, cover how these processes will be identified, performed, and controlled through the use of written documentation.

STEERING COMMITTEE

At the beginning of any systems selection or development project, it is necessary to form a high-level committee. This committee will, in effect, "steer" the project through its necessary phases and provide final approval (or disapproval) of the results. The data processing Steering Committee is usually composed of all of a company's vice presidents, or directors in the case of governmental units, and the data processing manager.

The formation of a Steering Committee assures that the viewpoint will be organization-wide rather than that of one vice president or director. The responsibilities of the committee are to establish specific objectives of the data processing effort, review proposals for new systems projects, recommend projects for acceptance, establish priorities of those projects, recommend data processing policies and procedures, and monitor and evaluate overall progress through periodic meetings. The committee steers the data processing efforts of the organization.

To accomplish this task, committee members must

Have sufficient knowledge of computer hardware to understand how it can serve the organization,

Learn new concepts regarding the capture and retention of information that was previously impractical to obtain without a computer, and

Learn to evaluate proposals presented to them so as to weigh the costs and risks against the benefits.

SYSTEM DEFINITION

For this chapter, a system is defined as a set of procedures and computer programs to handle a specific accounting task. More commonly, a system is one or more computer programs employed to handle a single accounting operation, or a complete application requiring many programs to enter data, manipulate data, update computer-maintained records and files, produce reports or other documents, and so on.

There are many reasons that new systems may be needed by an organization, such as the following:

Present programs are not compatible with new hardware being acquired.

Software programs are not adequate, difficult to maintain, patched too often, and too slow.

An installation is being merged with another, either by consolidation or by taking over another installation's work.

A need has arisen for on-line inquiry capablilities, such as in a bank, brokerage house, credit card operation, or for customer inquiries.

There is a need to be compatible with another data processing operation.

It is necessary to increase the internal speed of computer programs to handle a significant growth in the volume of business information being handled.

The organization may need a new system to match competition; for example, computerizing the checkout counters in supermarkets to increase efficiency and please customers.

The organization may wish to increase the amount of information beyond that which the present system can handle.

A manual application is to be computerized.

An entirely new way to handle a set of procedures is to be developed. An example is the automating of a warehouse to improve material handling, stock picking for customer orders and customer invoicing, and to reduce sales errors.

No matter the reason, there will always be a need for a formal process to develop a system in an accounting or similar environment.

SYSTEM DEVELOPMENT PROCESS

Figure 9.1 is an overview of a classic system development process consisting of six phases. Almost all system studies and changes since the advent of the modern business computer have followed this or a similar process. The six phases are the Initiation Phase, Overview Study, System Survey, System Design, System Development, and finally, Implementation. Each phase is followed by a decision to re-do the work, terminate the work, or proceed to the next phase.

I. Initiation Phase

The Initiation Phase, illustrated in Figure 9.2, starts when someone in the organization presents a request for new or changed data processing services to the Data Processing Steering Committee. If the requester desires certain information, the request should be written so that the problem (or the purpose) of the new information is clearly communicated. This will enable the data processing department to determine whether it can fill the need.

The data processing department's response to the request is prepared and recommendations are made regarding further action, after which the Steering Committee performs its review to determine the validity or reasonableness of the request. The committee then measures the benefits to be gained should the request be pursued further, versus the cost and risk of success. The committee then decides to:

1. Shelve, table, or deny the request,
2. Qualify the request prior to a decision, or
3. Proceed to Phase II, the Overview Study.

SYSTEM DEVELOPMENT PROCESS

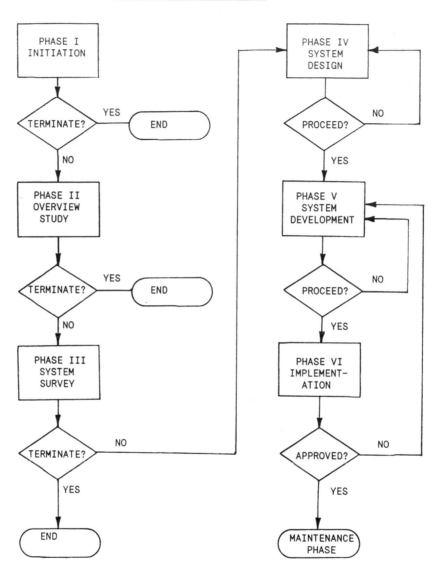

Figure 9.1. Six phases of the System Development Process.

II. Overview Study Phase

Phase II, shown in Figure 9.3, always starts with the written results of the Initiation Phase. The first step is to analyze the original request and extend the scope of the study to make sure that the proposal is not to patch a hole in the roof when a whole new roof is needed. This phase typically requires an analysis of more tasks than those identified in the original request.

PHASE I - INITIATION

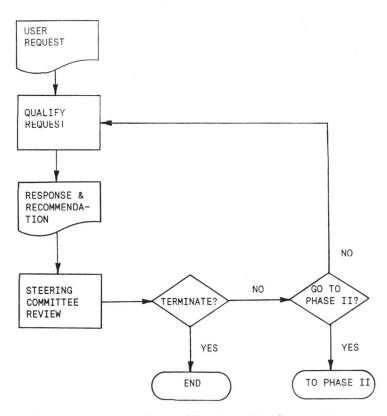

Figure 9.2. Initiation Phase of the System Development Process.

The results of the Overview Study are combined in a report analyzing the entire area under consideration and the recommended actions, which is then reviewed by the Steering Committee. The committee weighs the benefits, limitations, savings (if any), and the costs presented in the report. The decision, as in Phase I, is to:

1. Terminate the study,
2. Request additional information before making a decision, or
3. Approve or modify the recommendations in the report and recommend proceeding to Phase III, the System Survey.

If the original request is relatively simple and not part of a larger requirement, Phase II may be eliminated entirely.

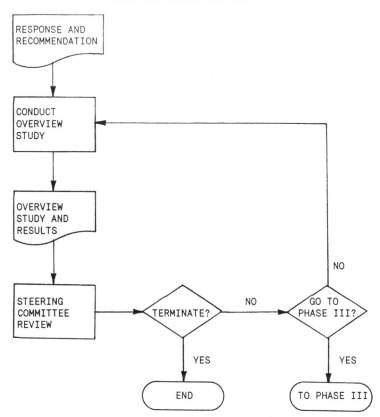

Figure 9.3. Overview Study Phase of the System Development Process.

III. System Survey Phase

Phase III, illustrated in Figure 9.4, is the System Survey, which begins with the approved report and all the documentation gathered so far. At this point, it is necessary to appoint a project team composed of both data processing and user department personnel. A typical team might have the following members:

1. Data processing manager or appointee
2. Accounting executive or appointee
3. Each user department director or appointee
4. Outside consultant, if one is employed
5. CPA from an outside auditing firm (optional)

The primary task of the team consists of conducting a system survey, which requires the gathering of all pertinent facts about the existing system, the system to be

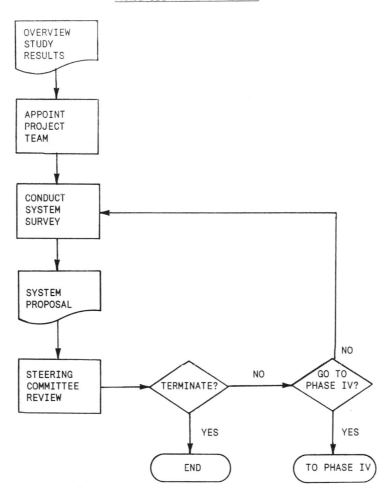

PHASE III – SYSTEM SURVEY

Figure 9.4. System Survey Phase of the System Development Process.

designed, and the development of a tentative design. The survey involves research, interviews, and other types of data-gathering activities.

The end result of the survey is a system proposal containing the tentative design of the new system, requirements for personnel and equipment, benefits and limitations, and a plan for development, implementation, and future operations. To control dollars to be expended in the next phase, a budget for the total task may be prepared.

The final proposal is submitted to the Steering Committee for review. The committee then weighs alternatives presented and recommends a course of action which may be to:

1. Terminate the work,
2. Obtain additional information prior to a decision, or
3. Proceed to the Phase IV, the Design Phase.

If the system proposal is approved, the committee should recommend a priority for its design and implementation as there will probably be other ongoing system development projects within the organization.

IV. System Design Phase

In the System Design Phase, shown in Figure 9.5, the new system is defined in its greatest possible detail. Consequently, this phase can be very time-consuming. The output is a detailed volume of System Specifications, consisting of at least six sections.

1. *System Summary*. The purpose and objectives of the system, the system flow-chart, and a complete narrative description of the system
2. *File Specifications*. File identification, file formats, and data descriptions
3. *Input Specifications*. Input identification, input formats, and editing requirements
4. *Output Specifications*. Output identification, output formats, and pro forma report layouts

PHASE IV - SYSTEM DESIGN

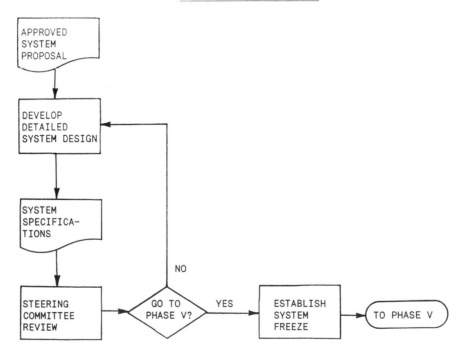

Figure 9.5. System Design Phase of the System Development Process.

5. *Processing Specifications.* The functions to be performed, rules of logic to be followed, tables, formulas, and so on

6. *System Test Plan.* The test objectives, validity criteria, and a test outline

In some respects, the System Specifications package can be compared to construction plans for a building, along with a bill of materials for the contractor. The package is reviewed by the users and data processing management. Only if there are considerable changes from the system proposed in Phase III does the Steering Committee review the details at this point.

After requested modifications have been made and approval is obtained, a system freeze is established. Any subsequent changes to the current system may not only increase the cost of implementing the new system, but will probably delay its implementation. The project now moves to Phase V, System Development.

V. System Development Phase

The System Development Phase, shown in Figure 9.6, which begins as soon as the system specifications receive final approval, probably requires more personnel hours than any other phase. The first task is to assign responsibilities and schedule the many people involved. This working group reports to the data processing manager during this phase.

The next step is planning the conversion of data, if this is a replacement system, and the planning of pilot and parallel operations. Adequate planning in these areas is vital, as the chances for problems are too great to risk.

At the same time, analysts and programmers are determining the logic to be used in the programs, coding and checking programs, and testing the programs. If the program chosen is a complete stand-alone package from an outside vendor, then the package is installed and tested. Individual program deletions and feature selections are made at this time.

Someone must be assigned to develop and write the instructions for both the people involved in the application and the users of the output reports. These instructions may be in the form of a *Procedures Manual, Information Releases*, or a separate *User's Guide*. When completed, the *Procedures Manual* is used to conduct orientation sessions with all who will be involved in the preparation of data and the use of the reports or other output.

Once the programs are ready, the users trained, and data conversion methods completed, the system test can be conducted. Again, this may be a time-consuming task as it is necessary to test the accuracy of the input, the usefulness of the output, and all the checks and balances included in the total procedure. Every program logic step must be incorporated into this test.

If the system test is satisfactory, it may be desirable to conduct a pilot test of actual data used in the replaced system to see whether it can be handled by the new

PHASE V - SYSTEM DEVELOPMENT

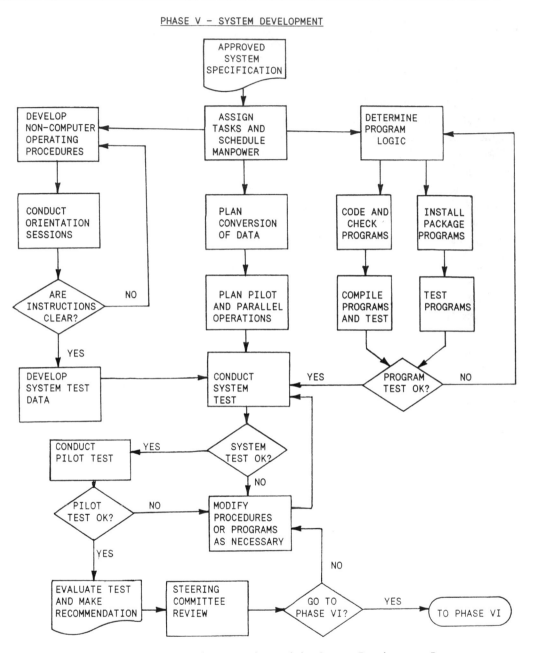

Figure 9.6. System Development Phase of the System Development Process

system. After this test, an evaluation report is prepared to compare the objectives in the system proposal with the actual results obtained with the new system. The evaluation report is reviewed by users and data processing management to determine whether they can accept the results and are ready to implement the system.

VI. Implementation Phase

The Implementation Phase, illustrated in Figure 9.7, begins with the conversion of data from its old form to its machine-readable form, or conversion from the current machine form to a new form. At the same time, it is necessary to complete the

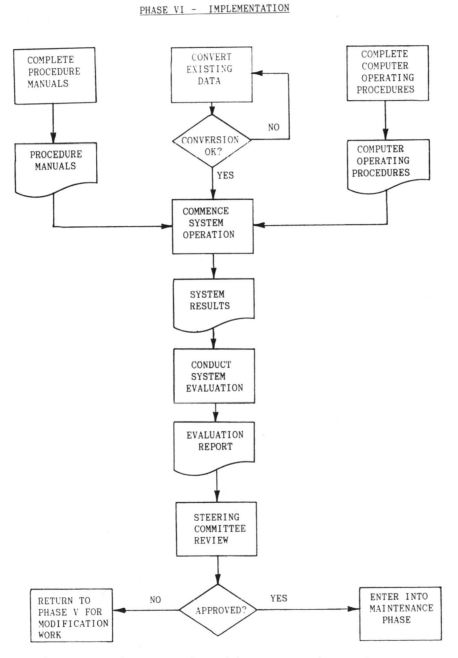

Figure 9.7. Implementation Phase of the System Development Process.

Procedures Manual and the data processing operating instructions, such as data entry procedures, input handling procedures, and output report procedures.

Now the new system can begin operation. After a brief period of operations, a study of the results is prepared. The Project Team appointed during the system survey phase conducts an evaluation of those results to determine whether the system is adequate and performing according to approved specifications. The evaluation report comments on any areas needing the attention of management.

Should modifications be necessary, the project working teams perform the same kind of work as in Phase V. After final review by the Steering Committee, the system enters a maintenance phase for continued operations.

SUMMARY OF THE SYSTEM DEVELOPMENT PROCESS

The six-phase System Development Process is a textbook method that allows for some tailoring to meet the individual needs and requirements of each organization. However, many good data processing operations do not follow this type of systematic development process. In too many cases, it was not felt necessary to perform some of the steps and, instead, shortcuts were taken. Many subsequent problems are caused by eliminating of one or more of the important steps as outlined, thereby increasing the risk of failure and decreasing the chances of success in developing computer systems.

THE COMPUTER REPORTS QUESTIONNAIRE

Business data processing generally consists of preparing data for machine entry, manipulating and storing data, and producing output for use in the business. Probably the largest part of the processing is the output: checks, invoices, master lists, and voluminous reports. Management sometimes feels that reports are not read, are not used properly, and therefore are a waste of time. The *Computer Reports Questionnaire* can be used to determine whether management may be right. See Figure 9.8.

The single-copy questionnaire is attached to output reports at predetermined intervals. The recipient of each copy of an output report is asked to complete the questionnaire and return it to a designated person, usually someone in data processing, or, possibly, the controller or internal auditor.

The basic purpose of the questionnaire is to determine whether the report is serving a useful purpose and is actually being employed to assist the user in a certain function of the company or organization. The report may be found to have outlived its usefulness as currently structured.

The answers to the first 10 questions will suggest several possible future actions concerning the particular output report. If a recipient's answer to Question 1 is "No," the report can be eliminated as far as this user is concerned. If the answer to Question 2 is "Read for information only," there may be a better way to provide the informa-

----

COMPUTER REPORTS QUESTIONNAIRE

Report Title _____

Report Number_____

Frequency of Issue:
☐ On Request   ☐ Daily   ☐ Weekly   ☐ Monthly   ☐ Quarterly   ☐ Semi-annually
☐ Annually   ☐ Other_____

1. Do you wish to continue to receive this report?
    ☐ Yes-----Answer all remaining questions.
    ☐ No------Do not answer remaining questions.

2. What do you do with this report after you receive it?
    ☐ Read and use to make decisions.
    ☐ Read for information only.
    ☐ Read and use for compiling other reports.
    ☐ Other (explain)_____

3. Do you pass this report on to others?
    ☐ Yes   } If yes, ☐ For their information.
    ☐ No   ☐ For them to take action.

4. How often do you use the information in this report?
    ☐ Daily   ☐ Weekly   ☐ Monthly   ☐ Quarterly   ☐ Never

5. How do you rank this report as to relative information in comparison to
    other reports you receive?
    ☐ Top one-third   ☐ Middle one-third   ☐ Bottom one-third

6. In view of the above ranking, should this report be issued:
    ☐ More frequently?   ☐ Less frequently?   ☐ At same frequency?
    If change is indicated what frequency of issue do you suggest?_____

7. Does this report reach you soon enough?   ☐ Yes   ☐ No

8. Would control of your operation or planning your responsibilities be materially
    impaired without this report?   ☐ Yes   ☐ No

9. Is this report suitable in its present form?   ☐ Yes   ☐ No
    Or should additional data be provided such as:
    ☐ Percentages?   ☐ Ratios?   ☐ Prior period figures?   ☐ Year-to-date figures?

10. If others who receive copies of this report agree to its discontinuance, would you
    still want it for your use only?
    ☐ Yes   ☐ No

11. Any other comments or suggestions as to form, scope, method of preparation, etc.?
    _____
    _____
    _____

Signed_____Department_____Date_____

Figure 9.8. Computer Reports Questionnaire.

tion, such as in a summary report. If the answer is "Read and use for compiling other reports," perhaps these other reports can be computerized or their information added to this report.

If Question 4 indicates that the reader never uses the information in the report, maybe it should be discontinued. In Question 5, if the report is ranked at the bottom third of the reports received, a study should be made to see whether it can be made more meaningful or should be discontinued.

Question 6 points out that a change in frequency of reporting should be studied. A "No" answer to Question 7 should alert the data processing staff that the system should be examined for ways to speed up the reporting process. Question 8 relates to the value of the reported information. A "No" answer suggests that either changes should be made in the information or the report should be discontinued. Question 9 allows the user of the report to enter his or her input into the reporting process. A "No" answer indicates that the contents of the report should be analyzed. Then a determination can be made as to whether additional data could and/or should be added to the report.

Question 10 provides one last chance to eliminate the report to this user. Although a user may answer the other questions in a way that shows the report is useful to him or her, a "No" answer here is a strong indication that this user feels the report is no longer necessary to the particular operation.

Periodic use of the *Computer Reports Questionnaire* may provide enough information for the Initiation Phase of another System Development Process.

INFORMATION SYSTEM WORK PLAN

The *Information System Work Plan*, Figure 9.9, was developed by a task force assembled to study five regional governmental units to determine whether some savings could be realized if changes were made in current operating methods. The governmental units consisted of a county, a city, a community college, a school district, and an intermediate school district. It could just as well be used by a company with several computer centers, or a governmental unit with several agencies or departments with computer operations.

This work plan covers both the acquisition of hardware and changes and additions to software programs. Parts of the plan would require the same studies as shown in the System Development Process discussed earlier. Phase I-1 asks that the organizational priorities of each unit be determined. This information is needed to ascertain whether any of the units already has a major change in the planning stage.

Phase I-6 develops criteria for an Initiation Phase. Phase II-1 is similar to Phases III and IV of the System Development Process. Phase III-3 and 4 determines the systems specifications for new systems.

The remaining sections deal with hardware selection. It is important that vendors not be included in the task force or any subcommittee until the final vendor or vendors are selected and approved. There are no unbiased vendors of computer equipment!

```
 ⊔ ⊔
 ▏ ▏ ▏
 ┌─┐
 H E C
 ┌┐┌ ┌┐┐
```
INFORMATION SYSTEMS GROUP

HAEUSSLER ENTERPRISES COMPANY

INFORMATION SYSTEM WORK PLAN

The following work plan will be discussed at our next meeting with the Chief Executive Officers of the entities involved in the study of both hardware and software upgrades.

PHASE I - INTERNAL SYSTEMS ASSESSMENT

1. Determine organizational priorities based on long range (three to five years) planning.

2. Identify key employees of the various functional areas to participate on the information systems project team. Distribute information system planning materials to help educate team members on the system planning process.

3. Prepare a summary of all currently used software:

    A. Operating system
    B. Application software
    C. Utility software

4. Prepare a summary of the hardware, including:

    A. CPU(s)
    B. Terminals
    C. Printers
    D. Storage devices
    E. Communication devices
    F. Other

5. Gather and condense all information from previous system planning sessions and distribute to team members.

6. Distribute and analyze a questionnaire to key system users to obtain their assessment and comments on the current system strengths and weaknesses.

PHASE II - EXTERNAL SYSTEMS ASSESSMENT

1. Analyze the various software options and determine which ones make sense. Options include:

    A. Custom designed programs.
    B. Integrated package programs.
    C. Non-integrated package programs.
    D. Modified packaged programs.

Figure 9.9. Information System Work Plan.

243

2. Analyze the various hardware options, including cable and communications needs, and determine which will be included in the investigation.

3. Analyze systems trends in the industry, both administrative and operational.

PHASE III - PREPARE SYSTEM SPECIFICATIONS

1. Identify those application areas where automation will be considered.

2. Prepare general hardware technical specifications, including:

   A. Communications specifications.
   B. Storage requirements.
   C. Cabling requirements.
   D. Current and projected number of users to be supported.
   E. Networking requirements.
   F. System administration requirements.
   G. Required access times and processing speed.

3. Prepare general software technical specifications, including:

   A. Ease of use
   B. "Look and feel" concerns
   C. Accessibility to data
   D. Audit trail
   E. System security
   F. Integration
   G. Training and support

4. Prepare application software specifications for each application area.

   A. Transaction volume
   B. File sizes, both master and transaction
   C. Data elements to be maintained
   D. Required outputs; daily, weekly, monthly
   E. Functional capabilities required

PHASE IV - SELECTION OF A SYSTEM VENDOR

1. Identify potential system vendors.

2. Based on the system specifications developed in Phase III, prepare a request for proposal and send to each prospective vendor.

3. Complete vendor evaluation, narrowing the prospective vendor list to between three to five vendors. Those selected will be analyzed in detail using the following process:

   A. Quantitive analysis
      1. Vendor capability
      2. Software capabilities
      3. Cost comparison
      4. Delivery time

Figure 9.9. Continued.

244

B. Qualitative analysis
    1. System demonstraion, either at a live site or in a vendor-
       controlled environment. Live site demonstrations are
       preferred.
    2. Vendor reference checks.

4. Project team recommendation.

5. Selected vendor notified.

PHASE V - IMPLEMENTATION PLANNING

1. Working with system vendor, develop a system implementation plan.
   Considerations would include:

   A. System priorities established in Phase I.
   B. Logical ordering required due to the database and file structures of
      the software.

2. System implementation begins.

Figure 9.9. Continued.

The details of this particular work plan are not discussed in detail in this text. It is shown merely to illustrate how a plan is developed for a comprehensive study of several data processing operations in order to consolidate operations where possible, determine whether current equipment is adequate or needs to be upgraded or replaced, and decide whether new application systems may be needed.

The task force that developed this work plan consisted of several professionals in accounting, data processing, human resources, and other departments. They were guided by a consulting firm that had performed similar consultations in other states.

There are a number of data processing terms, some of which are included in Phase IV of the work plan, that should be understood by members of a Steering Committee and a Project Team. A *request for proposal*, commonly called an RFP, outlines the total systems proposed in general terms and asks that each vendor submit its hardware and, sometimes, software solutions.

Before acceptance of a vendor's proposal, it is always desirable to have a *system demonstration* of the solution within an actual system already in use by the requesting unit. If this is not possible—sometimes because the cost of preparing a demonstration is significant to the vendor—a similar application chosen by the vendor may be demonstrated.

Integrated package programs are vendor program systems that include more than one application. For example, a vendor might sell a general ledger system, an accounts receivable system, an accounts payable module, and a payroll package that work with each other without additional programming. A *nonintegrated package* is a single set of programs that perform one function, such as payroll, for which the vendor offers no other related applications.

Utility software programs are generic programs that assist operations and are used in many applications. Examples are sort programs, report program generators that produce simple reports with limited programming, and file copy programs.

THE TOTAL SURVEY

Sometimes the major part of a development project is the survey of current data processing installations and practices. The following 10 forms were first developed and used in a major project to consolidate more than 20 state agency computer departments, each standing alone to serve a single agency, into six or seven larger and more capable computer systems to serve their own agencies and to act as service bureaus to handle other agencies' data processing needs. The primary purpose was to eliminate small, ineffective, and little-used computer hardware systems and to utilize larger equipment more intensively. Preliminary savings were estimated at two million dollars per year.

SURVEY METHOD

For the completion of the survey forms, four interview teams of two members each were selected. One member of each team was from the data processing management staff of a large state agency, the other from a consulting firm. All team members were quite knowledgeable in data processing. Each team visited an agency that used some type of computer processing. Within a few days, the team listed the hardware and the major applications, but only in sufficient depth to determine whether the applications could be easily moved to an internal service bureau operation at a larger agency. An accountant was employed to determine the potential cost savings for each contemplated change.

To assure that all team's output was similar in nature and readable by a third party, the special forms were designed and printed. Several copies of each form were packaged along with instructions. As each of the 10 forms has its own instructions for completion in some detail, the contents of these forms are discussed here only in a general way.

THE FORMS PACKAGE

The package used by the interview teams consisted of the following (see Figure 9.10):

DP1—Installation—Physical Layout
DP2—Data Processing Equipment Inventory
DP3—Other Equipment Inventory

DP4—Personnel Skill Inventory

DP5—Inquiries—Incoming

DP5A—Inquiries—Outgoing

DP6—Summary of Applications

DP7—Individual Application Details (large envelope)

DP8—Form Survey Worksheet

DP9—Narrative Memorandum of Job

Forms DP1 to DP6 were used to describe and define the installation, its equipment, its people, the inquiry capabilities, and a summary of all applications. One set of Forms DP7, DP8, and DP9 were used to describe each single application, its general processing methods, and its forms and files, and to provide a narrative description of the application.

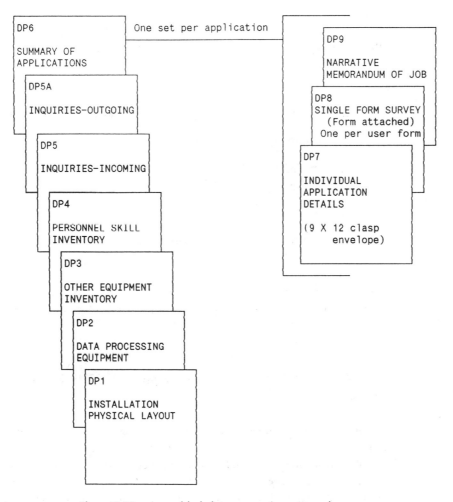

Figure 9.10. Assembled data processing survey forms.

Form DP1—Installation Physical Layout (Figures 9.11, 9.12)

The interview team was required to sketch the computer room, file storage area, and data entry room if it was at another location. The information recorded on Form DP1 describes the adequacy of the room for computer operations and can be used in determining the cost of dismantling its special features, as well as possible other uses of the room.

Form DP2—Data Processing Equipment Inventory (Figures 9.13, 9.14)

The information gathered on Form DP2 indicated the level of sophistication of the current operations and whether the equipment, or some of it, could be used elsewhere if this installation was to be closed. In this particular study more than 100 keypunch machines were located that were not being used at all, but were being stored in closets and unused rooms. Each machine was under full rental and no one had bothered to cancel the rental when the machines were no longer needed. Such survey, therefore, may reveal a variety of ways to decrease costs.

Form DP3—Other Equipment Inventory (Figures 9.15, 9.16)

Form DP3 provided for a listing of equipment, some of which might be needed and used elsewhere, or might be sold or scrapped.

Form DP4—Personnel Skill Inventory (Figures 9.17, 9.18)

DP4 was a very important form. Extra personnel would be needed at the consolidated computer centers, and this list provided knowledge of trained people who could be transferred.

Forms DP5 and DP5A—Inquiries (Figures 9.19, 9.20, 9.21, 9.22)

The survey sought to determine a variety of needs. Forms DP5 and DP5A provided an indication of what kind of paper reports were needed to answer inquiries and what kind of information was needed and obtained by inquiry of another department or person. They also gave an idea of the level of sophistication of communications and what kind of communications might be needed at the consolidated computer centers.

Form DP6—Summary of Applications (Figures 9.23, 9.24)

Form DP6 was simply a numbered index of the applications surveyed at this installation.

Form DP7—Individual Application Details (Figures 9.25, 9.26)

Form DP7 provided an overview of the input forms, output forms, files, and general processing methods used in this one application. It gave some indication of whether the applications could be handled on other equipment, whether there were special needs of the application, and the general size of the application. One form was used for each application reviewed.

Form DP8—Form Survey Worksheet (Figures 9.27, 9.28)

One DP8 form was used for each input and output form used in the one application. It described each form it accompanied and indicated whether there were special form requirements that the consolidated center would need.

Form DP9—Narrative Memorandum of Job (Figure 9.29)

Form DP9 was used as a write up of what the application does and what problems there might be if it were moved to another computer operation. Each memorandum necessarily included the opinion of the interviewers regarding the feasibility of moving the application and its necessary related operations.

COMPLETING FORM DP1 - PHYSICAL LAYOUT

1. Heading:
   Name of Company, Agency, or Institution.
   Name of Data Processing department.
   Location of Data Processing such as building, floor, room number.
   Name of Data Processing manager or director.
   Name of person preparing the layout form.
   Date the form is completed.

2. Scale. For small areas, one square indicates two square feet; in large areas, four square feet. As a guide for distances, suspended ceiling tiles are usually one square foot, two feet squares, or two by four feet rectangles.

3. Grid: Draw a sketch of the area using the following symbols.

   Wall is solid line.

   Window.

   Door with direction of opening.

   Support post.

   Electrical outlet.   E

   Show data entry areas by outlining such areas with dotted lines. Show areas not used for data processing but in the same room by blocking out such areas.

4. General information.

   Ceiling height. Estimated height in feet.
   Air Conditioning. Indicate yes or no.
   False flooring. Indicate yes or no.
   Supply room adjacent (to computer room). Indicate yes or no.
     If not adjacent, indicate where supply room is located. Enter building, floor, or room number.
   File Storage location. Enter building, floor, room number.
   Special wiring. Indicate yes or no.
   Backup power supply. Indicate yes or no.

5. Area sizes. Enter the approximate square feet of each of the following data processing areas.
   Processing area.
   Data Entry area.
   Supply Room area.
   File Storage area.
   Total square feet of all areas.

6. Provide any other information that may be useful.

Figure 9.11. Completing the physical layout form.

DP1 DATA PROCESSING INSTALLATION PHYSICAL LAYOUT	COMPANY

DP1

DATA PROCESSING INSTALLATION
PHYSICAL LAYOUT

Sketch of area including adjacent
  storage.

SCALE □=_____FT. SQ.
Include built-in cabinets.

COMPANY

DP DEPT.

LOCATION

NAME OF DP MANAGER

PREPARED: BY   DATE

CEILING HEIGHT_____FT.

AIR CONDITIONING   YES___   NO___

FALSE FLOORING   YES___   NO___

SUPPLY ROOM ADJACENT YES___   NO___

  IF NOT, WHERE LOCATED_____

FILE STORAGE LOCATION_____

SPECIAL WIRING   YES___   NO___

BACKUP POWER SUPPLY   YES___   NO___

PROCESSING AREA   _____SQ. fT.

DATA ENTRY AREA   _____SQ. FT.

SUPPLY ROOM AREA   _____SQ. FT.

FILE STORAGE AREA _____SQ. FT.

              TOTAL _____SQ. FT.

OTHER PERTINENT INFORMATION
_____
_____
_____

Figure 9.12. Physical layout.

251

COMPLETING FORM DP2 - DATA PROCESSING EQUIPMENT INVENTORY

1. Heading:
   Name of Company, Agency, or Institution.
   Name of Data Processing department.
   Location of Data Processing such as building, floor, room number.
   Name of Data Processing manager or director.
   Name of person preparing the Equipment Inventory form.
   Date the form is completed.

2. Name of Item. Enter name of item such as CPU, tape drives, disk drives, printers, other input or output devices. Also list terminals, PCs, modems, and so on connected to the mainframe by cable, even if in other departments or locations. Do not include Fax machines, special file cabinets, work tables, copy machines, or non-processing equipment which will be listed on Form DP3, Other Equipment Inventory.

3. Model No. Enter exact Model No. of each piece of equipment, including letter prefix or suffix.

4. Annual Rent. Complete for each piece of equipment, even if estimated. If purchased outright, so indicate.

5. Special Features and Attachments. Indicate core size, special read features such as Optical Character Recognition (OCR), external switches, special printer carriage widths, and so on.

Figure 9.13. Completing the data processing equipment inventory form.

DP2 DATA PROCESSING EQUIPMENT INVENTORY		COMPANY	
		DP DEPT.	
		LOCATION	
		NAME OF DP MANAGER	
		PREPARED: BY DATE	
NAME OF ITEM	MODEL NO.	ANNUAL RENT	SPECIAL FEATURES AND ATTACHMENTS

Figure 9.14. Data processing equipment inventory.

COMPLETING FORM DP3 — OTHER EQUIPMENT INVENTORY

1. Heading:
   Name of Company, Agency, or Institution.
   Name of Data Processing department.
   Location of Data Processing such as building, floor, room number.
   Name of Data Processing manager or director.
   Name of person preparing the Other Equipment Inventory form.
   Date the form is completed.

2. Name of Equipment Item. List copy machines, Fax machines, typewriters, modems, chairs, tables, cabinets, files, bursters, decollators, and so forth. List the number of telephones, main line and extension.

3. Quantity. Enter quantity of each listed item.

4. Descriptive Data. Enter any special features, model numbers, size, manufacturer, and so forth. List carriage width of typewriters.

Figure 9.15. Completing the other equipment inventory form.

DP3 DATA PROCESSING OTHER EQUIPMENT INVENTORY		COMPANY
		DP DEPT.
		LOCATION
		NAME OF DP MANAGER
		PREPARED: BY DATE
NAME OF EQUIPMENT ITEM (Decollators, bursters, copy machines, modems, etc.)	QUANTITY	DESCRIPTIVE DATA (MFR., MODEL NO., SIZE)

Figure 9.16. Other equipment inventory.

COMPLETING FORM DP4 - PERSONNEL SKILL INVENTORY

1. Heading:
    Name of Company, Agency, or Institution.
    Name of Data Processing department.
    Location of Data Processing such as building, floor, room number.
    Name of Data Processing manager or director.
    Name of person preparing the Personnel Skill Inventory form.
    Date the form is completed.

2. Name of Employee. Enter full name. Also list unfilled established positions.

3. Title (Level). Enter employee title used by Personnel or in budget. For government units, list civil service level.

4. Funct. Indicate percent of performance in each of the following job functions:

    OP - Operating
    PR - Programming
    SU - Supervision
    DE - Data Entry
    CL - Clerical
    ST - Staff

    (Example: DE 70%)
              CL 30%)

5. Type. Enter type of position as follows:

    F - Full time employee
    T - Temporary employee (indicate termination date)
    P - Part time employee (indicate weekly hours)

6. Sex. Male or Female.

7. Yrs. DP. Enter years of experience in data processing. Supervisor may have to estimate in some cases.

8. Highest DP Skill. List the highest data processing skill for each person such as Programmer, Operator, Data Entry, Supervision, System Analyst, and so on. Important secondary skills may be listed.

Note: In some surveys, additional important information may be included, such as budgeted overtime for this department, salaries for all employees and total salaries for the department, including unfilled positions. If substantial changes have been approved but not implemented, this fact should be noted.

Figure 9.17. Completing the personnel skill inventory form.

DP4 DATA PROCESSING INSTALLATION PERSONNEL SKILL INVENTORY	COMPANY
	DP DEPT.
	LOCATION
	NAME OF DP MANAGER
	PREPARED: BY DATE

NAME OF EMPLOYEE	TITLE (LEVEL)	FUNCT.	TYPE	SEX	YRS. DP	HIGHEST DP SKILL

COMMENTS:

Figure 9.18. Personnel skill inventory.

COMPLETING FORM DP5 - INQUIRIES--INCOMING

The purpose of this form is to determine the need for additional telephones, terminals, file clerks, or letter writers, or if the data must be kept at a special location in data processing to answer such inquiries. A high volume would indicate that an on-line inquiriy capability may be desirable.

1. Heading:
   Name of Company, Agency, or Institution.
   Name of User Department (may be Data Processing department).
   Location of Data Processing such as building, floor, room number.
   Name of Department manager or director.
   Name of person preparing the DP5 form.
   Date the form is completed.

2. Requested By: Name of Department, Division, Customer, Vendor, or Individual making the inquiry. This information is a summary of such inquiries over a period of time (at least a week, preferably one full month) by everyone in the department who answers a telephone or handles mail.

3. Mode. Indicate method of inquiring as follows:

   TEL   – telephone inquiry
   MAIL – mail inquiry
   TERM – terminal inquiry
   PER   – in person request (in Department or over-the-counter).
   IDC   – intra-department correspondence
   FAX   – fax machine

4. No. Per Day. Average number per day based on information obtained in item 2 above.

5. File Used for Reply. Indicate as follows:

   Paper File (Correspondence file or similar paper form file).
   Computer report.
   Terminal (Inquiry to computer).
   Microfilm

6. Data Required and How Quickly Answer Is Required. Use one or two words to describe data, such as Customer Number, Vendor Address, Employee Information, Part Number or Description, Telephone Number, Dollar Amount in Account, and so on.

   Time required can be instantly (on-line?), one hour, same day, within 24 hours, or by outgoing mail.

Figure 9.19. Completing the incoming inquiries form.

DP5 DATA PROCESSING INQUIRIES – INCOMING	COMPANY			
	USER DEPT.			
	LOCATION			
	NAME OF DEPT. MANAGER			
	PREPARED: BY DATE			
REQUESTED BY	MODE OF COMMUNICA-TION	NO. PER DAY	FILE USED FOR REPLY	DATA REQUIRED AND HOW QUICKLY ANSWER IS REQUIRED

Figure 9.20. Incoming inquiries.

COMPLETING FORM DP5A - INQUIRIES--OUTGOING

The purpose of this form is to determine whether this department needs a master report of some kind (alphabetic customer list with account numbers, account balances, and so on) to replace the need for inquiries to others. A high volume would indicate that an on-line inquiriy capability may be needed.

1. Heading:
   Name of Company, Agency, or Institution.
   Name of User Department (may be Data Processing department).
   Location of Data Processing such as building, floor, room number.
   Name of Department manager or director.
   Name of person preparing the DP5A form.
   Date the form is completed.

2. Request Sent To: Name of Department, Division, Customer, Vendor, or Individual making the inquiry. This information is a summary of such inquiries over a period of time (at least a week, preferably one full month) by everyone in the department who makes inquiries to outsiders.

3. Mode. Indicate method of inquiring as follows:

   TEL - telephone inquiry
   MAIL - mail inquiry
   TERM - terminal inquiry
   PER - in person request (to Department or over-the-counter).
   IDC - intra-department correspondence
   FAX - fax machine

4. No. Per Day. Average number per day based on information obtained in item 2 above.

5. Data Required and How Quickly Answer Is Required. Use one or two words to describe data, such as Customer Number, Vendor Address, Employee Information, Part Number or Description, Telephone Number, Dollar Amount in Account, and so on.

   Time required can be instantly (on-line?), one hour, same day, within 24 hours, or by incoming mail.

Figure 9.21. Completing the outgoing inquiries form.

DP5A DATA PROCESSING INQUIRIES – OUTGOING			COMPANY
			USER DEPT.
			LOCATION
			NAME OF DEPT. MANAGER
			PREPARED: BY DATE
REQUEST SENT TO	MODE OF COMMUNICA-TION	NO. PER DAY	DATA REQUIRED AND HOW QUICKLY ANSWER IS REQUIRED

Figure 9.22. Outgoing inquiries.

COMPLETING FORM DP6 - SUMMARY OF APPLICATIONS

1. Heading:
    Name of Company, Agency, or Institution.
    Name of Data Processing department.
    Location of Data Processing such as building, floor, room number.
    Name of Department manager or director.
    Name of person preparing the DP6 form.
    Date the form is completed.

2. Summary Reference Number.   A consecutive number beginning with "1" assigned to each application reviewed and documented with forms DP7 and DP8.

3. Individual Application Title.   A meaningful term describing the application being reviewed.   Such terms as "Updating Customer Files," or "Printing vendor checks" is adequate.   It may be helpful to add the Department's program number and working name.

Figure 9.23.   Completing the summary of applications form.

DP6	COMPANY
DATE PROCESSING INSTALLATION SUMMARY OF APPLICATIONS	DP DEPT.
	LOCATION
	NAME OF DP MANAGER
	PREPARED: BY DATE

SUMMARY REFERENCE NUMBER	INDIVIDUAL APPLICATION TITLE

COMMENTS:

Figure 9.24. Summary of applications.

COMPLETING FORM DP7 - INDIVIDUAL APPLICATION DETAILS

Note: This form can be printed on a 9 by 12 clasp envelope and the Survey Forms placed therein.

1. Heading:
   Summary Reference No. Assign number so that application can be traced from form DP6-Summary of Applications.
   Frequency. Enter average frequency that this job is run, such as daily, weekly, monthly, annually, and so forth.
   Name of Data Processing manager or director.
   Name of person preparing the DP7 form.
   Date the form is completed.

2. Input:
   A. Survey Form No. One line for each form listed and placed in the envelope with Form DP8-Form Survey Worksheet.
   B. Name of Form. Actual title of form if known, or a simple description such as check, deposit slip, remittance advice, purchase order, and so on.
   C. Method of Input. Enter type of input such as paper, direct terminal entry, floppy disk, magnetic tape, hard disk file, and so forth.
   D. Dept. Form No. Enter, if known.
   E. Average Input Quantity. Approximate number of entries each time this job is run.
   F. Characters per Entry. Average number of characters of the input form used in the processing.
   G. Other. Any other information concerning the input that may be useful.

3. Output:
   A. Survey Form No. One line for each form listed and placed in the envelope with Form DP8-Form Survey Worksheet.
   B. Name of Form or Other Output. Actual title of form, if known, or name of printed report, or name of machine-generated file.
   C. Type of Form. Indicate whether output is paper, printed report, disk file, tape file, or other.
   D. Dept. Form No. If output is a form used by another department, enter the form number such as "AR8-Accounts Receivable Statement."
   E. Average Output Quantity. Approximate number of forms, printed report lines, or transaction records on tape or disk.
   F. Other Information.

4. Files Maintained:
   A. Name of File. Briefly describe each file kept on a current basis.
   B. Type of File. Enter disk, floppy disk, magnetic tape, paper forms, and so on.
   C. Size of File. Emter number of forms, number of transaction records, number of master file records, and so forth.
   D. Basis for Retention or Purging. Estimate the retention or purging time such as "until employee leaves", "until next update", "monthly when summary report is printed", and so forth.

5. Short Job Description:
   Provide a simple general flow chart showing input and output with Survey form numbers. Form DP9 provides a narrative description.

Figure 9.25. Completing the individual application details form.

264

DP7	SUMMARY REFERENCE NO.	FREQUENCY
DATA PROCESSING INSTALLATION **INDIVIDUAL APPLICATION DETAILS**	JOB TITLE	
	NAME OF DP MANAGER	
	PREPARED: BY	DATE

INPUT

SURVEY FORM NO.	NAME OF FORM	METHOD OF INPUT	DEPT. FORM NO.	AVERAGE INPUT QN.	CHAR. PER ENTRY	OTHER
1						
2						
3						
4						
5						

OUTPUT

SURVEY FORM NO.	NAME OF FORM OR OTHER OUTPUT	TYPE OF FORM	DEPT. FORM NO.	AVERAGE OUTPUT QN	OTHER INFORMATION
6					
7					
8					
9					
10					

FILES MAINTAINED

NAME OF FILE	TYPE OF FILE	SIZE OF FILE	BASIS FOR RETENTION (OR PURGING)

SHORT JOB DESCRIPTION:

Figure 9.26. Individual application details.

COMPLETING FORM DP8 - FORM SURVEY WORKSHEET

An original or a copy of the form being described should be attached to each Form DP8.

1. Heading:
   Enter the Summary Reference Number assigned on Form DP7.
   Enter the Input No. or Output No. assigned on Form DP7.
   Enter name of person providing information about this form. This
      person may be in Data Processing or User Department.
   Name of person preparing the DP8 form.
   Date the form is completed.

2. Name of Form. Enter the official name of the form or descriptive heading on form.

3. Form No. Enter form number, if known, and date of last revision, if known.

4. Copies and Destination or Use. For each copy of the form (Original is copy 1), enter the color of the form and the final destination of that copy or the use of the copy. An example might be an invoice form, as follows:

1	White	To customer
2	Yellow	To Accounts Receivable Department
3	Pink	To Shipping as authorization to ship

5. Is the Form Prenumbered? Check yes or no.

6. Source of Supply. Can be purchased, printed in own print shop, supplied by another department or agency, photocopied in originating department, and so on.

7. Estimated Quantity Used Per Month. Enter quantity determined. Check if this is about the same as the input entries to the Data Processing application.

8. How is Form Completed. Check method such as handwritten based on personal contact with individual, typewriter, computer output (i.e., turnaround remittance advice),   on a terminal or personal computer, or other ways.

9. Remarks. Enter any other information which may be of interest in understanding the application.

Figure 9.27. Completing the form survey worksheet.

DP8	SUMMARY	INPUT NO. _____
	REFERENCE NO.	OUTPUT NO._____
FORM SURVEY WORKSHEET	INFORMATION PROVIDED BY:	
	PREPARED: BY	DATE

NAME OF FORM_____

FORM NO._____DATE OF LAST REVISION, IF KNOWN_____

COPIES AND DESTINATION OR USE:

COPY   COLOR   DESTINATION OR USE

  1   _____   _____

  2   _____   _____

  3   _____   _____

  4   _____   _____

  5   _____   _____

IS THE FORM PRENUMBERED?   YES___   NO___

SOURCE OF SUPPLY: _____   PURCHASED. NAME OF PRINTER, IF KNOWN_____

                     _____   OWN PRINT SHOP

                     _____   FROM ANOTHER DEPARTMENT. WHICH_____

                     _____   OTHER. DESCRIBE_____

ESTIMATED QUANTITY USED PER MONTH _____

ORIGINATING DEPARTMENT_____

HOW IS FORM COMPLETED: ____ HANDWRITTEN
                          ____ TYPEWRITER
                          ____ COMPUTER OUTPUT
                          ____ TERMINAL OR PERSONAL COMPUTER
                          ____ OTHER _____

REMARKS:_____
_____

     ATTACH ORIGINAL OR COPY OF FORM

Figure 9.28. Form survey worksheet.

DP9	SUMMARY REFERENCE NO.
NARRATIVE MEMORANDUM OF JOB	JOB : DESCRIPTION:
	PREPARED: BY DATE

The surveyor should indicate in brief, narrative form, what the job consists of and whether there are any requirements which would be difficult to fulfill if application is moved. Also whether, in his or her opinion, the job is suitable for processing at another location, and, if not, why not?

Figure 9.29. Narrative memorandum of job.

SUMMARY OF THE FORMS PACKAGE

These forms and their proper use proved quite helpful in surveying 20 data processing centers and eventually closing 15 of them and disposing of most of the equipment at those locations. Of the consolidated centers remaining after the project was finished, almost all had newer and larger equipment, benefitted from staffs that were better trained overall, and enjoyed much longer and heavier usage of equipment. The interview packages were used to help determine where each closed agency operation was to have its processing done. At the completion of the project, savings were estimated at more than $2 million annually, more than $4 million in current dollars.

The cost of the forms is negligible. Those shown here were generated by the author on an IBM-compatible PC, an Epson 24-pin dot matrix printer, and the *Column/Table*, *Graphics*, and *Line Draw* features of the WordPerfect 5.1 word-processing system. Any number of similar forms can be designed easily and photo-copied for use in a similar situation.

CHAPTER 10
STYLE:
THE EASY WRITER

First, don't worry! This chapter is not going to cover all the rules of grammar, spelling, style, and other English rules you learned between the fifth and twelfth grades. It will try to cover the problem areas for those of you who have been asked to prepare a formal document of an operation in an accounting environment. Here is the most important rule of all:

Clarity and readability are much more important than style, perfect grammar, and a large vocabulary.

Certainly, all the rules of grammar cannot be covered in one chapter of a book not devoted to the study of the English language. However, there are a few basic rules that nonprofessional writers stumble over. There are consistent errors in spelling. There is misuse of verbs and use of passive verbs that do not motivate the reader, and there is poor use of sound, basic writing techniques such as outlining.

So this chapter will cover, in order, a good outlining method, commonly misspelled and misused words, a list of action verbs, common grammar mistakes and how to avoid them, sexism in writing, number usage, and the *Fog Index*.

THE OUTLINING HABIT

The writer should learn how to outline written material and get into the outlining habit as quickly as possible. Whenever any technical material is longer than four or five handwritten pages or two typewritten pages, outlining the material before writing the first draft helps.

Outlining is a fast and effective way to show a great amount of information in a concise, effective manner with a minimum of writing. Much narrative documentation begins with an outline. Word processing outlining programs are available to aid writers and speakers to formulate ideas in a logical pattern.

Outlining Technique

Effective outlining has few rules. These rules concern indentation and numbering. Standard outline formatting is as follows:

```
I.
        A.
                1.
                2.
                        a.
                        b.
        B.
II.
```

The four characters to mark each section level, Roman numerals, capital letters, arabic numerals, and lower case letters, are followed by a period. Line up the periods vertically for each type of character. Thus, Roman numerals are shown:

```
  I.
 II.
VIII.
XVII.
```

Arabic numerals are lined up as follows:

```
  1.
  2.
 12.
 48.
102.
```

By aligning the periods, the text is a pleasing, straight vertical line.

Indention should be uniform, usually three to five spaces for each change in type of line. The part of a single line carried to a second line should be indented two spaces. For example:

I. Explaining the use of indention in developing a working outline.
    A. When changing line identifiers.
    B. When a long line must be continued to a subsequent line.

Minimum Line Identifiers

The last rule is: There must be at least two of each type of character. There cannot be a *I* without a *II*, an *A* without a *B*, a *1* without a *2*, and an *a* without at least a *b*. If, for example, outline step "V. Completing the form" was followed with "A. Accounting Department," there must be a B. If not, line A would be eliminated and line V changed to "V. Accounting completes form." The next outline step, in this case, would be a VI.

Outlining is the written version of a flowchart. Figure 10.1 shows a simple flowchart of an accounting operation and its outline counterpart. Outlining is faster than flowcharting and changes can be made more easily.

SPELLING

Misspelling has always been, and always will be, a problem. You can no longer depend on the secretary, typist, or word processing specialist to be a good speller. You, the writer, are responsible for the accuracy of your material. When in doubt, use a dictionary. If you are lucky enough to have a good word processor, there are spelling programs available that will read a data file and list all words that are not found in their dictionaries.

The English language is difficult because of its many changes in plural usage or in endings. Thus certain words are frequently misspelled by many people. See Figure 10.2 for nearly 200 words commonly misspelled. Figure 10.3 lists several groups of similar words frequently misued.

ACTIVE VERBS

Nothing makes reading more tiresome and difficult than using passive verbs. The writer is whispering when he should be speaking boldly, particularly when documenting professional and technical material. The reader of such material is reluctant to become involved in narratives which are meant to be informative instead of interesting. Action verbs help.

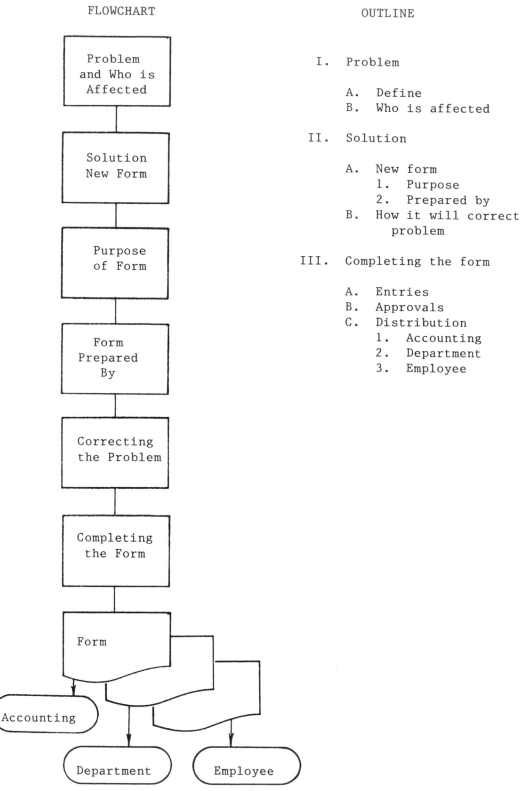

FLOWCHART

OUTLINE

Problem
and Who is
Affected

Solution
New Form

Purpose
of Form

Form
Prepared
By

Correcting
the Problem

Completing
the Form

Form

Accounting

Department

Employee

I.   Problem

A.   Define
B.   Who is affected

II.   Solution

A.   New form
     1.   Purpose
     2.   Prepared by
B.   How it will correct
     problem

III.   Completing the form

A.   Entries
B.   Approvals
C.   Distribution
     1.   Accounting
     2.   Department
     3.   Employee

Figure 10.1. A flowchart of an accounting operation and its outline counterpart.

absence	dealt	imaginary	precede
accessible	deceit	immediately	prerogative
accidentally	definite	incidentally	prevalent
acclaim	dependent	indispensable	privilege
accommodate	desirability	ingenious	probably
accompanied	despair	interpret	procedure
accrue	desperate	interrupt	proceed
accumulate	develop	irrelevant	prominent
accustom	dilemma	irresistible	pronounce
acknowledgment	disappoint		pronunciation
acquire	discipline	judgment	pursue
across	dissatisfied		
actuality	dissent	knowledge	quantity
address	dissension		
aggravate	doesn´t	laboratory	really
allotted	dominant	laid	recommend
all right	donor	library	relief
already		likelihood	rhythm
amateur	eighth	literature	roommate
analysis	embarrass	livelihood	
anticipate	eminent	losing	satisfactorily
apparatus	emphasize		schedule
appreciate	endeavor	maintain	seize
appropriate	environment	maintenance	separate
approximately	equipped	manageable	shining
arguing	erroneous	meant	similar
ascend	especially	mileage	sponsor
	exaggerate	miniature	strength
basically	exhaust		subtle
basis	exhilarate	necessarily	succeed
beginning	existence	ninety	successful
belief	extraordinary	ninth	surprise
benefited		noticeable	
	familiar		
calendar	fascinate	occasion	temperament
canceled	February	occasionally	thorough
candidate	finally	occurred	transferred
category	financial	occurrence	tries
changeable	financier	opponent	
chief	forty		
column	forward	paid	unnecessary
committed	fulfill	parallel	useful
conceivable		particularly	using
condemn	generally	passed	
conscience	government	past	
conscientious	guaranteed	perceive	various
conscious	guard	persistent	villain
consistently		pertain	volume
continually	height	phase	
continuous	hindrance	phenomenon	
controlled	hundred	possess	weird

Figure 10.2. Words frequently misspelled.

```
--------------------------------------------------------------
buses  - vehicle
busses - kisses

capitol - a building
capital - (all other uses of the word)

complementary - relating to or adding to
complimentary - free, admiration

continual  - without interruption
continuous - extension in space, time, or sequence

discreet - good judgment, prudent
discrete - individually distinct, separate entity

personal  - private
personnel - people

pore - read studiously, small opening
pour - to move with a continuous flow, rain

principal - authority or sum of money
principle - a rule of conduct

stationary - fixed in place
stationery - paper

therefor  - in return for
therefore - for that

cite - to refer to, to name, or to quote
site - place or position
--------------------------------------------------------------
```
Figure 10.3. Words frequently misused.

Compare the following:

The employee maintains a compilation of the daily production.
The employee compiles the daily production.

The senior clerk will be assisting the payroll clerk.
The senior clerk assists the payroll clerk.

Look for verbs ending in -ation, -ing, -ed and -tion. These are signs of tired, passive verbs. Here is a short list of active verbs used most frequently by accountants.

accrues	accumulates	approves
authorizes	cancels	charges
checks	compares	corrects

credits	decides	enters
extends	files	issues
locates	obtains	prepares
receives	reconciles	records
requests	reviews	runs
sends	totals	uses
verifies	writes off	

Figure 10.4 is a list of active verbs found most useful to the writer involved in the documentation of accounting manuals.

COMMON GRAMMAR AND USAGE PROBLEMS

There are hundreds of grammar rules. Only a few will be discussed here. Good grammar is a writing tool. The writer should know good grammar and should not violate a rule without a good reason. However, good grammar should not override good writing.

Comma. Generally, when in doubt, leave it out. No comma is used after the year when specific dates are used: "The letter of May 2, 1986 covered the problem." An expression that could be left out of a sentence should be enclosed in commas: "The boy, tall and skinny, stood at the door."

Apostrophe. In possessives, the apostrophe is before the final *s* if singular, after the final *s* if plural.

"The boy's shoes were dirty." (one boy)

"The girls' shoes were wet." (more than one girl)

Omit in numeral dates: 1970s, the 1800s. Use the apostrophe when numerals are omitted in dates: '78, '60s. Omit the apostrophe when an acronym is plural: TVs, VCRs.

Split Infinitives. Avoid splitting the "to" infinitive. However, it is permissible today for a single word to split an infinitive: "To graciously accept." "To never complain."

Exclamation Points. Use sparingly, if at all. Exclamation points are very jarring to the reader. You are, in effect, shouting a message.

Between, Among. Between two items, among more than two.

Of. Generally avoid *of* after *all, outside, inside,* and so on.

There is, There are. May usually be deleted when used at the beginning of a sentence.

Accepts	Edits	Obtains	Schedules
Accrues	Enforces	Operates	Secures
Advises	Enters	Orders	Sends
Aids	Establishes	Originates	Separates
Allows	Evaluates		Serves
Analyzes	Executes	Participates	Ships
Approves	Explains	Performs	Shows
Asks		Picks up	Signs
Assigns	Files	Places	Sorts
Assists	Follows up	Plans	Stamps
Attaches	Forecasts	Prepares	Starts
Audits	Forwards	Prescribes	Stops
Authorizes		Prevents	Studies
	Gathers up	Prints	Submits
Buys	Gets	Processes	Supervises
	Gives	Procures	Supplies
Calculates		Produces	Surveys
Changes	Handles	Protects	
Charges	Helps	Proves	Tabulates
Checks		Provides	Takes
Combines	Identifies	Pulls	Tells
Compiles	Indicates	Purchases	Terminates
Conducts	Initiates		Totals
Confers	Inserts	Reads	Transcribes
Controls	Inspects	Recalls	Transfers
Corrects	Installs	Receives	
Counts	Interviews	Recommends	Uses
Creates	Investigates	Reconciles	
Credits	Issues	Records	Verifies
		Rejects	
Decides	Keeps	Releases	Weighs
Deletes		Reports	Withdraws
Delivers	Lists	Requests	Works
Describes	Locates	Requires	Writes
Destroys	Logs	Restricts	
Determines		Retains	
Develops	Mails	Returns	
Devises	Maintains	Reviews	
Directs	Makes available	Routes	
Distributes	Marks	Runs	
	Measures		
	Moves		

Figure 10.4. Active verbs for accounting procedures.

Poor: "There is a problem which may arise."

Good: "A problem may arise."

If, Whether. *If* is used when introducing a simple condition. *Whether* is used for an indirect question or when expressing a doubt. "Whether he will be there is not known." Also use when alternatives are connected by "or" or "or not"; "Whether he comes or goes is not important."

Quotation marks. In the United States, quotation marks are *always outside* an ending comma, period, exclamation point, or question mark.

Publication Titles. The titles of books and periodicals are underlined in typewritten materials. When typesetting, the underlinings indicate the words should be in italics. An article title should be enclosed in quotation marks. For example, "Saving Your Money," by G.R. Brown, appeared in *Reader's Almanac*.

Which, That. If an expression could be placed between parentheses, use *which* and place commas on both sides of it. If the expression relates to something specific, use *that* with no commas.

Almost, Only, Nearly. Place these modifiers immediately before the words they modify. "This house nearly costs $25,000" should be changed to "This house costs nearly $25,000."

Farther, Further. Farther means more distant; further means "in addition" or "to a greater degree or extent."

Abbreviations. The abbreviations *lb., oz., ft., in.* should be spelled out as *pound, ounce, foot* or *feet*, and *inches*. However, some common abbreviations are permitted when used with numbers, such as 50 mph, 1800 rpm, 50 hp, and so on. The ampersand (&) is used only in organization names that use the abbreviation in their official titles.

ELABORATE OR REDUNDANT PHRASES

Sometimes substituting a word for a phrase gives the writing more directness. Many of the following phrases are out-of-date, even archaic for modern business. Here are some examples and replacement words:

Phrase	Replace With
as hereinbefore indicated	as shown above
as related to	about
assuming that	if
at this time	now
at your earliest convenience	(delete)
based on the fact that	because

because of the	because the
during the time that	while
enclosed please find	here is, here are
for the purpose of	for
I would like to	I will
in the amount of	for
in the event of	if
in view of the above	therefore
in order to	to
out of (the door)	out (the door)

SEXISM IN WRITING

Webster's New Collegiate Dictionary defines *he* as *used in the generic sense or when the sex of the person is unspecified*. Purists will continue this practice. However, the new feminists will not accept *he* being used when referring to people in general. There have been suggestions that the generic *he* be replaced with *he or she*, and *him* with *him or her*. Other suggested changes are *he/she* or the new pronoun, *s/he*. Luckily, this abominable replacement has not caught on.

The writer cannot eliminate so-called sexism completely, but can soften it somewhat by switching to generic nouns or, in some cases, by recasting sentences. In accounting, we are lucky to have many job titles which are generic, such as:

Accountant	Officer
Applicant	Operator
Chair (for Chairman)	Provider
Clerk	Secretary
Customer	Signer
Director	Traveler
Employee	User

There is another tendency to switch to a plural pronoun with a singular subject such as "When someone makes their payment to the . . ." The purist will say that *their* cannot refer to *someone*, yet this use is gaining acceptance with the singular subjects *one, no one, anyone, everyone, each*, and so on. The path of least resistance, when possible, is to recast the sentence. For example: "The company urges everyone to submit their suggestions." Change to ". . . submit suggestions." Try it. You may like it.

Another method, particularly if examples are presented, is to begin with a person's name to denote the specific sex. "Take the case of Betty Brown. When she completes the program . . ." will read quite easily and no one will object.

NUMBER USAGE

Accountants use numbers, and writing for accountants will contain many references to numbers. The following rules cover how numbers are to be used in print.

1. Never begin a sentence with numbers. "50 states have approved this act" should be written "Fifty states have approved this act."
2. Spell numbers one through nine in words, 10 or larger in numerals. "Five or six people collected more than 75 signatures on the petitions."
3. Compound numbers are in numerals. Examples are fractions, 2×4, 3×5 card.
4. When showing odds, use hyphens such as 3-to-1, 7-to-5.
5. Decimals of less than one should be preceded by a zero, for example, 0.7 percent.
6. Large number examples: "One million dollars." "More than $50 million." Use zeros with less than one million. Example: "300,000 people."
7. Dates: "the 1980s"; "during the '80s."
8. Compound numbers from 21 to 99 are hyphenated.
9. Spell % as "percent."
10. Spell ¢ as "cents."
11. Use numbers with A.M. and P.M., a.m. and p.m., or AM, PM.

THE FOG INDEX

The Fog Index* (*How to Take the FOG Out of Writing*, Robert Gunning and Douglas Mueller, Dartnell Press, 1985) can be a useful tool to measure complexity. It is based on sentence length and difficult words, both related to how well readers will understand a written passage.

To calculate the Fog Index, pick a sample of your writing 100 to 125 words long. Count the average number of words per sentence. An independent clause with a subject and verb is treated as a separate sentence. Then count the words of three syllables or more. Do not count capitalized words, combination words like *bookkeeper* or *manpower*, or verbs made into three syllables by adding *-es* or *-ed*. Divide the number of long words by the passage length (100 to 125) to get the percentage.

Add the count of number of words per sentence to the percentage of long words and multiply the sum by 0.4. Ignore the digits after the decimal point.

The result is the years of schooling needed to understand the writing tested. Few readers have over 17 years' schooling, so any passage over 17 gets a Fog Index of

*Fog Index is a service mark of Gunning-Mueller Clear Writing Institute, Inc., Santa Barbara, CA 93110.

17-plus. Test your writing occasionally. If your Fog Index is over 12, you are giving your writers a handicap.

As stated before, you are writing for an average reader you may never meet. If in doubt about a long sentence, change it to two short sentences. A paragraph containing only one sentence is a warning of a possible sentence-length problem.

While a good vocabulary is helpful, a large number of words over two syllables, over 20 percent for instance, might make the material difficult for the average reader to comprehend. Dependence on a thesaurus for unique words may be hazardous to your writing health.

CHAPTER 11
MECHANICS:
BLACK AND WHITE AND
READ ALL OVER

The mechanics of writing include the paper, type style, hardware, method of reproduction, use of logos, numbering schemes, indexes, headlining, editing, and distribution. Remember that you are not a publishing company; you are not writing the "great novel"; you *are* a disseminator of accounting information to those within the company who are involved in the accounting process or are affected by the policies and procedures related to accounting.

You have chosen to be a *documentor*. *Documentation* has always been the weakest link in the accounting system. Professionals like to *do*, not document how it is to be done. In many organizations, there is reluctance to document a policy or procedure because the "hard copy" becomes a restriction that hampers freedom to change directions without being noticed.

Documentation provides the consistency that accounting needs. It is part of the third leg of the accounting trio: accuracy, fairness, and consistency. In the early 1960s, many bookkeepers and accountants dropped out of the accounting environment because they could not tolerate the demands of the computer-generated accounting procedures that demanded errors be reported and corrected before acceptance into the accounting process. Before data processing, many accounting errors were quiet errors, such as misposting, coding errors, and so forth. Everyone knew they were there but the effort to discover and correct the errors was not worth the cost. The computer has eliminated most quiet errors.

There will be nothing in this chapter about accounting. What will be covered are the rules for producing a financial manual for professionals and paraprofessionals, starting with the rough draft of information and ending with distribution to those who need to have the information. It is the mechanical procedure that will be covered.

PAPER

Unless the information is to be printed on both sides of a page, the quality of paper used is not critical. It should not be too flimsy or too expensive. It may or may not be in color to denote purpose. If printing on both sides of a paper, a practice not generally recommended, check the paper for opacity. If you see the characters on the back when reading the front, the paper is not heavy enough. In this case, use at least 24-pound bond. Most photocopy paper is adequate for single-sided printing and may be adequate for double-sided printing.

Some people like to use color to denote purpose. For example, pale blue to denote policy, pale pink for personnel procedures, yellow for action requests, and so forth. This practice is fine as long as the ink and the paper are in contrasting colors. Do not use blue ink on blue, or brown on brown or similar paper, or black on a dark gray. The lack of contrast will discourage the reader. Nothing is better than black ink on white paper. Any paper color other than white creates problems with some photocopy machines.

TYPE SIZE AND STYLE

Any good electric typewriter or letter-quality printer with an elite type size (12 characters to the inch) is adequate for documentation. The preferred type style is Prestige 12 or Prestige 72, a roman typeface. Do not, under any circumstances, use cursives which imitate handwriting, fancy old-English type, square-faced type, or all-capital type used by most mainframe computers, probably the hardest of all typefaces to read. (The rough drafts of this book and many of the printed figures were written on a Systel word processor, a Canon 400 typewriter with Prestige 12 print wheel, the Wordstar word processing program, and film ribbon.)

USE OF LOGOS

Logos on all forms and documentation are highly recommended. The logo tends to make the reader accept the material as *our* procedure rather than just a procedure. The logo may be just the name of the company or organization, possibly with special print style or layout. Or it may be a trademark, seal, or special art. The acceptable logos of the University of Southern Mississippi are the official seal or an abstract rendition of the Administration Building with the name of the University under or encircling the drawing. The logo also lends an official status to the contents of the report or document.

NUMBERING SCHEMES

Several numbering schemes can be used for manuals. The simplest one, and probably the one preferred by most people, is arabic numerals. Readers are used to this style since it is used in all books, magazines, and newspapers. The only objection to arabic numerals occurs when the document is unusually long, more than 50 pages or so. The primary reason for objecting to arabic numerals under this condition is maintenance. If errors or changes are made on page 4 or 5 of a document 150 pages long, and the changes add one or more additional pages, the alternative to issuing pages numbered 5a, 5b, and so forth is to reissue the entire 150 pages. So the first rule is: Break large manuals into sections of 20 to 30 pages.

When dividing a large manual into sections, three methods of defining sections are available. The first method is to provide separator pages between sections which show the name of the section such as *Chart of Accounts* and *Account Definitions*, each with pages beginning with number 1.

The second method is to assign a section name to each section and repeat this name on every page of that section. Thus the fifth page of "Section A - Chart of Accounts" would show "Section A" in the upper right-hand corner and arabic numeral 5 immediately following or at the bottom of the page.

The third method is to use Roman numerals for sections. Thus "Section I - Chart of Accounts" would have every subsequent page labeled with I and the page number, for example, I-5. However, do not switch to the outlining method and use more than one roman numeral and one arabic number. A page marked "I-C-4-b" will lose the reader immediately.

One of the worst methods is the Dewey decimal method, yet this method is still seen frequently, particularly in government documents. While this method allows unlimited expansion, imagine the frustration of the reader when encountering page number 4.22.5.3 in a book or manual that is written to be constructive. In this example, the next page number could be 4.22.5.4, 4.22.6, 4.23 or 5.1. These numbers are even more frustrating when referred to in writing. The only system worse than the decimal system is the Internal Revenue system which uses numbers interspersed with capital letters.

In summary, the preferred numbering scheme is arabic numerals with sections of materials not longer than 20 or 30 pages. However, when short documentation is to be issued sporadically, such as policy pronouncements, replacement procedures, or action requests, the preferred system would be retrieval numbers. Such numbers permit excellent indexing of pronouncements over time, can indicate that the current document supersedes a previous one, and is easy to refer to.

RETRIEVAL NUMBERS

Retrieval numbers are assigned when the document is issued. They can be preassigned in groups of four or five to indicate the general purpose of each group. While a 4-digit number is adequate, five digits are preferred. In an accounting operation, the number groups might be assigned as follows.

Purpose	4-digit	5-digit
Corporate policy	0001–0999	00001–09999
General accounting	1000–1999	10000–19999
Procedures	2000–2999	20000–29999
Information releases	3000–3999	30000–39999
Action requests	4000–4999	40000–49999

The 5-digit retrieval number system permits further subdivision within one series. An example might be to divide general accounting numbers 10000–19999 into groups as follows:

Group	Retrieval
Controller	10000–10999
Payroll	11000–11999
Accounts payable	12000–12999
Budget	13000–13999
Cost accounting	14000–14999
Accounts receivable	15000–15999
Purchasing	16000–16999

More on this method of numbering was discussed in Chapter 3 on policy/procedure statements.

ROUGH DRAFT

Every manual or procedure starts with a group of ideas. The easiest way to begin writing is to outline the project. Outlining permits easy movement of similar ideas into like groups, emphasizes highlights, and provides a consistent structure to the finished manual. Once the outline is acceptable, the writing can begin.

At this point, the main effort is to get something in writing. The writer can use dictating equipment, longhand, typing, or word processing equipment. The object is to get a workable first draft. Forget sentence structure, grammar, style, and possibly everything else you learned until a stream of paragraphs is on paper and ready to be edited to completion. If you get writer's block, insert a word or two about the idea and start a new paragraph about a new subject. The rule: Spit it out, get it typed double-spaced (triple-spaced if it is a barely more than an outline), and cook it later to perfection.

The next step is to add information to provide more strength to the document. Full sentences and possibly even paragraphs might be added at this stage. If it becomes hard to read, get another typed rough draft. Then start the final editing. Keep in mind your spelling and grammar habits, and, most importantly, the audience this document is designed to reach. Use short sentences, paragraphs with only one major idea, and determine whether a form or list should be attached for additional information or clarity.

To enable the typist to make sense of your changes, you will need to establish some kind of code to be followed. Because this single manual is not going to be a book, you will not need the dozens of special marks used to communicate to typesetters. However, you will need some communication codes.

EDITING CODES

The typist or word processor should be informed of your handwriting style. For example, if a heading is printed in all capital letters, the typist should type the heading in capitals. Regular handwriting indicates upper and lower case typing as shown. Handwritten material should show the spacing between paragraphs, between numbered lines, and so forth.

If your first draft is handwritten, the following information should be added to the upper-left corner. If dictating equipment is used, the information should be given at the start of the dictation.

Rough Draft. This tells the typist to double space the typed output. If you are using block style, then triple spaces are needed between paragraphs.

Which Manual. Name the manual this procedure is to be added to. The specific manual will determine the style to follow.

EDITING THE ROUGH DRAFT

You have received the rough draft and now must indicate changes to the typist. The instructions must be kept simple. The easiest method is to make the change where needed and place a small "x" in the left margin where the change was made. To replace a word, cross out the old word and write the new one above. If a word is to be capitalized, cross out the lower-case letter and write the capital letter above. If a word is misspelled or transposed, draw a single line through the word and write in the correct word.

If there are multiple corrections in one line, add an "x" for each change or correction in the margin. The other changes consist of moving words or sentences left or right, spacing between lines, starting a new paragraph, eliminating a paragraph start, and inserting additional material. Figure 11.1 shows how these editing corrections can be made.

HEADLINING

Most manuals require either a subject title or a headline. You must decide the most important information contained in the material. Is it a new form? Is it a revised procedure? Is it a new or revised policy statement? In newspaper writing, every news article is *slugged* with a single word or, at most, two words. This *slug* describes the most important fact in the news article. Think like a newspaper writer. Keep the subject short and meaningful. Generally, a subject title or a section name should not contain more than five or six words and never be longer than one line.

FINISHED COPY

The finished copy depends on the method of printing. The three most common printing methods are photocopying, typesetting, and multilith printing. Photocopying and multilith printing are photographic processes that do not require editing again and therefore are preferred to typesetting. Also, typesetting is much more expensive than the other two methods. Unless the volume of output is large, photocopying is the preferred method. This method allows you to control the process.

Good copy machines will produce from 20 to 60 copies a minute. Thus a 10-page issue to 100 employees, a total of 1000 sheets, will require one hour or less, plus collating and stapling. Multilith machines generally run at 100 copies per minute and the same output can be printed in a little over 10 minutes.

If you are going to reproduce the copies for distribution to the users, the final typed draft must be on the form used for that particular manual. After selecting the format for a specified manual, have 100 or more sheets reproduced by a printing

Meaning	Marked in Manuscript
Set in all capitals	*Caps* (The Accounting Manual)
Capitalize word	✗ The ʒnited States is the
Set in lower case	*lc* The U(NITED) States
Move left	✗ ⟵ However, the principle rests with the government.
Line up flush left	✗ 1. When the form is sent it is given to the clerk.
No paragraph or indent	✗ then given to the clerk. The clerk reviews
New line, flush left	✗ to the clerk. The clerk
New line, paragraph indent	*¶* to the clerk. The clerk
Paragraph indent	*Indent* Before the form can be approved and paid, the
Insert space	*Space* Dear Mr. Brown: Here is the paper I
Insert 2 spaces	*2 spaces* CHAPTER 9 CREATING A NEW FORM
Delete	✗ and ~~that~~ is the reason to
Insert copy	✗ and will provide ^good response
Close up	✗ write‿offs are made in
Misspelled word or transposed letters	✗ ✗ It is ~~difficlut~~ *difficult* if ~~there~~ *their*

Figure 11.1. Correcting rough draft material for retyping.

company. The final draft is typed on one sheet of this special form. The rest will be reproduced.

FINAL LAYOUT

The layout for all manuals requires 1-inch margins on both sides and at the bottom of an $8\frac{1}{2} \times 11$ inch sheet. If plain paper is used, the top margin should also be one inch. If a standard form has been designed, the top margin will contain a logo, name of manual, and other information, and the top margin can be one-half inch. See Figure 11.2 for layout.

Most modern electric typewriters and word processing printers provide for three type sizes: pica, 10 characters to the inch; elite, 12 characters to the inch; and micro, 15 characters to the inch. Today, pica is used only for TV, film, and stage manuscripts. Elite is the standard type for almost all other uses. Micro is sometimes used if a multiple-column report will not fit on a standard page. To provide 1-inch margins on standard typing paper, the margins for these type sizes are as follows:

Type	Left Margin	Right Margin	Characters per Line
Pica (10)	10	75	66
Elite (12)	12	86	75
Micro (15)	15	110	96

DISTRIBUTION

Each manual has its own normal distribution, usually based on a need-to-know or need-to-use basis. There are only three basic distributions: *Restricted, Designated,* or *All*.

The *Restricted* distribution is seldom used in accounting. One example might be a policy on the type of entertainment allowed and how the expenses are to be reported. The organization might not want employees below a certain classification level to entertain or be reimbursed for such expenditures. Restricted implies that only those on the restricted list can have access to the policy.

The *Designated* distribution is very common. The use of this distribution requires that the person authorizing the issuance must provide the names of specific persons or departments to receive it. For example, a distribution might be to accounting managers, purchasing, and receiving. Or it might be to all department supervisors and officers. Another example might be a new policy regarding retirement and the distribution would be to company officers and those eligible for retirement under the new rules.

Policy/Procedure Statement

3-Hole
Punched

◯

1" Margin

| LOGO |

L. O. GRANT ORGANIZATION, INC.

- RETRIEVAL NO. (Assigned when released)
- PAGE (Style 1 of, 2 of, ...)
- ISSUE DATE (Month, day, year)
- ORIGINATOR (Person or Unit)
- SUPERSEDES (Retrieval No. of replaced statement, if applicable)

1" Margin

SUBJECT: (All capital letters) (Used for Indexing)

Background or Problem

Narrative explaining cause of problem and need for revision.

Revised Policy or Procedure

Narrative explanation, effective date, and enforcement.

Revised or New Form (If Applicable)

Uses of the form and general instructions.

Completing the Form (If Applicable)

Detailed instructions for completing each area of the form.

Summary

Name, address, telephone number where assistance can be obtained.

Attachments: (Use exact name of attachments)

Distribution: (Optional)

Figure 11.2. Policy/procedure statement layout specifications.

The *All* distribution is to all employees, all departments, and so on. For example, an announcement of a new payroll system might be sent to all employees. A new authorization policy could be sent to all departments.

Whenever a new document relating to any of the manuals is distributed, the issuer must maintain a card file showing the name of the document, the date issued, the retrieval number if any, and the distribution used.

It is recommended that additional copies be run, usually 5 to 10 percent of the required number, because invariably someone may be missed or additional copies may be requested by certain recipients. The master copy is retained intact and unbound so quick photocopies can be provided on request.

CHAPTER 12
MAINTENANCE:
AS TIME GOES BY

As soon as a documentation system is in place, maintenance is not far behind. Accounting manual changes consist of adding or deleting something, changing a record, account, or procedure, or clarifying a previous release. Maintenance of documentation can vary considerably, from a minor change that may affect only a few people to a massive change such as the installation of new systems or major overhaul of the existing systems.

Figure 12.1 lists the different accounting manuals and the general method of maintaining each one. Note that there are three levels of change and several ways to announce or publish changes. Minor changes, such as adding or deleting one or a few account numbers, income or expense codes, approval authorizations, and so on, can be reported by interoffice correspondence or memoranda to those departments or employees affected by the change.

Intermediate changes, such as the replacement of a significant portion of a section of one of the manuals, the introduction of a new form, a significant change in an existing form, or a policy or procedural change which may affect most operations

General Accounting Manual

    Minor change – Memorandum to user departments.
    Intermediate change – Use Policy/Procedure Statement.
    Major change – Reissue Manual or major sections.

Policy/Procedure Statements

    Any change – Issue new P/PS and supersede old P/PS if
      appropriate.

Forms Manual

    Minor change – Memorandum.
    Intermediate change – Use P/PS.
    Major change – Reissue Manual or specific forms sections.

Year-End Manual

    Any change – Revise and publish new manual each fiscal year.

Data Processing Manual

    Minor change – Internal memorandum to accounting personnel.
    Intermediate change – Memo to department users.
    Major change – Reissue sections or entire manual.

User Manual

    Minor and intermediate changes – Memo to department users.
    Major change – Reissue manual annually or if substantial
      change such as a new accounting system or significant
      procedural changes.

Information Releases

    Any change – Issue new Information Release.

Figure 12.1. Maintenance methods.

within the company, are disclosed through the policy/procedure statement system, possibly in conjunction with replacement sections of the manual as attachments.

A major change, such as a new accounting system, a new data processing system affecting users, a replacement of several action forms or transaction forms, and so forth, would require the rewriting and reissue of the manual, or major sections thereof if the change affected only one or two separate sections of a manual.

Note in Figure 12.1 that two documenting systems maintain themselves. Policy/procedure statement changes can only be updated by a replacement P/PS which shows supersession of the replaced P/PS. The information release also stands alone. Each information release relates to a single issue or event and if a prior release was in error or needs clarification, a new release is issued without reference to the prior release. There is no provision for superseding an information release.

In all cases, the determination that maintenance is required and the level of reporting changes is both subjective and judgmental. The person or group most closely related to each manual is probably the best source for determining the impact of an addition, deletion, or other change to that manual.

Each of the seven manuals previously covered will be discussed in turn, with the levels and methods of reporting changes related to typical maintenance items. The three levels of reporting are the memorandum or letter, the policy/procedure statement or information release, and the reissue of a new manual or substantial sections of the manual.

The memorandum would specify the change and the reason therefor such as new account, account deleted or inactive, and so on. The change would be related to a specific manual or prior release with enough information to enable the recipient to enter the change in his or her copy of the proper manual.

MAINTAINING THE GENERAL ACCOUNTING MANUAL

Typical minor changes consist of adding one or a few accounts or expense codes, or deleting some accounts. A minor change might also be a change in a form or in what data are entered in some area of a form. In most cases, changes of this type affect only one or two persons or departments so the logical method of reporting the change is a memorandum to the users affected.

The introduction of a new form or replacement of an existing form, changing many account numbers or expense codes, or changes in organization structure with little impact on the general accounting procedures are best reported through the P/PS system. It is here that the background information can be reported, the changes described in any amount of detail desired, and the distribution handled in an effective manner.

However, if several P/PSs are issued over a relatively short period, you should consider reissuing the manual or substantial sections thereof—a major change.

A major change in the general accounting manual, then, would be the introduction of many new accounts, a new general accounting system or major subsystem, a reorganization of a significant portion of the operations of the company, or substantial changes in data entry processing or processing methods and reports.

MAINTAINING POLICY/PROCEDURE STATEMENTS

As stated earlier, policy/procedure statements are *never* updated; they are superseded and a new P/PS released. The heading of the new P/PS would indicate the retrieval number of the one superseded; the body of the new P/PS would only mention the superseded one in the background information section in general terms.

MAINTAINING THE FORMS MANUAL

The forms manual is a series of forms and instructions for completing accounting forms. Updating usually consists of replacing the instructions or the form, or both. This procedure is an exception to the rule that asking the user to update a manual by removing and replacing pages is to be avoided. If the forms manual has a known sequence, such as form number or official title, inserting new pages is not burdensome. When issuing a new form or a replacement form, the covering memorandum should explain its purpose and location in the forms manual. If deleting a form from the accounting system, the interoffice memorandum is the only method available for informing holders of the forms manual of the deletion.

If the forms manual has a published index, then the index should be reissued after two or three changes have been made to the contents of the manual.

MAINTAINING THE YEAR-END MANUAL

The year-end manual is rewritten and reissued prior to the end of each fiscal year, and no interim maintenance is required. It is important that some changes be made every year in the manual or users will stop referring to it as a year-end closing guide and it will become useless as an action program manual.

MAINTAINING THE DATA PROCESSING MANUAL

The data processing (DP) manual resembles the forms manual in style and content. DP manual changes in record layouts, batch input or processing forms, and output report layouts are handled by asking the holder to remove existing pages and insert the new record or report layouts. If the changes are many, or the system is being drastically altered or replaced, then a new DP manual would be compiled and issued, along with instructions to destroy the old manual.

MAINTAINING THE USER MANUAL

The user manual is a periodic-release type of manual, essentially to inform new employees following a period of employee turnover. However, if the manual remains substantially unchanged, then maintenance is handled like that for the general accounting manual. In fact, changes in the general accounting manual should be noted in this manual to determine whether the holders of user manuals should be informed. It is assumed that this manual has a much wider distribution than the general accounting manual.

Minor maintenance need not be reported because the people affected are informed through a memorandum or letter. If a new or replacement form included in the user manual is being issued, the holders of the user manual should be informed by memo or through the P/PS system. If the change is major, such as a new accounting system or substantial changes thereto, or a major policy change negates a large portion of the manual, then a new manual should be written and published and the holders notified to destroy the old manual. It was stressed that the user manuals should be dated so if a user makes an inquiry to accounting, both parties would be referring to the same publication.

If newly hired employees need the user manual, they should receive the latest manual with updates noted or copies of the change letters or memos included. If the manual is used as the basis of a short training session for new employees, the changes would be discussed as an integral part of the instruction.

MAINTAINING THE INFORMATION RELEASE SYSTEM

Like the policy/procedure statement, the information release (IR) updates itself. The information release is event-driven, reporting information on a need-to-know basis. This information is neither major policy or procedure but may be a minor clarification or minor change thereto. Retrieval numbers are used only to communicate the existence of an IR and they are never superseded. Even if a prior IR was in error, the replacement release would not need to refer to the prior one. The new release would give all the necessary details and related information as though the old one never existed. To remember this, keep in mind how newspapers handle an event. A newspaper article seldom states that the "event reported last Tuesday on page 3, column 4 is now being changed to read. . . ." Neither should an information release provide a rehash of the prior one and the changes this new release is reporting.

DETERMINING MAINTENANCE REQUIREMENTS

Updating manuals and sections of manuals is highly judgmental. Indications of the need for the release of new information to the holders of any of the manuals are the increase in transaction errors, sudden disregard of company policy or procedure, consistently faulty transaction coding indicating the preparer has not been informed of a change in the coding structure, and so on.

We have been discussing seven manuals and many references have been made to the holders, the users, the recipients, and so forth. The preparer of the manuals or systems documentation must maintain a record of the distribution of each type of release if updates and changes are to be distributed to the original recipients of that manual. For each release, the minimum record is a 3 × 5 index card with the exact name of the release, date published, retrieval number if any, and the distribution list. Subsequent issues of an item to other employees or departments should be noted on the appropriate card.

For small-issue releases, such as the general accounting manual with limited distribution, specific names and titles may be recorded. For larger, more general releases, the general name of the employee group may be listed. For example, if a P/PS were released to supervisors, department heads, and senior management, names would not be needed because the next release, even if it is an update of a previous publication, would be addressed the same way.

Large lists of names are difficult to maintain because of employee turnover in most organizations. At all times, the primary objective of releasing information is to get the information to the right department or designated level of personnel. The distribution list should be fairly definitive. For example, if a P/PS is used to announce a special change in the retirement plan for employees over 60 years of age, the distribution list should have that description. Maintaining specific names is not important because it is unlikely that a similar release will be issued to exactly the same employees. Thus designated group names become an important part of the distribution system.

CHAPTER 13
MANUAL
DOCUMENTATION
SUMMARY:
IT HAS TO BE YOU

When the decision has been made to document an accounting system, the primary question is "Who is to be given the responsibility to monitor and control the production of the final manual(s)?" Certainly, the selected writer should have a fairly comprehensive knowledge of modern accounting practices, some knowledge of the organization, *and a strong desire to complete the assignment*.

In a very large organization, a specialist may be employed in a staff position to the controller or chief financial officer. This *inside* consultant should be given as much authority as an internal auditor, with full access to the officers and department heads, documents, and the current procedures in use. The position title should indicate the span of authority, such as Director of Accounting Systems, Director of Management Systems, or, more specifically, Director of Systems Documentation.

Two specific employee types immediately come to mind: the recent college graduate with a major or minor in accounting, or an older person within two or three years of retirement—an excellent use of an experienced person with prior management-level experience in an accounting function.

In many organizations, the task of documenting accounting systems can be assigned to the controller who can assign specific areas or tasks to knowledgeable unit managers reporting to him or her. The controller is then the editor, approver, and publisher.

In any case, the assignment should be closely allied with, and monitored by, the controller's office for it is here that the highest level of knowledge of the *working* accounting procedures are controlled, changed when necessary, and maintained appropriately.

Following is a brief summary of appropriate documentors for each of the seven manuals discussed in this book.

GENERAL ACCOUNTING MANUAL

The controller is the logical choice to develop this manual. Department or unit managers of payroll, payables, cash receipts, investments, cost accounting, fixed assets, and so on can be assigned specific documentation tasks related to their operation or to the general operations of accounting. The controller would supervise the editing, printing, and publishing. In a large organization, a staff position could be added to handle these tasks.

For a nominal fee, a high school or college English teacher or professor can be hired to check grammar, spelling, and current English usage.

POLICY/PROCEDURE STATEMENTS

Because P/PSs are the heart of an ongoing accounting operation, these should be under the controller's jurisdiction. Most P/PSs are originated in departments, and the system of bringing the policy or procedure to the controller with the request to publish it, as described in Chapter 3, is a most satisfactory solution.

FORMS MANUAL

Again, the controller is selected to centralize the accumulation of forms and forms descriptions. A small working task force can be organized to bring all current forms up to date and then describe how each form is to be completed and used. Once the total forms manual is in place, it is not difficult to make additions or deletions for the relatively infrequent changes in operating forms.

YEAR-END MANUAL

The logical preparer of the year-end manual is the director of internal audit or a knowledgeable audit manager, particularly if the person works closely with the external auditors to facilitate a speedy, effective financial audit of the organization. The audit specialist should be able to write effective programs of examination for specific audit functions.

Effectively handled, a comprehensive preaudit review and a detailed year-end manual can reduce the costs of an independent audit significantly.

DATA PROCESSING MANUAL

The writer of this documentation should have some knowledge of basic business data processing. However, much of the required manual contents can be determined with extensive interviews with user personnel and computer analysts and programmers. Suppliers of packaged accounting systems provide user documentation. In most cases, this documentation must be customized to the specific organization's methods and procedures.

USER MANUAL

This manual is ideally suited to be a cooperative department or unit project, headed by the controller or staff assistant to the controller. Each department or unit knows the forms in use, the proper data to be included, approvals, and the related problems based on prior outside user questions and complaints. The user manual is a *Reader's Digest* version of the total departments' operations.

Each preliminary writer should be instructed to write only what is necessary for the user to know. It is not necessary to describe all the inner workings, controls, or procedures employed to edit, enter, summarize, and report the data or produce a final output report. Here we are talking basic input forms and procedures related to user-provided information required by the forms.

INFORMATION RELEASE SYSTEM

No start-up is required. The first release of written information can be done at any time and it is never necessary to back up in time to report history. The information release is a close relative of the daily newspaper; it is the who, what, where, when, and how of a particular event and the reporting of the event to interested parties. The logical person for this system is the controller or chief financial officer.

THE JOB DESCRIPTION

Following is a job description showing the traits desirable in an employee who will be assigned the writing and compiling tasks, and the criteria for selecting an outside consultant who may be employed to produce specific accounting manuals.

DOCUMENTOR JOB DESCRIPTION

1. Degree in accounting.
2. Large-company business experience.
3. Knowledge of internal accounting controls.
4. Good writing ability (style).
5. Desire to spend one or two years in this job.
6. Good interviewing techniques.

CONSULTANT SELECTION CRITERIA

1. Significant experience in writing documentation for accounting, data processing, or similar operations.
2. Well-designed plan to utilize internal employees as much as possible for start-up materials.
3. Good, readable writing style. (Review several recent reports or actual documentation prepared by the consultant who will be assigned to the job.)
4. Receive assurance that the consultant understands fully the exact requirements of the specific manuals he or she is to complete.
5. Determine any other specific needs such as office space, photocopying, and printing to be provided, typing or word processing services, and so forth.

SUMMARY OF RULES

Throughout this book, several rules and guidelines were suggested. The principal rules are repeated here as a convenient reminder to you, the writer. However, a rule can be broken if you feel differently about it. As stated in the Preface, you will develop a documentation style that fits your situation.

DOs
Do write in simple sentences.
Do outline a manual, major policy, or procedure before starting the actual writing.

Do present the problem or the background of the situation before stating a new policy, procedure, or other solution.

Do provide a contents page or index for every manual.

Do use active verbs.

Do strive for uniformity in presenting similar materials.

Do have at least one other experienced employee read new material before releasing it to others.

Do provide the name of a person, unit, or department on every release so readers know where to call for clarification or an answer to a problem.

Do put the manual where the action is. A manual not available when and where needed is of little value.

Do use only one side of the paper.

AVOIDs

Avoid colored paper, unique or unusual printing styles, and nonstandard paper sizes.

Avoid Dewey decimal-type numbering systems.

Avoid numbering copies of manuals for control purposes.

Avoid flowcharts and decision tables. Most readers only scan this type of material.

Avoid replacing or inserting individual pages within an existing manual.

Avoid issuing a replacement policy or procedure with the obsolete material and new material marked with special codes or letters. This style is difficult to read and comprehend. The opening purpose or background paragraph should point to the areas changed.

Avoid negative statements in policies and procedures. Stress *will* rather than *will not*.

Avoid accounting jargon and special industry terminology unless terms are explained when first used.

Of the seven manuals discussed in this book, two are present in some form in every accounting operation. These are the general accounting manual—at least the chart of accounts, and the policy/procedure statements or their equivalent. While the other five may be optional, parts of them will show up in the general manual or as retained copies of correspondence, informal releases, or memorandum notes.

The following figures (13.1 through 13.7), in the form of information releases, summarize the general specifications of the seven manuals discussed in the previous chapters.

Information Release

FINANCIAL AFFAIRS

L. O. GRANT ORGANIZATION, INC.

GENERAL ACCOUNTING MANUAL - SPECIFICATIONS

Mechanics

Printed or photocopied on 8½ by 11 white paper on one side only, and punched for a 3-ring binder.

Content

Minimum contents are the chart of accounts, description of the numbering scheme, and definitions of income and expense or expenditure codes. Optional items are the basic accounting forms if no Forms Manual is maintained, batch or job control record formats, major accounting principles followed, and layouts of all major financial statements and schedules.

Updating

Major updating is required if major changes in systems or new computer application programs are installed. Reissued by section after several minor updates have been published.

Minor updating is by Policy/Procedure Statement, memorandum, or letter. Minor updates are defined as adding or deleting one or two new accounts or object codes, changing the definition of an income or expense code, or adding a new accounting form or schedule.

Numbering and Indexing

Numbered sequentially by section, beginning with "1" in each section. Because both the chart of accounts and definitions are in account number order by type of account, indexing consists only of a list of sections by title.

Normal Distribution and Retention

Distribution is to accounting staff and outside department personnel who initiate a large volume of variable accounting transactions. Retention is mandatory.

Figure 13.1. General accounting manual—specifications.

<table>
<tr><td>
LOGO

L. O. GRANT ORGANIZATION, INC.
</td><td>
Information Release

FINANCIAL AFFAIRS
</td><td>
- RETRIEVAL NO. 5002
- PAGE 1 of 1
- ISSUE DATE January 2, 1987
- ORIGINATOR Controller
</td></tr>
</table>

POLICY/PROCEDURE STATEMENTS - SPECIFICATIONS

Mechanics

Printed or photocopied on 8½ by 11 white paper, punched for 3-ring binder, but corner-stapled when issued. Use of standardized first sheet with full company name and logo is recommended.

Content

Each Policy/Procedure Statement stands alone and is referenced to a former P/PS only if it supersedes that P/PS. The P/PS announces policy additions or changes, major procedures, new forms, and any other significant management pronouncement affecting company operations.

Updating

There is no updating as such in the P/PS system. Each P/PS is complete as issued with the problem or background information stated, the policy and/or procedure defined, the effective date if required, and instructions for compliance.

Numbering and Indexing

The use of Retrieval Numbers used in sequential order is recommended. Retrieval Number groups should be assigned a permanent 4- or 5-digit series.

A new index should be isued after every 10 or so P/PSs are released. Minimum indexing is annually. The Index contains Retrieval Number, Date Issued, and Subject. A superseded P/PS should be included on the next Index with "Purged" or "Superseded" as the subject, and not printed at all on the following index. The Index itself does not use a Retrieval Number.

Normal Distribution and Retention

Each P/PS is issued to the accounting staff (sometimes only at the manager or supervisor level and above), and all outside departments affected by the policy or procedure or with the need to know, such as upper level management.

Permanent retention is assumed until a P/PS is superseded by a replacement P/PS.

Figure 13.2. Policy/procedure statements—specifications.

Information Release

FINANCIAL AFFAIRS

• RETRIEVAL NO.   5003

• PAGE   1 of 1

• ISSUE DATE   January 2, 1987

• ORIGINATOR   Controller

L. O. GRANT ORGANIZATION, INC.

FORMS MANUAL - SPECIFICATIONS

Mechanics

Printed or photocopied on 8½ by 11 white paper, 3-hole punched for a loose-leaf binder.

Content

Each form is described in a three-page-per-form layout. The first page describes the mechanics of the form, number of copies, use of each copy, retention and filing information, how obtained for use, and which department controls the distribution of blank forms. The second page contains the numbered instructions for completing the form. The last page is a copy of the actual form with every space for entering data numbered for reference to the instructions.

Updating

Generally, no updating is required unless the form is revised or discontinued, in which case a new set of form uses and descriptions is issued through the Policy/Procedure Statement system to those involved in its preparation and use. Certain forms may be included in the User Manual and holders of that manual should be notified if an included form is changed or replaced.

Numbering and Indexing

All forms should have a number and revision date affixed thereon. If not, the form is described by the actual name of the form as printed in the heading.

Indexing is normally done by principal area of use such as payroll forms, accounts payable forms, cashier forms, accounts receivable forms, and so on. Under each section, the name and number of the form is shown. Sequential page numbers may be used, in which case the index would show the locations as pages 7-9 or 13-15.

Normal Distribution and Retention

Each unit within and outside the accounting department should receive information about the forms they prepare, edit, approve, complete, or process. It is expected that recipients of the Forms Manual retain it indefinitely. This manual is usually updated piecemeal rather than replaced in its entirety.

Figure 13.3. Forms manual—specifications.

Information Release

FINANCIAL AFFAIRS

L. O. GRANT ORGANIZATION, INC.

- RETRIEVAL NO. 5004
- PAGE 1 of 1
- ISSUE DATE January 2, 1987
- ORIGINATOR Controller

YEAR-END MANUAL - SPECIFICATIONS

Mechanics

Photocopied on 8½ by 11 white paper, corner-stapled.

Content

The Year-End Manual contains a list of all accounting procedures
required to close the books at the end of the fiscal year and the person
assigned to complete each procedure, schedule, or financial statement
and related information.

Updating

A new Year-End manual is prepared before each fiscal year-end, usually
one or two months prior to the year end date.

Numbering and Indexing

The pages are numbered consecutively. No indexing is usually required
because of the manual's limited size and sequence by major accounting
operation of balance sheet, operating accounts, and statements and
schedules.

Normal Distribution and Retention

Distributed to every person assigned to complete one or more listed
tasks. Retained until the books are closed and the statements
published. One copy should be filed with the year-end working papers
and another clean copy retained for review and updating for the next
year-end closing.

Figure 13.4. Year-end manual—specifications.

Information Release

FINANCIAL AFFAIRS

L. O. GRANT ORGANIZATION, INC.

- RETRIEVAL NO.   5005
- PAGE   1 of 1
- ISSUE DATE   January 2, 1987
- ORIGINATOR   Controller

DATA PROCESSING MANUAL - SPECIFICATIONS

<u>Mechanics</u>

Batch control forms and report descriptions are typed on 8½ by 11 white paper, punched for a 3-ring binder. Tables, data dictionary, and output reports are usually printed by computer on standard 14 by 11 continuous paper and bound into computer output binders.

<u>Content</u>

If not included in the General Accounting Manual, batch control forms are included here. Tables, if available, are needed for reference and updating purposes. Descriptions of reports and the reports themselves (generally reduced photocopies of typical reports) are optional.

<u>Updating</u>

The forms and descriptions are replaced when computer changes require changes in forms used for data entry. Generally, there is very little updating of batch control forms or reports unless significant systems changes are made to the related programs.

<u>Numbering</u> <u>and</u> <u>Indexing</u>

Batch control forms and output reports are usually identified with a program number. These numbers can be used to index the materials. Tables are described by title and number and a simple index of the titles is usually sufficient as they are used only by accountants experienced with the data processing systems.

<u>Normal</u> <u>Distribution</u> <u>and</u> <u>Retention</u>

Because of their complexity, the contents of the Data Processing Manual are distributed only within the accounting and data processing staffs, usually one reference copy in each department.

These documents are retained until a new report is printed and checked for accuracy, at which time the replaced tables and forms are destroyed.

Figure 13.5. Data processing manual—specifications.

	Information Release	• RETRIEVAL NO.	5006
LOGO		• PAGE	1 of 1
	FINANCIAL AFFAIRS	• ISSUE DATE	January 2, 1987
		• ORIGINATOR	Controller

L. O. GRANT ORGANIZATION, INC.

USER MANUAL - SPECIFICATIONS

Mechanics

Printed or photocopied on 8½ by 11 white paper, corner-stapled. May be prepunched for 3-ring binder and bound in Accopress binders. Index is printed on the cover of the manual. May be printed on both sides of paper but printing on only one side is recommended.

Content

Included are the index, major forms prepared outside of accounting, departmental procedures such as reporting time and attendance, sick leave, vacation, and so forth, list of accounting personnel and area of accounting handled by each, instructions for preparing budgets, and instructions for reading reports furnished by accounting for deparmental management use.

Updating

Updating materials for holders of the User Manual usually consist of Interoffice Correspondence, Information Releases, or Policy/Procedure Statements. When changes are significant a new manual is prepared and distributed, usually required after a significant system change occurs.

Numbering and Indexing

Pages numbered consecutively. Index of contents should be on cover of manual with consecutive page number references.

Normal Distribution and Retention

As the manuals are intended for users who need the information for supplying coded forms and data to accounting, retention by the users is required.

Distribution is made to those operating units or departments who provide accounting information on forms or turnaround documents such as time reports and clock cards. An office copy should be provided for secretarial and clerical use in each department.

Figure 13.6. User manual—specifications.

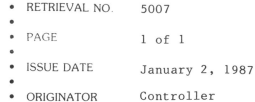

	Information Release	• RETRIEVAL NO.	5007
LOGO	FINANCIAL AFFAIRS	• PAGE	1 of 1
		• ISSUE DATE	January 2, 1987
		• ORIGINATOR	Controller

L. O. GRANT ORGANIZATION, INC.

INFORMATION RELEASES - SPECIFICATIONS

Mechanics

Printed or photocopied on 8½ by 11 white paper, corner-stapled if more than one page. Use of standardized first sheet with full company name, logo, and accounting department name is recommended.

Content

Individually issued standard layout releases to keep staff informed of events or information that may affect their function or routine. Each release covers one subject and does not relate to any other Release.

Updating

No updating permitted or required. If a prior Release is to be corrected or expanded upon, the new Release should cover the entire subject independently of the prior Release.

Numbering and Indexing

Information Releases should be numbered consecutively only for reference purposes. The use of a formal Retrieval Number series is recommended. An index may be prepared to inform employees who may have been missed during the initial distribution that information on the subject was made available. A photocopy of the Information Release is sent to anyone in the company when requested.

If many releases are issued, a monthly index of the Information Releases issued during the preceding month may be helpful. One copy of this monthly index would be sent to each department with the request that it be circulated or posted in a prominent location.

Normal Distribution and Retention

Distribution is usually limited to all employees in the accounting department and possibly to supervisors of departments closely related to accounting, such as purchasing, receiving, warehousing and stores, treasurer, investment function, and so forth.

Retention of the Information Release by the reader is optional. No formal retention of these event-oriented documents is required.

Figure 13.7. Information release—specifications.

INDEX